Fairy Tales

&

Horror Stories

A Memoir

Eye of the Dove

by Jerry Barry

When you're flying and you look down on all that's below you

At people and pets and the places you go to

They'll all look up at you crying

They'll all look up at you flying around

They'll all swear that they knew you

When you were a child, long before you flew

But you'll swear they never knew you at all

When you're flying and you look down at all of the green trees

And do dances in the air with the greatest of ease

Please don't, don't travel too high

Or you might burn your wings on the sun

Please think of me while you're up there

Flying around lighter than air

Most of all just make sure to have fun.

Acknowledgements

We all have a story. We are all unique and it's because of that difference, that we all offer a piece of the puzzle to share. You have a piece to add, just like your next door neighbor, or your old lover does. Life is one big, jigsaw puzzle.

My life story so far has been sometimes bizarre, sometimes comical, sometimes very scary. I have been led to send it out to the Universe, so that there will be room for new and wonderful things to continue to enter in. I hope you enjoy the ride and it encourages you for the better.

These events have led to me being fearless on stage, and now I am feeling fearless on the page, as well. I encourage you to be your own wonderful fearless self too.

I want to thank Wayne Fuller and David Underwood who are wonderful men, been good husbands and friends, and encouraged me to "find my voice." They have put up with a lot because of it along the way.

To my children, Jesse and Shawna, from whom I know about being a mother, first hand. The moments I've experienced with you in my life are epic, and were necessary for me to learn to love myself and the world more. You are loved and needed.

To my friends: Diana Baretsky, Christine Bonvino and Lorie (O'Donnell) Finger, for reading reams of fodder and helping with their editing thoughts.

To friends: Val Chism and Heidi Nightengale for their moral support.

To my friend, Book Marshall, for his talents with graphics and cover art.

To Chrissy Clancy for the cover picture. This was taken when we were out magically playing as big children in the surf and woods.

To my friend Russ Tarby, a great copy editor, a professional writer and friend. Thank you for being objective and so supportive. You were ruthless, right on the money and yet, kind.

Thanks to Stephen King, who gave great tips on how to write memoir in his book, "On Writing." It really helped me to follow that advice.

To Louise Hay and Doreen Virtue who have given me spiritual instruction for many years ever since I found your wisdom on your pages.

To my sisters and brothers who have had to accept a weird changeling sister. This is offered with remembrance of some of our shared life with parents we loved.

To my parents, Bernice and Earl, to whom I owe my safety, musical talent, eclectic spirituality, belief in myself and the determination to get back up and try again.

To all the fans of my music and Merry Mischief, you make me want to keep on singing and hanging it out there.

I also thank you, Dear Reader, for supporting me with the purchase of this book and with your word of mouth to keep it going forward. Go forth, acknowledge, forgive, and make good ripples.

Hugs,
Merlyn

Contents

The Calling of My Name

There was a bright eyed, mischievous girl...

She lived in a safe and quaint cottage filled with love, family and animals.

Yet a demon came to live within in the walls.

It would torment her walks and while climbing trees, and at night it would torment the family's dreams. No one knew why it came to live there, it just did.

The girl was, by nature, an energetic child; but she became increasingly fearful of sleep. So menacing were the energies of the demon, that the girl feigned sleep at all costs.

The demon followed her day and night, just looking for an opportunity, but night was the worst. It turned doorknobs. It whispered through the keyholes. It rattled the windowpanes of the cottage. Its glowing eyes watched her, its clawed hands waited for her feet under the bed. It stepped into her sleep with screaming nightmares.

Yet through it all, the day would dawn brightly again, and the girl saw the world filled with wonder and hope. Enchantment flowed through her veins; magic came to her and sparkled in her sky blue eyes. Power came to her in the form of magical tricks. She exuded innocence and at the same time seemed like an old soul and filled the hearts of those around her with dreams and melodies.

In the wild wood, her imagination blossomed with color and shadow boxes and pollywogs and story writing. She found freedom by running through green pastures, the hem of her skirt getting wet while picking cowslips and Queen Anne's lace in the bog. It was all to make bouquets for fairies. She calmed herself by snuzzling velvety horse muzzles and soaking up the purring motors of kittens dressed in her doll's lace dresses.

This girl was the appointed leader of a pack of unruly, wild and carefree children who made up plays and wars and who baked extravagant gourmet pies in the mud.

So revered was she, that when the demon found a crack to wedge its way in, it poisoned her and she became ill. All movement stopped in their village. For days on end, the cicadas hummed their hot song and the butterflies paused and pulsed, waiting for her recovery.

The lass's fever flowed like lava through the channels of her body. Her mother worried and fretted and gave her cold ice rubs trying to break the heat of her tortured body. The child had many dreams. Odd dreams. Wild horrific dreams. Wondrous dreams. The demon had caught her in a world of mystic realms and would not let her go.

She was caught somewhere between ether and earth….

She roamed. Dreamlike. The fever raged on for days. The demon finally got its taloned grip on her and refused to let her live. It wanted her Power.

The mother called for the Doctor God. The Doctor sent word and prescribed a strong drink of deadly nightshade for the wee child. The mother regarded it heavily.

She thought that the dose must be correct because he was, indeed, a learned man.

She made up the drink as given and noted its strength in color.

The mother then listened to the Goddess within her and asked for a sign.

Then the mother did something outrageous. She dared defy the will of the Physician God.

She followed her nagging heart and made up her own remedy. It featured a hearty dose of motherly compassion tempered with a watered down version of the nightshade. The mother administered it to the feverish girl soaked in delirious sweat. The Goddess Mother within her instructed her well. The girl continued to dream in her hazy, drugged, fever dream-

land.

The Dream

She dreamed of monsters. She dreamed of the end of the world. She dreamed that she was a magical witch. She was capable of both Grand Good and Mischievous Evil. The girl rode a broom in her dream through the rooms of her cottage. She dreamed that she did magical healing spells for any that made a plea. With a poof of smoke from her wand, they were cured. She flew her broom through the kitchen, with her dream mother following fast, trying to grasp her as she flew.

The lass sailed past and out the front door. It banged shut behind her. She was now a creature of the air.

Now that she was outside, the exhilaration of riding the wind made her stomach lurch and yet thrilled her. She heard the sound of applause somehow. She adjusted to the dip and flop of her stomach as she flew to rooftop heights... then swooped down to touch the herbs and flowers with her fingertips as she tickled the grassy tops. Oh! The adventure of flying!

The lass thought another thought and immediately she was at the back of the house. Her floating steed hovered steadily over the top of the house, then flew her to where she willed...to the apple tree. Here she magically scooped up all new fallen apples lying there at the base of the tree.

Now she had ammunition. Her broom was armed with a magic weapon which pelted any wrongdoers like a cannon. Apples were aimed and fired from her cannon broom and targeted the scum of the earth in her new cause of protecting the underdog. And somehow she felt powerful like a crimson, jingly, burly pirate. A pirate armed with Eve's magical love apples as cannonballs.

The demon fled.

The good witch pirate girl of wonder knew the apple was her entry to the Faerie World. Anyone knows that apple is what opens the doorway into the world of the Fae. She knew it like the calling of her own name. The girl felt oh so much older than her years. There was now a Power that would reside within her... to help others with illumination. Immediately, the knowledge struck her that some skill, love, harmony, beauty, harvest, and the magic of divine, shamanic madness and visionary experience would be hers.

While feeling powerful though, there lived a thorn of poison within her always, as a sometimes weakness and Achilles heel to remind her of her own mortality.

The girl then flew up to the crook of a gnarled, old cedar tree. She sat there and pondered the sturdy weathered tree and felt at home. All negativity that had previously bound the house had to be swept away with a cedar broom. She flew round the house on her broom, three times clockwise thusly to ensure it. She didn't know why she did this, but it seemed to feel right to *her. The house felt cleansed.*

It was then, when the last wisp of cedar smudge cleared the air that she found herself waking up back in bed, eyes adjusting to the afternoon sun, wrapped in her sweat-soaked sheets. It was a hot summer day when the child awoke from her fever.

And somehow…she knew who she was.

A New Old Soul

I heard tell that before we are born into this world, we get a glimpse of this new life from the other side. Sort of like a preview of coming attractions. This must be where "déjà vu" is born. Those magical early riff tracks of our life sneak-peeked before birth are what we used to decide on our choice for this life experience. These previews then come back to us as a flashback later on in life when they occur again, as the déjà vu feeling.

So if that's the case, just keep reminding yourself that you've picked this life, for whatever reason, to experience certain things.

What have I needed to learn? Well, some of the same things as you, and maybe a few other things along the way. OK, some really bizarre shit has happened to me, and I'm going to tell you about it in my stories. This book is as true as it gets, and I'm sure you won't believe the half of it, but I'll tell you anyway. But who am I to know anything? I'm a musician with a life of weirdness, with shocking stories to tell, which make me the odd "Merlyn-bird" I am today.

You will see yourself in some of these stories, or maybe you will simply be thankful that you chose the life you are living now.

While I currently like being prompt as an adult, when making my own debut into this world, I dragged my wee baby feet. I was a whole month late. The due day was right, but I was just way overdue. A MONTH overdue. I guess I didn't want to leave my mother. I was soaking her up and had her all to myself. I guess I knew that this was the closest I'd ever be to her and wanted to stay as long as I could. I adored my mother, but always felt that there was a part of her that was a bit aloof and distracted, like she was calculating math or something while talking to me. I never seemed to get her full focus. While I longed for her total undivided attention, there seemed to be some far off thought always calling her away, even though she was physically present.

When I finally chose to be born a flighty Gemini *(and not a stubborn Taurus),* I arrived on May 26, 1960. I came into the wide world with much ado and entrance of a grand dame. I'd stayed behind the curtains waiting to make a spectacular entrance for so long, that when I was finally born, I was heralded as "a Gift from God." As an immediate result of the length of time incubating, pondering if I did, indeed, want to be born into all this, I got all pruney. Just like a wrinkled up raisin for a whole week after. My body, head to toe, fingers and toes were crinkled as if I'd been in the bath tub too long. A wee, little old lady. I was officially born as a citizen of Earth and deemed "an old soul." Always mentioned with my baby pictures was the following: "You looked like a wrinkled little old lady. We couldn't give you baths with soap and water as it would be too drying to your little old lady skin. So for a whole month, the nurses suggested that we bathe you in baby oil," said Mom.

Thus, I have the softest skin, yet I am tough as leather. I have had to be and it has come in quite handy over the years.

There was much rejoicing over that soft, little, old-wizened baby at the time of my birth. I was given the moniker of "Marilyn Lucy." I was named after a combination of my mother's middle name, my sweet Godmother, Marilyn, and also my bittersweet, blatantly outspoken Great Aunt Lucy. I've also identified with those names over the years by thinking of Marilyn Monroe and her longing for identity, and her wishing to bond with her elusive self, as well as Lucy Ball's anything for a joke and daring outrageousness.

Marilyn and Lucy, Two very old-fashioned names for a

brand new baby girl, are ones that I didn't hear growing up named for any other girls my age. From the very beginning, being named after those particular ladies, I was a split sort of character. I was destined to be both sweet and tangy. Wonderful and Wicked. Earthy and Comical. Mannerly and Unruly. Sexy and Unarming. Such is the accompanying luggage that the mercurial Gemini brings with her upon arrival.

The whole family was elated and their joy filled the house. It was within this excitement and the need to get back to business at home, that followed the sensible notion with which I was raised: "The house does not get used to the baby. The baby gets used to the house."

So life got back to normal as soon as possible after I was born, without much fanfare after the first hullabaloo. My baby bassinet was placed in the busy kitchen for all to watch and monitor. I definitely got used to being around a lot of people and activity always swirling around me. Much ado and then… well…nothing. I don't remember being held much. I think my brothers and sisters mostly got that job.

My mother, Bernie Brown, matriarch of our family, delegated what chores needed to be done and managed the farm to run like a well-oiled tractor. After all, there were now five children to raise, animals that needed tending and dinner to get on the stove. There was no time to nurse a baby, and besides, the family physician, told my mother that her "milk was no good." This was a common ploy back in the 1960's, set forth by the formula advertising companies in order to sell the new-fangled formula to women who had perfectly good breastfeeding equipment. However, in this case, it worked out in mom's favor because she really didn't have time for nursing an infant anyway, nor could she sit still much. I was number five in a line of ultimately, six children.

Fortunately, there was a dairy farm next door with lots of cows, which, of course, meant lots of available milk. My frugal, problem-solving parents decided that milk is milk, and they could make their own formula and save money at the same time. They read somewhere that *cow's milk + corn syrup = baby formula*. It was simple Scottish problem solving at its finest! They set about nourishing this new mouth with the homemade formula and started saving money right away as soon as they brought me home from the hospital.

Then there is Mom's next story that immediately follows that one: "All went well giving you the fresh cow's milk formula for about three days until all *Hell* broke loose. Marilyn, your legs were drawn up, your belly was hard as a rock, you convulsed, and well, in all my years of having babies, I never heard a baby SCREAM like you."

So, only a few days after I was released, they rushed me right back to the hospital. Always a Diva, I guess. "Milk Allergy" was quickly pronounced and the family breathed a heavy sigh of relief that it was something easily cured. There was an immediate call put in to "The Goat Lady" for my daily sustenance of life giving milk.

The Goat Lady was aptly named because she lived with goats. Not next to goats in a barn on her property, but WITH goats. The goats lived in her house, *with* her, as pets. Not diapered and dressed in frilly dresses as my friend, Mimi, has with her visiting and educational pet goat. No. These were the sleep in your bed, eat off the table, bleating watchdog, and mow the lawn sort of goats. The Goat Lady was of a mysterious personage, elusive, and seldom seen. The only thing that was known about her was that she was odd and the goats were her pets. Even back then, in the sixties, that was wonderfully weird.

My parents approached her and a deal was struck on my needy behalf. In exchange for groceries, the diligent Goat Lady milked her goats every morning, just for me. However, the Goat Lady had no electricity. I'm not sure if it was by frugal necessity or by eccentric choice, so "She would put the milk in a mason jar and then screw top ring tighten the lid. The jar was then placed carefully in a pan of cold well water at the end of her driveway to await pick up. We had to get there bright and early to get it, or else it'd curdle," said my father matter-of-factly. The result of all this was…that I lived.

I had four older siblings ready and waiting for me when I

came home from the hospital. The first born was my brother, Rick, who was 13 and "in charge" as the oldest. He was also a Boy Scout and well on his way to being an Eagle Scout. Then there was Gary who was 12. Next was Chris, who was always a prankster and a practical joker. He was 10 when I was born. He was a tall beanpole of a kid and into science projects, mostly those that had to do with magnets, electricity and copper wire. Next came the only girl so far, my older sister, Adele, who was 9 years old when I was born. She was hoping for a baby sister, and her dream had come true! She was my closest sibling in age and I became her real baby doll. Del couldn't wait until I was born, and she carted me around in an antique stroller. She was like a second mother to me.

I imagine that it was hard for my older brothers and sister, who had chores to do and had to be responsible, to be faced with a needy infant. I grew into a mischief-maker of a toddler, who got a lot of the attention. My brothers and sisters ended up nicknaming me "Bub," which was, of course, short for "Beelzebub." You know… the devil? So, if you add up the story so far, it translates to this: I was an adorable Mercurial old soul, Angel-baby, Demon-child who suckled from goats. Now, that's a lot of leeway for behavior.

How do you make sense out of life when it starts off like this and throws more curve balls along the way? Day by day.

My father, Earl, was a quiet, kind, passive, smart man. When he was inducted into the Air Force during WWII, after taking the aptitude testing, he went straight into being an officer and skipped private rank altogether. He became a pilot flying B-29s, the "Flying Fortress" and the biggest warplane of that time. After the war, he liked to quietly garden and putter on building things and was often found outside or in the barn or basement if you had to look for him. He played chromatic harmonica very well. Pop had a harp in every key.

My mother, Bernie, was as overworked as Cinderella. She had no wicked step-mother instead, her mother was bed-ridden for most of Bernice's childhood, and she took care of her mother. Bernie said she was "Chief Cook & Bottle Washer" and had always been since she could remember. Bernie cracked the whip on herself. Four kids in five years, then me nine years later, she had a farm to manage and a home to create and sustain. I imagine that she must've dreamt of a Prince Charming. Mom's joy was music and writing. Music seemed to be Bernie's ticket away from drudgery starting way back when she was a teenager. Thinking about it, she would say, "I was in a country trio group called 'The Cowgirls' and we were on the radio in the late 1930s. We had matching skirt outfits and cowboy hats to go with it." She reveled in the memory. She said that she'd played guitar in the trio and they sang "the old songs." I realized later on, that mom's story was much like Loretta Lynn's in a way, except Bernie didn't get a big break.

Earl was a smart and handsome and he and Bernie had music, youth and physical attraction in common. She said that one of her best memories of dating Earl was this: "We would go to different friends homes 'Round Robin' every Friday night. Then we'd pick up and move all the furniture out of the parlor, roll up the rugs and we'd play music, and everyone would dance, and we'd play cards and drink beer." Partying with friends is my family tradition, it seems.

After Bernie and Earl married and had the kids, mom would get out her guitar and play and sing in the afternoons sometimes, and she and dad would play music together too. She would do all her favorites, "Your Cheatin' Heart," "Cold, Cold Heart," "Prison without Any Walls" and "Heartaches."

My music came from my parents and from the great role models that they were to me in how much enjoyment they derived from it. After big family dinners, we'd clear the plates and all play music for hours. Bernie would lead off the songs playing rhythm guitar and singing and everyone else would fill in with playing spoons, wash tub bass, banjo or whatever instrument they wished to be good at.

On Saturday mornings, Mom would crack the whip early and get everyone up to do chores. The jobs were doled out: feeding the farm animals, dusting, washing woodwork, gardening, the constant wringer washer being carefully fed. One thing was for certain. WSEN's Old Time Country radio show would be on and cranked every Saturday morning. It vied for attention up against Saturday morning cartoons. I'm happy to say that while Bugs Bunny and Tom & Jerry did ultimately win my young adoration, I also grew up knowing who Ernest Tubbs and Tennessee Ernie Ford, and Roy Acuff were.

Family Home

When pop came home from the war, they bought a quiet, pastoral, safe, 62-acre rolling field farm outside of Watertown, NY in the hamlet of Brownville. The price? $5,000. It was an idyllic place. Washington Irving previously waxed poetic about landscapes such as this. It was beautiful but it sure wasn't Easy Street. The property had a lot of potential. In addition to its several barns, it also came with a "fixer upper" house *(to put it mildly)*. Their new homestead featured no running water, no plumbing, and sported a rat infestation, which also coincided with a large nest of rat feasting snakes under the front porch. *(deep breath)* "Ah, nature."

Evidently, there is an old wives' tale that says: "Rats are elusive; they hide for much of their time. But for every rat you actually see, there's a hundred you don't see." After sharing that little bit of kitchen witchery logic, Bernie would remind us that, "We had to chop the knots out of the kitchen floor to even it, and your father would take his .22 and pick off the rats swarming on the compost pile in the evening by the burning barrel. He'd toss the rats onto the fire." These were some of the heartwarming lovely stories of the beginning of my family home.

Obviously with a house in that kind of shape, there was much to do to make this house a home. Having a big Catholic family was a good first step to conquering the land and living the life they wanted. That meant, pump 'em out if you can, so they can help run the farm. Neighbors of ours, the Connors, had nineteen children in all. I can't possibly fathom having that many kids come out of my womb. Not to mention carrying them and squishing up all your organs. That means that Mrs. Connor was pregnant for nearly every year of her married life by the time she was just forty. Whoa. My parents didn't have that many, but they did have four kids in five years. And then I came along, a spontaneous gift from heaven after a nine-year hiatus due to problems with Dad's diabetes.

Fortune smiled upon me when I was 3, when my younger sister, Dorothy, was born. I don't really remember her birth or any of that time frame at all, I have no memory of my little baby sister until she was about 3 and I was 6. It's missing and I'm not sure why. I can only remember a couple things from my baby years. One is the recollection of a balloon clown doll that scared the bejesus out of me. Another is a pink bunny baby bottle that I adored and was my friend and lifeline.

Pop was a kind and quiet man but was not averse to taking a shotgun to a sick, injured or unruly animal. Justice was swift for a dog that killed neighbors' sheep or our own livestock. Such animals did not live long under Dad's roof. A tomcat of mine once came in from outside and marked his territory by peeing on Pop's leg inside the house. That kitty, too, had a short-lived life and an impetuous end. Unfortunately for me, though, I watched that altercation happen and then ran to the window and watched my meow get suddenly blasted in the snow for his tomboy sins. Thus is the way of farm life and animal husbandry. Ask anyone who grows up on a farm. It seems cruel, and it may be, but it's the lay of the land.

My father worked very hard at his day job running machines at the Air Brake in Watertown. His job always sounded so vague and mysterious and very difficult to me. Assembly line work I think. When he came home, Pop smelled like a combination of metal and oil and iron filings and mustard and bologna and wax paper. His lunchbox was like a shiny silver treasure chest with a rounded lid with latching buckles. It sometimes contained the rare treat for me and Dorothy: a vending machine candy bar. Mmmmm!

Dad wore big, heavy, clunker steel-toed boots every day,

even in 100-degree summer weather. I couldn't wait for him to come home, as sometimes he would let me stand on his steel toes and dance with me. I'm sure he looked forward to this coming home time more than I did. Sitting with my mom, listening to her day, recanting his, with a beer in hand at the kitchen table was his daily habit before dinner. Sometimes he would even pour a bit of ale into my special wee German stein cup for me. I felt special and got some much-needed attention from him during these moments. I guess I must get my love of beer from my dad. Sometimes, at the end of the day, Mom would also allow herself to have a glass of beer in her special mug too. They were social drinkers. I have kept this tradition although I have, at some points in my life, been more than just social. But surely, I digress.

After work, Pop would go outside into the fresh night air, away from his daily, noisy, oily grind and saunter out to putter in his serene garden. He adored nature. Earl Brown was a thoughtful, quiet man who liked his solitude and his plants. He would try to grow anything and he succeeded. We had huge field of a garden and cold cellar in the basement. Mom would can all the vegetables we couldn't eat during the summer. I remember picking miles and miles and miles of green beans. Evidently, I inherited his green thumb. Years later, when I was a teenager and was observed to be growing some "suspicious plants" in my room; my mother called the State Troopers to "ask their advice." They came to our farm house, and my mother showed the cops three plants that I had been nursing. They were about two and a half-feet tall, luscious, healthy marijuana plants. The police advised Mom to "destroy the plants and have a talk with your daughter at once." I was underage and thankfully, not there at the time. The cops left and, when I was present next, Mom and Dad sat me down at the kitchen table for "a talk." I, of course, totally lied about where I got the seeds. I did admit that I enjoyed growing them. I said I thought that two or three plants for an individuals' home use should not be a problem. It's a healing herb, after all, and no worse than smoking anything else. I told this matter-of-factly to my parents. Mom then calmly lit a cigarette and told me about the evils of drugs. Pop, however, took me and my plants over to the garbage can. He made me watch him while he cut up my beautiful pot plants with their dark green, saw-toothed, pretty leaves. The only thing he said to me about the event, with a gardener's voice made sad by the scissors was: "Nice plants, Marilyn."

Both my parents were helpful members of the community and it seemed that everyone knew their neighbors. Mom would often go for coffee, or have neighbors in for a cup with fresh baked treats from the oven. Mom's office was her kitchen and she was justly proud of it. It was a real farm kitchen, with a Lazy Susan in the middle of the table that offered you handy choices: spoons, sugar, salt, pepper and, of course, toothpicks for after. There was always a full pitcher of milk in the fridge; if you wanted cream you just had to pour it off the top of the milk jug.

Every day mom baked for us. The smell of fresh-baked goods steaming from the oven was as much of a constant fixture as the checkered gingham tablecloth. Dinnertime was firm. Mom tried to keep Dad on a predictable eating schedule to help manage his diabetes. Pop got insulin shots every day, usually by my mother in his arm, or by himself in his thigh, just before breakfast. He'd come down to the kitchen table and have a cup of coffee with her. If his arm was sore from earlier shots, he'd discreetly drop his trousers and give himself an injection in his upper thigh for his regular dose of life. I admired him for this painful daily reality check. He just seemed so resigned and stoic about it. I know I wouldn't have been.

Mornings had a couple of rules: make your bed when you get up and get the chores done first. This is the Golden Rule of all farmers: "You ALWAYS feed the livestock first before yourself." Then there was a guaranteed big country breakfast of eggs, bacon, stacks of toast and fresh percolated coffee. In winter a big pot of oatmeal, cream and brown sugar was added to the morning table. I learned about priorities by living them.

It was an idyllic storybook existence for a child. I would

run barefoot *(often at the chagrin of my parents)* and romp for hours in the pines up the road, climbing the trees until I was at the tippy top, making the trees sway and bend just a little under my weight, and that's where I could see as far as a robin could. I would pretend I was a bird. I wanted to fly so badly I would dream about it. My hands would get all sappy-sticky from the trees. I breathed in balsam and pine needles and I came alive! Climbing trees was one of my favorite things, and I was particularly fond of the willow tree in our backyard. It was indeed magical and I'm sure fairies frolicked there. I would scour the tree for treasures and often found cardinal and robin nests, praying mantises and walking stick bugs. I made doll heads from nuts the squirrels had stashed away. I covered their heads with hair of milkweed silk. I fostered my fairy-tale spirit with ingenuity from living in the now with what was on hand. Climbing trees and sitting in them like a wild bird was almost as good as sitting on the freshly tarred road out front and popping tar bubbles with my thumb and fingers. It was tar that boiled up like road pimples in the summer sunshine. Smelling the hot tar just made me giddy. The way it oozed when you squeezed the tar juice out of its pus face fascinated me. It was so pliable and ooey-gooey. The highway road crew had recently come through our country lane and widened it so that two cars could pass each other. I liked lying on the side of the newly paved road feeling the summer heat bake me and the tar together.

I also had an imaginary friend. He was magic, and I would tell you even today, with a straight and true face, that he was an Angel. Later on, he went away and I'm not sure why. I was so lonely without him that I replaced my longing for him with a mop handle with empty triangle mop head and named it "Ben Peacher." I would drag that thing up and down the road for hours, talking to it, running with it, making up games to play with it. It was my friend and we went everywhere together around the house, barn and yard.

I had a few kid friends out there in the boonies, and we would pal around sometimes. But most of the time, I was left to my own way to entertain myself. My imagination was great so it was no problem. As long as I was home by suppertime, all was well with the world. I was safe and the world was a happy, carefree place for me.

Around this time, when my siblings were older and independent, Mom decided that she needed to get out of the house. She was having a bit of an "empty nest" and felt that with less kids around, she needed more to do. She wanted a job. She was a good homemaker and the family could use the extra money, so she asked the parish priest what she could do for a job.

He said, "You could clean the church rectory and the sanctuary here at The Immaculate Conception. We can always use help. I also hear that St. Patrick's Church in Watertown is looking for a cleaning woman there."

Part-time Orphan

My mother got the older kids off to school, a sitter for my wee baby sister, and determined that I would have to go with her to her job when she went to clean the sanctuary and the rectory. I was old enough to "wait and be good" while she cleaned the restrooms, the priest's office, polished candlesticks, dusted the altar, washed and pressed the altar cloths, and dusted the statues of Jesus, Mary and Joseph. Waiting wasn't that easy for me as a 4-year-old. I found that I was even more lonely sitting in a big, empty, echo-ey church. After looking around quietly for what seemed like forever, checking out all the stained glass, brass and statues five times, I would start to hum to pass the time. I found that the echo was interesting and that led to speaking aloud in the empty church, which led to a song. *(Even as a baby, I sang in my crib until someone would come to get me)*. I started singing whatever tune I knew. I thought I had quite a voice.

"Where Have all the Flowers Gone" and "Day is Done" were big then. Sometimes, I would sing for my Mom while she drove to Church, with me riding in the back seat, standing and straddling the hump. Mom liked my songs. It was during "Up with People" days, and there was lots of pop singing in

Catholic churches back then. When I was waiting for her in St. Patrick's Church, I started to like the way I sounded in there, singing away. The priest who offered confessions also offered a solution: "Why don't you have Marilyn stay at the Catholic Orphanage next door when you are working here? There are other children there for her to play with and she will be able to be watched by the nuns." *(His rebuff made me learn that everyone is a critic).* A new plan was hatched. So the next day, I was dropped off at…the orphanage.

Let me tell you, that if you ever get dropped off at an orphanage, and your mother tells you that she is coming back, you desperately want to believe her! But you become afraid because all the orphans that also got dropped off there tell you that they also got told the same thing by those that dumped them there, oh so long ago.

"Who are you?" the orphans asked me. "I'm Marilyn. I'm not staying. My mother has to work at church next door. She's picking me up soon." The kids would give me a knowing look and then would say something like: "Yah? My mother told me that too. She never came back and yours won't either." These kids were practical and implemented a savage honesty that was heart wrenching, and they told me in a manner almost gleeful to break the news that now, I was one of them. I'm sure the kids were just trying to break it to me easy, or maybe it was their way of trying to haze the new kid, but it surely didn't help. Their candor sent me into fits of tears. *(I learned not to trust anyone at this very moment and am positive that my fears of abandonment came from this time in my life.)* Then the nun came over. I thought I could get some comfort from this woman of faith. Instead, this servant of God shook me hard by the arm and said, "No crying. You will upset the other children. Come sit down and be quiet and eat your breakfast." She gave me a bowl of oatmeal. Actually, the whole place smelled of oatmeal. There was white grainy sugar for it, not dark brown sugar that we always had at home. The oatmeal was already cold. There was milk in the cup set on my paper placemat. I poured the milk on my cold oatmeal and I ate it, with tears running down my cheeks as quietly as they could. The kids gave me my lonely first-day space. I didn't want to play with them. No way.

All I could think of was… **"I am NOT an orphan! I have a mom and dad."** I started chanting that to myself.

The good news was that my mother finally DID come back for me later that day. The bad news was that the other orphans saw that she did come back for me, and theirs didn't. While I did tell them the truth about me going to an actual home, it was a truth that they didn't want to see and they now hated me for it. When my mother dropped me off AGAIN the next day, none of the kids would talk to me. They distanced themselves from me for my sin of being able to go home. I spent my time sitting in the window seat, waiting for my mother, looking out the window. I didn't play with anyone. I can't tell you what the orphanage was like. I really don't remember anything but the hard window seat and the oatmeal. Every morning it was the same. "Orphanage oatmeal is best served cold and lonely" must have been their motto there. On one hand, I felt sorry for the kids there, and actually bonded with one waif of a girl. On the other hand, I disliked the rest of them for segregating me. My display of emotion was deemed "unnecessary moping." The inability for the other children to bond with me as a transient drop-off was not acceptable to the nuns. They soon told my mom that she couldn't bring me to the orphanage anymore. About the time that this happened, I had made one good friend there, but, alas, we were soon parted. "It's too hard on the other children," the nun confided as I left for the last time, No one thought to ask me or my one friend there what we thought about it as we clung to each others' reflection in the window. I would later talk to her in my reflection at home, much like an Anne of Green Gables moment that I would read about later on in my life.

I learned that there is one constant thing in life, and that, my friend, is Change.

Miss Glasier

It was September and I was 4 years old and at the tricky calendar spot when it was time to go to kindergarten or stay home for another year. It was decided that I was ready for school, and I was very brave as I boarded the yellow school bus. I was going to Glen Park Elementary in the General Brown School District. I knew who my teacher was, and she came highly recommended by all my older brothers and sister.

Miss Glasier was pleasant but firm and strict in a schoolmarm sort of way. I was a little scared of her. But then again, maybe it was all those drills that set us off. At certain points in the school week, we heard an air-raid alarm and were instructed to immediately drop what we were doing and get down under our desks and cover our heads. It was the Cold War. We were told that we were being watched and to do a good job. As a matter of fact, the whole world was watching us. I daydreamed a lot. I wondered about the big All-Seeing God Eye in the Sky. I wondered if I covered my head under the desk or not, if God really COULD see me and my Fear.

But I soon learned that there was something even more important than having you bombed to Kingdom Come. That was the Report Card. It was a BIG DEAL. There were three categories on the report card:

S-Satisfactory
N-Needs Improvement
I-Improvement Shown

By the looks of my kindergarten report card, I got ALL "S"s. So I guess I was satisfactory after all. I lived through kindergarten *and* the air raids. We never did have an actual bomb dropped on us, so our compliance avoided nuclear destruction for our part of the world. I was rewarded with Life, because The All Seeing Eye knew that I was good. Whew.

The colors of the autumn were riotous; red and gold tree leaves seemed like hands waving to us playfully from the outside as we were directed to sit erect and still at our desks. The wind whipped up a frenzy which shook the trees in time. The wind howled to us to come and play, but the windows rattled a locked tight answer to the winds lonely call.

Amazingly enough, we all excelled at music time! This was our class's favorite part of the school week and my personal favorite part of Fridays, in particular. Miss Glasier would bring out the box of musical instruments that we would be playing. She called it the music box and it was brought out only once a week. The music box was like a magical Dr. Seuss Box within its mysterious depths. There were bangers and clangors and boppers and thumb-strummers, pluckers and pickers and clackers and hummers.

We put away our lined writing tablets and construction paper as neatly as possible, and stowed away our number 2's in the plastic zippered bag with our name on it, along with the new crayons in our desk. Some days the entire class was bade to stand in a big circle. A magic thespian circle formed, and we held hands to act out "The Farmer in the Dell." We were prompted to sing: "The farmer takes a wife, the wife takes a child, the child takes the dog"…and so on down the line. It was a big class, so we had to make up postmen and milkmaids and plowboys and cooks and however many it took, to include all of our classmates in the song "just to be fair." I never wanted to be the Cheese, though. No one did. That's because, "The Cheese stands ALONE." After the Orphanage, I didn't like being alone.

Miss Glasier liked to mix things up from week to week at music time so that none of us got the same instrument too many times in a row. Evidently, she didn't want any of us to become a child prodigy on the comb and tissue paper so that the other kids would feel bad about their irregular tambourine shaking. When she saw one of us was getting "too good" on any one style, or song, or started to continue to ask for the same bongos or kazoo consistently, she would surely assign us something vastly different in shape and size and sound. "It was only fair," she said. Miss Glasier wanted us all to excel evenly. She wanted us all to be on a level playing field. We picked up our chosen instrument and looked to our Master Conductor to lead us. Miss Glasier had our attention.

(Miss Glasier reminded me of a stern Olive Oyl. I often wondered if she had a boyfriend and wondered if he would be Bluto or Popeye. I hoped it was Bluto. He seemed so strong and I liked his muscles and his big black beard. He was sort of a Super-Jesus, only tougher and meaner. And BIG. Popeye's arms always looked sort of weirdly disfigured to me. I didn't like his tattoo. But there's the rub: Popeye was a sweetheart and a nice man and he brought Olive Oyl pretty flowers for their dates. Bluto always seemed to have an agenda. He always made her kiss him when she didn't want to and Bluto WAS mean sometimes. OK. A lot of the time.)

"Marilyn?"

"Yes, I am paying attention, Miss Glasier." She made sure we were looking as she led us off and we all followed along while she bopped out a rhythm on the small multicolored xylophone she held in her talented hands. Our conductor led us in "Three Blind Mice" and "Taps."

(While we played, I remembered that my father always said that "Taps" was a funeral song. I always thought there must be a connection, that Miss Glasier was making a statement somehow with these two songs. I knew I could decipher it if I thought about it really hard. Like maybe we were playing "Taps" for all the mice and rats we had in the barn that we found dead with missing parts (some without those tails) on our doorstep. These dead rodents were from the barn cats, given as funeral gifts in the morning. Why just that morning, I had stepped over our black-and-white long-haired mouser named Patches as she was gnawing the hind end off what must've been a particularly delicious mouse. At least she made the mouse seem scrumptious the way she was crunching and purring and defensively guarding her meal at the same time. Better than being the lonely cheese though….)

"What? Yes ma'am. I'm paying attention. Yessiree, I am."

We were an ORCHESTRA. We were AMAZING. I'm sure we all had thoughts of grandeur and stage performance at the Spring Concert. I knew then that I was going to be a musician. I just knew it. I was going to be onstage someday and entertain the crowds waiting to hear me sing. I was kind of sad that we didn't have more Music class to practice our burgeoning talents. I'm pretty sure it was because Miss Glasier suffered headaches on Fridays after music class.

Cassie

Our next-door neighbors lived about a quarter-mile away. Cassie was younger than me, but older than my little sister, Dorothy, so she sort of filled the gap between our ages. She was also weird. Nowadays, when I think back on it, I figure she must've suffered from Pica like her mother. I had marveled in amazement as Cassie's mother would wet the end of her pinky finger and dip it into the ashtray, pick up some ashes and lick it. She liked it. She told us kids not to do it as it was bad, but she really wasn't kidding us about how much she enjoyed it. It was certainly bizarre to see someone's mother do this in front of us.

One day my Mom cleaned out her cupboards and I found myself the proud owner of a few old pots and pans that were too beat for mom to cook with anymore, and now they graced my toy cupboard with my plastic tea set. I was becoming a young lady and no one could argue with that. My dad was even going to build me a hope chest someday to store all the great things I was bound to amass for My Own House.

I loved making mud pies. I was damn good at them too. Simple Simon had nothing on me as a pie man. Now, I was no Bernie Brown in the real, "savory-make your own-prize winning-Mom pie crust-with fresh rhubarb and strawberries" kind of baker yet. But I could make an awesome mud pie. A dirt cake with strategically placed rocks and grass garnish that makes you weep and shout out "Brava!" And worm crisps. OK, so these were an accidental invention all of my own making. I am sorry to say that quite a few worms met their wiggly maker while under my watch.

It all started with me digging bait with my dad before he went fishing. "Let's go get some night crawlers, Bub," he say. We'd walk to the "hot bed" and lift up the cast off house window that he'd placed over the raised bed he made to start seedlings. Under the glass was a tiny fairy greenhouse. Moisture droplets beaded up on the window panes and moss grew in the corners. Pop would take a shovel and, with one foot placed squarely on the spade, he'd bring up about 20 earthworms. Big fat ones.

Teeny little ones. Pop and I would grab all the big ones in an old tomato soup can and he'd take them for his bait box and fishing trip. Sometimes I'd go with him to fish. And sometimes I stayed behind just to play with the worms. After seeing them crawl around in the dirt, I decided that they were fun to watch and I'd like to continue eyeing them, but not kneeling uncomfortably over the hot bed with the wood railing digging into my armpits. So I'd run and grab an old cake pan from my dirt dish cupboard and bring it back to put in a few worms to observe. They were interesting. My pop told me that they had seven hearts. SEVEN! I wondered if one got heartbroken, would it feel sad? I watched how they moved and investigated the world without eyes. How could they see? They really seemed to have some sort of sight the way they pushed their faces into things and obviously made decisions on the next path. Weird, weird worms. Then I was called away to pick beans or went off to chase a kitten. When I came back hours later, the sun had set and I remembered my worms. Too late. All my wiggly worms had been transformed into worm potato sticks. Worm chips. I was horrified when I found them. I imagined with horror and shame that they just slowly and painfully baked in the hot sun on that silver, metal, round cake pan. I had become a killer. I fried worms. I hated myself for it. Can worms scream, I wondered? But seeing as how they were sentient beings, I couldn't just let them go to waste. I decided that they would make an interesting garnish for my next fabulous mud pie. Cassie was there watching me make it. It was a thing of beauty. Then the really weird thing happened when I turned it out and said it was done

Cassie wanted a slice.

I have to admit that I was pleasantly *(but shockingly)* glad she appreciated my culinary artistry. We spread a towel out on the grass, I got a tea party plate and cut her a nice triangular wedge and served it to her. Worm chips and all. And eat it, she did. Yummed it right up. Just like her mom, she just loved the taste of dirt. She said it was delicious, and I believed her as she smiled a muddy grin. But then again, she would bite her own toenails, so the compliment really didn't count.

I realized then, that you could sometimes get followers, who would do damn near anything you asked them to do. Whether or not it was a good thing, though, was yet to be determined.

Avocation Vocation

We didn't watch much TV so I grew up using my imagination for entertainment. I loved to write and create for hours on end. In my mind, I was a newspaper journalist writing columns for the paper, or being a storyteller. I would painstakingly write one of my stories into columns and then replicate it onto several sheets of paper, just like a news sheet. My Scottish nature bade me to sell it to my family members and neighbors for a dime a sheet. I think I made a whole dollar before I tired of the hand-copying. But most of the time I was a famous singer in a show. At Christmastime, I would snag the special edition center pullout of the daily paper when it came. It had all the Christmas carols' lyrics in it, with several verses each. I would sit Dorothy down, and I would be her teacher, sing to her and teach her all the songs, all the while sitting on the imagined theater stage, which of course was really the top step of the staircase. But you can't stay inside singing on a stage or writing forever, so after my chores were done; I fed the chickens, pigs, dogs and cats, Mom told me to "go outside and play."

I so enjoyed our farm! The old farmhouse was our castle. Adventures ensued in the big, rambly barn, rustic pig pen, several little barns, a creek lush with cowslips and tadpoles and acres of fields and cow pastures.

I spent hours wading in the creek, dressing up my cat in doll clothes, playing with milkweed seed fluff and pods, and putting on my regular "shows" in the garage when the car was absent. It was mostly for my mother's benefit. I so wanted her to come out and see. It was always hard to get mom to take a break from her chores to come out and give me any attention.

There were always other more important things for her to attend to. Basically, it was "Mommy! Look at me! See me? See me?" And that, my dears, is how *all* performers are born.

Laundry Day

At one time, my family had several milk cows, 200 laying hens, pigs, a pair of breeding Dutch rabbits with their harvestable minions, dogs, assorted cats and resulting kittens, a fat and silly hamster, a vicious gerbil, an aquarium of colorful fish and a superbly singing parakeet who would bite. My mother's realm was a busy house full of kids, with bunches of relatives on Sunday visits and holidays, neighbors for morning coffee and a barn full of needy animals.

One fine summer day my frequently over-worked mother needed to hang the wash. She had just finished putting it through the ringer washer, and it was ready to dry. I loved watching Mom stop the tub and pick an article of clothing and carefully send it through the ringer. I was told to watch and learn but not to touch. In very direct language I was informed often that the wringer was a VERY dangerous machine. But it was also sort of fun, and if you did it right, the ringer squeezed all the water out of the garment so that it would dry faster. Mom was a pro at it.

For instance, I learned that you had to feed in the shirt, one sleeve at a time. You should never start with the collar as it would be too thick. Same goes for pants. Start by putting in one leg at a time. Never start with the waistband. Some things needed to be ironed after they came out of the ringer. Those were rolled into little bundles and placed into the 'ironing hamper" for the next stage of the process…or it would go into the Mangle. To "mangle" something, you would assume it means to crumple it or to destroy it somehow, wouldn't you? But here's another meaning. To "mangle" means to "straighten" or to "make flat."

My mom had a Mangle and knew how to use it. It was a

large rectangular machine consisting of a padded roller that heated with steam with a metal cover that came down in front when not in use. It was a savagely dangerous machine. While its name, "The Mangle" was fun to say, it was also ominous enough to scare someone away from ever using the damn thing. People had been killed. God forbid your hair or sleeve or tie got drawn into The Mangle, then you too were drawn in to the rollers to be crushed. I was told in no uncertain terms, to keep BACK from the Mangle, and to not interrupt Mom when she used it. She wanted to have no distractions she might regret.

When it was time for pressing laundry, Mom remained undaunted. Tuesday was designated Laundry Day. After washing and sorting the clothes to line dry or to mangle, she would pull out the machine. It had a pretty decorative sleeve casing on the padded rollers that Mom made of the pretty, cotton feed-bag material. The casing could be pulled off and washed and replaced. Then just pull out the machine, remove the cover, put the water in the steamer reservoir, plug it in, and wait until it was "up to steam." Mom could run my Dad's pants through it to give them creases on the trousers. There was a trick to it. It was "all in the lining up of the item." If you lined everything up "just so" and then sent it through The Mangle, it would cough you out a pair of perfectly pressed pants, sheets, tablecloths, curtains, pillow cases or bedspreads. I remember Mom sitting at it like Rosy the Riveter feeding in the fabric ever so precisely. Then hot padded rollers would deftly whisk it away to some Neverland of hot steamy ironing magic and send it back to you all smooth and flat and warm.

Mom was very happy when she sat at The Mangle. I think it's because there was some instant gratification to the huge workload that she handled. She could turn out some quantity of work with this instant machine. That was back when pressed sheets were a must for any self-respecting housewife. Everything was either rolled in the laundry basket to await sprinkling from the Tab soda bottle filled with water *(with the special sprinkler nozzle that dad had made out of a cork and a watering can sprinkler nozzle)* in preparation for individual ironing, or it was sent through

The Mangle. I learned from all this that "work" was a four-letter word, but it could be enjoyable, just be safe about it, OK?

Our kitchen filled up with a hot, steamy-clean heat when The Mangle was in use. The radio was on and a pot of coffee was at the ready to inspire her to tackle the piles of folded fresh laundry, which stacked behind her on the kitchen table.

When I remember this moment, I am treated to a smorgasbord of the senses: Mom's cigarette growing ashes while impatiently waiting in the ashtray, the sound of country music warbling on the radio, the smell of fresh coffee, and hot, freshly starched, cotton laundry. The steamy room made me sweat. These things all paint a fine and fearless picture of my hard-working mother.

While she worked, the rest of the wet laundry was thrown into a large, oval wicker basket to be hung on the line. Dad had made a helpful clothespin can by punching holes in it and threading through a wire hanger. When filled with clothes pins, it could be dragged along the clothesline at fingertip readiness.

Armed and ready, with loaded basket, Bernie went out to hang clothes. The sheets always smelled so fresh and even felt different on the bed when they'd been dried in the sun. They felt crisp and I swear you could smell summertime on them. This must be how wine connoisseurs can detect the hint of lavender or rosemary in their goblet. In the same way, I could definitely pick out the scent of mown grass and herbs on the sheets at night.

Mom stepped out the back door and headed to the clothesline, between the house and dad's garden. She scattered lummox dogs and skittered hens out of the way. Lately one damn rooster had turned into a real nightmare. He was a big Rhode Island Red, a ten-pounder if he was an ounce. He had earned a bad reputation for being mean to his hens, and all his girls had the bald heads to prove it. But stupid girl chickens will be chickens, and mean boy roosters will be roosters.

Mom set her basket down in the grass and started filling the wind with clean, wet laundry, lining the lengths of the line with white cotton sheets to flap in the breeze. Suddenly, the rooster had enough of this tantalizing display of feminine wiles and flew up to her and grabbed her shoulders with his talons and dug in. He clung to her standing form and started to peck her head, giving her stars.

What did this undaunted, fearless farm woman do? She didn't have time for this shit! There was too much work to do, and frankly, she'd HAD it with this particular cock's behavior! Undaunted, Bernie reached round behind her head, grabbed the bony chicken legs of this violent fowl and ripped him off her shoulders. Blood began to seep through her calico short sleeved shirt, but she thought nothing of that. Right now, she had bigger fish to fry in the form of an abusive Rhode Island Red that had bitten the hand that fed him! Holding the rooster, now squawking, upside down, she took a length of extra clothesline and wrapped it round his legs several times and made a knot tight. She hung him on the end of the clothesline, still squawking and protesting and flapping his nuisance while she finished hanging up the clothes. When dad got home, she told him her tale, and he went out and chopped off the rooster's head and we had an impromptu chicken dinner that night.

Here is the lesson I learned from that awful rooster:

Respect claws. This was one sharp-taloned fowl. He brought terrible harming love to his "ladies," always posturing, conniving and aggressive. Yes, this chicken was all these things. But in the end, when all was said and done, after all his drama had concluded, you had to enjoy it for what it was. Damn good chicken. Also, you just have to do the laundry of life, no matter what it entails.

Basilisk

It was a very hot, oppressive dog day of August. Dorothy and I had gone off on an afternoon walkabout on a bit of an adventure. We left the farmhouse and walked off the road, stepped down into the ditch, up into the pasture and jumped the fence into the dry, tall grass. We walked a bit farther and came to the creek, or where the creek was supposed to be *(and by the way, that's officially pronounced "crick".)*

The creek bed was now totally bone dry as we walked along the bank and stepped on and off the rock floor and sideline grassy edges. The cicadas hummed a rise-and-fall crescendo, a loud song of heat vibrating in the air. The flat, grey bedrock was smooth, almost like a road, out in the middle of the field. No fish, frogs or tadpoles now. It was this way only a short time out of every year. Almost as though the tide had gone out and had never returned. It was interesting to walk where just a couple of months before, we had spent hours wading thigh-high in the cool water catching tadpoles and frogs in our mason jars.

It was a world apart.

And then….That was when we saw it. A large, moving, rolling, green ball of writhing life!

It took us several moments to try to distinguish what exactly it was. We dropped down onto our bellies in the meadow overlooking this wild occasion to peer quietly and stealthily into nature's unfolding secret. Comfortable and yet fascinated, we paused on our adventurous journey to stop and study this bizarre carnival of nature. Our eyes squinted in the sunshine and we tried to make out the shapes that were coming through the hot, rippley waves of heat emanating off the creek bed. It felt hot as molten lava. What was this thing? This moving thing? This wild, odd thing?

And then we knew. SNAKES.

It was a squirming, twisting ball of at least a hundred, sexually-engaged snakes, there on the hot rock of the dry creek bed. There they were, in broad daylight, scandalously mating, copulating, squirming, orgasming, jockeying to be the next one chosen by the female. Or females? Who knew what the hell was happening in this outrageous orgy of reptilian intercourse. It was difficult to tell just how many snakes this mating ball actually contained in its mysterious, ever changing shape. It is hard to describe, but I'll tell you, it was about a yard wide, and ever-shifting and changing, breathing, twirling. It looked to be rolling down the creek bed like some kind of alien crawling monster. A weird, burgeoning life form!

We lay there in the tall grass, watching, mesmerized by this oddity in nature. Our eyes were sending patterns inconceivable to our brain, where the synapses must have popped and snapped trying to comprehend. We tried to make sense of it all. It was like trying to translate a foreign language on the spot. Or maybe like trying to transpose music into a different key instantaneously during a stage performance. It did not make sense immediately to the surroundings. We were transfixed by the enormity of this magical serpentine event. Never had we ever seen anything like this!

We would have still been there, to this day, gape-mouthed and slack-jawed until the next thing happened. Two sentry snakes spotted us. Their spy network had picked us up! I swear they "stood" up on their tails, like rods standing alone, to peer up over the tall grass and pin pointed us on their snakey-protective security system. We were on their horizon. I heard my mind say, "Centurion Guard Snakes!" YES. They were coming after us just like scouting gladiators on a mission! Up until this point, neither of us had been afraid. We'd been wandering God's green acres in peace and wonder. But now, terror paralyzed us.

These warrior snakes sprinted towards us. They were moving through the dry grass as fast as an African Olympic runner would've been racing to a finish line. This is when reality finally kicked in and the adrenalin started coursing through our child veins with adult protectiveness to MOVE NOW! We sprang to our feet and took off running down the path towards the barn. I yelled for my little sister to follow me and fast. My mind was willing my legs and feet to do what they were told. Dorothy, being smaller and more vulnerable, kept looking back. She was not watching where she was running, like the proverbial girl in the monster movie. The tall grass moved in swishes and jumps from the approaching centurion snakes cutting a swath quickly, deftly and directly towards us. Now, in every good horror movie, it is inevitable that one of the heroines falls while being pursued by evil. Somehow I became aware that my sister had fallen along that path. (*Here is where I would like to tell you that I, unselfishly and bravely, went back to help her, just like in a movie. But all I could do was motivate my own scared self to safety. "Every man for himself while being chased by snakes or zombies" was my survival motivation.*)

When I hit the edge of the lawn, it felt like I was coming to the Grand Finish Line. It was where the mowed grass divided the world from the wild, untamed chaos. It transformed the jungle to organized culture and civilization. Dorothy came up behind me, livid at me, for abandoning her to what was seemingly, certain and imminent doom at the coils of a real life Basilisk. We prided ourselves on our stalwart constitutions and our aching, quivering legs and pounding hearts.

Dad was sitting on the porch, on this hot day off, with a cold beer in hand, swatting flies in his chair on the porch. My sister and I spilled out of the field, yelling, lungs heaving, legs sweating and quivering with recent effort. We told Dad our story, with gasps of air and while trying to catch our breath. In his dry, calm and logical manner, he said: "Well, don't go back there anymore." (I can honestly say that the thought to go back there, was the furthest thing from my mind.)

I guess there are some things in this life that are sacred and secret and not always meant for you to know about sometimes. If you learn about them, you will have to pay a price. Now, don't get me wrong. I appreciate snakes. Snakes are amazing creatures and are necessary for the environment. But this memory and another have colored my wholehearted love for snakes into serious heebie jeebies

On a summer day not long after the snake orgy, I was helping my mother unload the groceries and hoping for one of the treats that came in with the bags. Ice cream on a hot day sounded great! But mom wanted to sort things just so, and told me to go outside and wait. I grabbed my current Nancy Drew and walked outside while reading and turning pages on this exciting mystery. I was intending on sitting in the front yard underneath the maple trees in the shade. I turned the page and also turned to sit down on the grass to spend some time in shady contemplation when I looked under myself the last minute before I plopped down. There…curled up directly beneath me… was the biggest blackest snake I'd ever seen! It was all coiled up and looking at me oddly, like he was just waking up. Of course I was about to sit on him, so I should think he was concerned as well. I froze and put my thigh muscles into reverse and then into overdrive. I ran into the house, yelling: "Mom! Mom! There's a HUGE snake outside! Come quick!"

Bernie was in the middle of putting away groceries and didn't want to be bothered. She said, "It's probably just a garter snake. Don't be afraid."

"NO Mom. It isn't. It's BLACK. It's BIG. It's alive! It's curled up like a rope under the front maple tree. He's fat. Has a big head." I said while trying to catch my breath and shiver the willies off of me. "Oh, alright." *(heavy sigh)* "I'll go see."

Bernie dried her hands on her apron and followed me out front. And there it was. Just as I said. She stopped dead in her tracks and said calmly, "Stay ON the porch." She turned around, went into the garage and came out with a cement shovel and approached said snake. She then calmly, sincerely and forcefully chopped off its head while it writhed and its coils flailed.

"Water moccasin from the creek. Something was obviously wrong with it to curl up here in the middle of the day," she said as she put away the grisly shovel.

There is just something strangely poetic, fierce and empowering about seeing your calico-aproned mother chop up and kill a big black poisonous snake with a farm shovel before your eyes. There is also something very creepy, risky and unsafe knowing that it was gonna bite your ass too. It sinks into your soul somehow. To this day, I appreciate snakes, but they are not a pet in my eyes. They are risky business indeed.

The Sampsons

I have a tolerance for oddity. When I was bored and tired of playing by myself so much, I would go visit the Sampsons, who lived towards the village, right on the way to church. In retrospect, I will say, that this was way before "Early Intervention" and common knowledge of the "Developmentally Disabled Adult" programs and awareness that we have today. I believe now, that the Sampsons were a functional developmentally disabled couple that had children. Two of the kids turned out to be typical but one was disabled.

Beatrice was a kind, old, daft, squeezable grandmotherly type neighbor lady who was a bit "slow." She was a good Catholic and went to the same church we did at the time. Beatrice would never come right out and ask for a ride to church. Instead, she would just start walking and hope that someone would pick her up on the way by. In a sort of a passive-aggressive sympathy plea, Beatrice would walk and sort of shuffle and look so pitiful that my mother would always pick her up, and Beatrice would always turn around and act surprised when our car pulled up behind her. Like she didn't know Bernie would be coming by at exactly 8:15 a.m. every day.

Other than that, Beatrice was a nice lady and she was kind to me when I came to visit. Beatrice's disabled daughter was Sandy. She and I hung out as friends and even though she was 28 and I was 12, it seemed right somehow.

Sandy had a room in that old comfy, crooked farm house of theirs. They had given her some privacy with blanket "walls" strung on clothesline to separate it from another room and divided it in half with her younger brother. Sandy and I would listen to The Partridge Family songs on her record player in her room. We'd eat warm cookies that her mother had just made and we'd dance to "Come On World, Get Happy!"

I was pretty good with being a part of their extended family, until one day of epiphany. I was helping Beatrice make sugar cookies in the kitchen by the toasty wood stove. They also had a hand pump for the water over the sink. It was a rustic and cozy kitchen, with cats under the table and a kettle of water always on the boil for tea. Beatrice's cookies were always so good, thick with granulated sugar sprinkled on the outside. She seemed to make them every time I came down. They were wonderful and warm and delicious and comforting, straight from the woodstove oven in the familial safe kitchen. That is, until the day that I saw Beatrice pick her nose while handling the cookie dough and then, without thinking, pulled out a big snotty booger, and without wiping off her hands or blowing her nose, she, without thinking, included it right in with the dough. Needless to say, I never ate cookies there again. OH HELL NO.

After that, it started to dawn on me that they were different, and I realized how different they were. I suppose it made me more aware of others with disabilities. Because of Beatrice and Sandy, it was easy for me to accept others and I learned tolerance and self-preservation at a very early age.

One really amazing thing about the Sampsons' house, *(besides being a bit like the crooked man's house, with the crooked wife and the crooked cat)* was the crooked attic. I asked Mrs. Sampson if she had any old clothes that I could wear to be a witch for Halloween one year. She said I could look around in her attic.

Now, to get to the attic you had to crawl up these really narrow stairs with high walls on the side. There was so much clothing on the stairs that you had to creep up it like you were mountain climbing. It would be an episode on *Hoarders* today. The wood creaked and it all seemed so very musty. The attic itself was more like a room that they used as storage. It was brightly lit, and it was full of stuff. It was like a White Elephant Sale and you had a pocket full of cash. I pawed around for several days up there, peeking in trunks, opening bags and boxes. I found TREASURE.

Find #1 was a pair of old vintage hook & eye pointy "witch" shoes. Black and tiny fancy old lady shoes that fit me! Mrs. Sampson even had a button hook for me to use!

Find #2 was a velvet dress with silver and black brocade top. I still have it to this day. It's about a size 2, but it fit me then, because I was little.

Find #3 was the best of all. It was a muskrat coat. OK, so it was a bit tatty, and there was a rip in it, but it was awesome!

Mrs. Sampson let me keep them all! My mom said that the shoes were antique, however and I shouldn't keep them, and that Mrs. Sampson "didn't understand that what she was giving me was quite valuable as she was "slow." Mom said that I should give them back as they were worth money. So I did. But she let me keep the dress and coat, and I was a fabulous witch that year for Halloween.

This was my first delicious swim in the world of costuming (garb.) I even wore the coat later on to high school until it died a thousand ratty deaths. But it rocked when I wore it in then, and those were some of the favorite things that anyone has ever given me. While I did give back the shoes, I would wear them and tromp around at the Sampsons house for a few weeks, just because the shoes were so COOL. The attic and the clothes filled my head with possibilities! I could dress up like anything! A hobo! A pirate! A witch! A glamorous starlet! I will always be grateful for that carefree adventure in Mrs. Sampson's musty, dusty, creepy, fun old treasure trove of a room. Junk from someone's attic can be an amazing treasure to a young witchy pirate. This was my first adventure into my lifelong love of second hand clothing!

I also found a nest of baby mice, a live bat, and a dead cat up there. They had been wondering what had happened to that cat. Yes, the Sampsons were a very different sort of family.

Mr. Sampson was an aloof man and full-time farmer whom I never liked much. He just creeped me out and thankfully he was always busy with sharpening tools, mowing, or plowing to have much of an interaction. When we did talk, he was a bit short-tempered and cruel. Once he told me that their barn-cat was having kittens. Would I like one? Well, I would ask my parents, but probably no, because our barn cats also gave constant kittens and we currently had plenty of cats. This is when he told me that he would just drown them. Or maybe he'd put them in a burlap bag, hang the bag on a tree and just chop it up with an axe or throw the bag in the road for folks to run over. Was I <u>SURE</u> I didn't want one?

I learned that disabilities run the gamut. Some folks, like Beatrice and Sandy were just harmless and ignorant. They hadn't been given the gift of the abilities or education that others had. And some folks' disability like Mr. Sampson's, was just a cruel disposition.

Post script: The Sampsons also had a son named Curtis who was always terribly embarrassed about his family. He joined the military immediately out of high school. Curtis kissed his mother lovingly goodbye. He sent her money but was never seen again. That too, says a lot.

Janitor in a Drum

Donny was my next-door neighbor down the road. We used to go adventuring on our bikes. He was about two years younger than me but a wild, fun, Peter Pan Lost Boy always up for adventure. He used to kiss me for what seemed like hours at a time. The first penis I ever saw was Donny Farr's. He pulled his pants down in the backyard and ran around chasing us for fun, and we all turned into screaming girls as we ran away from it. I couldn't help but look back while I was running and all the time wondered what the hell that thing was that was bobbing around over the waistband of his dropped swim shorts. One time he let me see it for real. It was the weirdest thing. So strange. I told him to put it away and we went for a bike ride instead. *(I couldn't help thinking then, how weird looking it was, and wondering if all boys had them. Euw.)*

We wound up down past the Sampsons' house, where we found a brand new dirt road that we'd never seen before. A couple of large dump trucks came out of it that said on the side of the truck they were from the paper mill. But it wasn't the paper mill's property. What was going on down back in there? We let curiosity get the most of us, and we dropped our bikes and walked back in to find out what all the activity was about in this secret place.

In the rolling beautiful pasture land back there was a cluster of trees with a pond. Frogs were aplenty in the water. But the strange thing was that there were big steel drums all around the pond. I'd seen cans like that before. They looked like "Janitor in a Drum" cans only bigger! There were at least a dozen full cans and some empty. It looked like they'd been emptied right into the pond. The pond was really different than any pond I'd ever seen. It was a glowing lime green just like the color of the cleaning fluid that my mom used in the laundry room. There were also a lot of dead frogs on the side of the pond and some were still swimming in the ripe water.

Donny splashed right into the stinky water to catch frogs. Something about this didn't seem quite right. I told him that I thought something bad was in the water. He didn't care, it was slimy and he was green and thought it was fun. He only wanted to catch the frogs. There was even a two-headed frog he caught. It didn't live long. Everything was dying in and around the water.

I went home and told my dad about the dump trucks and the color of the water and the janitor in the drum cans that made the water smell funny. He said that it wasn't our property and that even though the Sampsons weren't that smart, they could do whatever they wanted on their land and for me not to worry about it. Back then we didn't know or worry about aquifers and unsafe business practices.

I sometimes wonder now if Donny ever got cancer. I really can't imagine that he is alive today after swimming in fluorescent glowing toxic waste water. Instead, I like to imagine that he's a mutant Super Hero with Special Powers making the Earth a safer place to live in.

Artie

This is probably where I should tell you that I also lived next door to person who was a predator. Nay, not just dangerous, but deadly…and eventually infamous. Down the road on the opposite end of our street, lived a twisted man who tried to bait me when I was young. By the grace of God, I managed to avoid his plans for me and got away from him several times.

We had all heard stories in the community about one of our neighbors. He was a kid named Artie. He lived down the road from us on Shawcross Corners with his dad and his mom. The parents were quiet and kept to themselves, but his mom, Betty, would sometimes come and have coffee with my mom. Evidently, Artie was always in trouble, his mom would say. She hoped he would "grow out of it." I guess he had gotten in trouble for starting some fires. People thought he was just a kid with too much time on his hands. He seemed to be a bit of a loner, got into trouble on the bus, and would sometimes get off the bus at our corner and walk home on the long, narrow road to his house. I don't think he liked school because he dropped out when he was 15 or so. He walked a lot or rode his bike around the neighborhood

One time he was walking past our house. It was a beautiful summer day, and I was about 8 or so and sitting with my cat at the edge of the yard. He must have been about 20 then. He stopped and asked me about my cat and said, "Can I sit for a minute and pet your cat?" I nodded yes. He was walking home from Brownville and was tired. He didn't say much, but he plucked a bunch of grass and gently put it on top of my cats' head. The cat purred at the new game. I did the same, and we just sat and covered my kitty with grass pulled from the lawn. It was fun and the kitty liked it. Before Art got up he pulled a big fistful of grass and chucked it down my sleeveless blouse to be funny. I was surprised! Ugh, now I had all this grass down my shirt! He laughed, got up and brushed off his hands and started walking home. I guessed that he was just being silly like boys do, by picking on me a bit. I did like the game of covering my cat in grass, though, and continued to lightly tease him and my future pets in this way with that silly game. It was fun!

Artie was odd. He always seemed neat, clean and quiet, but there was always just something about him that put you on edge. Artie still wasn't working but still living at home. He walked into Brownville and walked back past our house for something to do. That must be why he walked the long way past our house instead of straight into the village from his house.

Anyways, it wasn't long until he stopped again at the house before he continued his walk home. I really didn't like Artie much, I don't know why. Other than the game we played with the cat, he always seemed sort of "off." He sometimes would come out and say the most bizarre and cruel things.

We had lots of pets and livestock at the farm, and it seems I was always holding or petting a dog or cat. One day, Artie was sitting on the front steps and he said to me, "I hate really cats and dogs."

"Well, I thought you liked them because we played that grass game with my cat."

"Nah, I just did that so I could put grass down your shirt," he said with a wry grin.

"I love them" I said, and I tenderly kissed my darling kitty.

Artie said, "I hate them. You know what I think is fun? I like to take two tom cats and tie their tails together to each other, with twine, and then I like to throw them over the fence so that they can fight it out. They always kill each other. I love watching them scratch and claw each other to death!" He laughed heartily.

I looked at him with wide eyes full of tears, "Why? Why would you do that?!"

I couldn't imagine somebody doing that! I couldn't comprehend the inhumanity or callousness. I never heard such a horrid thing. It didn't make sense to my young mind. I looked at him quizzically and with fear.

"Because…. I said… I HATE CATS, you little, stupid shit." He said it in a very mean voice. He looked me in the eyes, lowered his voice and said, "I hate kids too." He looked at me with eyes so hard, it took my breath away. First he was kind, and then he snapped and was cruel. I started to cry. My stomach started to do all kinds of flip flops then. I wanted to run. Artie just always looked at me weird and made me feel like my skin would crawl whenever he was around. It was like he was looking at me, but not seeing me. He was seeing something else. Even when he did look at me, I couldn't tell what he was thinking, but I knew it wasn't good. Even as young as I was, there was something warning me. Then Artie would soften, and try to be friends again, and I almost wanted to like him. He would be instantly nice again. He wanted me to sit on his lap, but I didn't want to. He would try to touch me, and pick me up, his grip was strong and swift, but I didn't want to be close to him after he said he hated kids and cats. He didn't seem to be a nice person on the inside. I can't explain it, other than to say I knew something was terribly wrong.

Once I told my brother, "I don't like Artie. He scares me. I think he's going to hurt me."

He replied innocently enough, "Oh, he's just having fun trying to scare you. You know how boys are." I did know how boys are. I had three older brothers who liked to good-heartedly tease me for fun. My brother thought I was just being a baby. Until one day, he understood. He finally saw what I saw. Anyways, once, when my brother was in the house, Artie caught hold of my wrist and grabbed me with an iron grip and said, "Come here and sit on my lap. Want to have some fun?"

I said, "No, I don't," and I started to wrench my hand out of his clutched fist and tried to get away to go into the house. But Artie didn't let me go. Instead, he flipped me upside down, and dangled me over the porch railing! It was about a five-foot drop to the stones below. Artie's strong hands gripped my ankles. My sundress was over my head, and I was screaming, terrified not only because was I upside down, but because my panties were showing! My mother had told me that this was unladylike! Nobody was supposed to see my panties or my privates! And yet, here I was, out of control and being held in a way that showed the whole neighborhood!

I heard him laugh and say, "What if I dropped you, and your head cracked open and I could see your brains?" Then he jerked me like he was going to drop me, let go just a little, and I could feel my weight being pulled to plummet down, free falling, then he would catch me at the last second. I was terrified that he was really going to do it! I just knew that I would be hurt, and soon! All the blood was rushing to my head, and I was starting to feel fuzzy. My blood-curdling screams sent my brother running out to the porch. When he saw my predicament he told Artie to put me down.

Artie laughed and said, "Awww, it's just a little fun!" while still dangling me, one-handed holding my foot. My muffled cries were turning into anguished screams as I realized that Artie wasn't going to do as my brother had told him.

So my brother said again, "Come on, she's afraid. It isn't fun for her! Put her down!" Finally, Artie hauled me up, squirming, crying and hysterical and before I ran off, Artie said, loud enough for me to be sure to hear him: "Your dad's got rope, right? I bet he does. Come on, let's go get some rope and hang your little sister in the barn. Just to scare her. Let's strangle her."

Right then, my brother (thank God) was my saving angel; he told Artie to go home and to not to come back again.

It was interesting. Artie later stopped by to apologize. He said, "I was just fooling." He smiled a chameleon smile. It was hard not to like him, sometimes. He was just a regular guy with a hard life, he said. One minute threatening you, the next minute nice as the guy-next-door.

I blocked out Artie and his malice. I went back to my child's life of play and innocence. We lived in rural upstate New York, outside of Brownville, just a few miles from Watertown. Life was good again. I dressed up my cats in doll clothes and carted them around in an old baby carriage I found in the barn. The cats didn't like it, but they tolerated it. The best part was seeing them sit, complete with baby bonnet, ears down, mad, yet, obeying me. I loved my cats. I wanted someone to love. I wanted someone to care for. Then the cats would wait for their moment of escape, and make a mad dash for it, lunging and bolting a hobbled escape across the lawn (despite being hindered with a long christening gown.) I loved to watch them, and would finally rescue them, defrock them of their foreign garb and let them go chase mice and rabbits. I thanked them for their tolerance.

I was still not afraid of the barn *(even if there were ropes there that could hang you)* because it was my safe dad's old barn and I loved it. The smell of the old wood and animals, the hay and straw, the barn owl who had made a surprising nest at the door, my dad's old Allis-Chalmers tractor, the secret stalls, the darkness of the many areas, the musty, golden straw-filled hay mow, the streams of light filtering in through the cracks in the roof, the shafts of light yellow and warm sunshine filled with the sight of seed and bits of hay in the very air.

One day, I saw another disturbing sign. Artie was coming down the road towards the house. He was kicking something, like a tin can, along the road as he walked it. As he got closer to the house and was pleased to see me sitting on the porch, I made out the object he was kicking. It was a puppy. My neighbor's new puppy.

It was dead. It was now being kicked at intervals along the road. I was horrified, and my throat closed up tight and tears welled in my eyes. I had petted that puppy just yesterday. The only thing that Artie said with a grin, as he walked by, kicking the dead dog was: "Your dog is next." I went to my room, hugged my dog and cried the rest of the day.

His full name was Arthur Shawcross. He was someone who knew us, had been at our house, went to our school and menaced me as a child. Later on, Arthur was arrested for the murder of two local children. Sometime previous to those murders, someone tried to abduct me. I known now it was Artie trying to bait me, the way he did to those future murdered kids.

You see, I loved to play in the pine trees and I spent as much free time there as possible. My Dad and brothers and I had participated in a "reforestation" plan on the property. We planted lots of trees. It was a lot of work, but fun to tromp out in the fields planting the seedlings.

There was one section that had a lot of taller pine trees already there. This was a favorite spot of mine. There were always cardinals and blue jays and squirrels. The ground was a soft, quiet, safe bed of pine needles and it smelled heavenly. I would meet neighbor kids there, and we'd climb the trees for hours on end or make forts under the branches.

One day as we were laughing and playing and just being kids, I noticed, from my high vantage point in the top of one tree, that a car had slowed down just a few feet away from us. All of a sudden, I realized the driver was watching us.

The car stopped and sat there dead still for quite a while. Instantly, hairs on the back of my neck stood up. The Peter Pan Pirate in me tried to hush the other kids to become "quiet Indians" as I felt an ambush ready to take place. I knew that we were being hunted. A predator was stalking us, somehow, even though I knew nothing about such things. I just "knew." The other kids didn't listen to me, but kept up their raucous play, swinging from the trees. They didn't have the sixth sense that I was developing. Unbeknownst to me, the driver of the car also just "knew" that this was a hot spot for catching children. The hunting would be good here, he thought. The car's engine started up and slowly drove away, but the spot was noted and marked for future reference.

One day I went to play in the pines on my own. The minute I entered the protected clearing I knew someone had been there. Maybe even was there still, as there was a "presence" I could feel. There was also an offering left for me *(or which- ever child was the first to find it)*. It was a straight, tall, foot-high stack of magazines. They were piled up neat and straight. I approached the mysterious delivery with trepidation. Who had put this here? What was it? I looked around and did not see anyone, even though I could feel as though someone was there. No, no one was standing on the pine needles or lurking close by. I felt like a skittish deer in headlights. So I walked up closer to let my curiosity probe the sudden and unlikely delivery. *[Now, today, I would call them some of the worst pornographic magazines, and that's speaking as an ADULT who knows what that means.]*

The picture of the woman on the cover was beautiful but bizarre, like a wondrous freak of nature. She had no clothes on, but more than that, she had enormous breasts. Breasts as big as the size of your kitchen table! Trembling, I curiously opened the cover and looked, delicately, but shockingly so, at the pictures I saw within those magazines. There were depictions of things that I never would have dreamed existed. There were pictures of strangely-endowed women and men, with their enormous bodies and exposed private parts. I had no idea before what they even looked like much less than how they were used in such ways. I had never seen nor even imagined it. I saw the sex act for the very first time that day. There in the beautiful, quiet woods, in my safe place of childhood fun. I saw women tantalized, teased, having fun being chained up and beaten. It all ran together with white fluid that ran out of a man's penis. It didn't look like anything I'd ever seen before. Was it real? The women displayed obvious pleasure, but it was mixed up with torture, rape, multiple partners, bondage, even blood. My heart was racing and pounding in my ears. My breath came in short gasps as I was riveted by this awful display. I knew it was bad. I knew I shouldn't be seeing it! But I could not remove my innocent eyes from this amazing and awful train wreck. I felt sorry for the women. But some of them looked as if they were enjoying it. I was so confused. There were advertisements of things to buy in the back. Strange things like horse whips, like those in our barn, which were used, not on horses in these pages, but on women. There were bridles and crops and so many more animal-discipline training things.

My mind was a whirling dervish of imaginings that I had never even known existed. I was a child of Sunday school and Catholic upbringing, who said her prayers on her knees every night. I must have been there for quite a while absorbing this sensual circus. My trembling fingers turning pages, my mind terrified, my body reacting in ways I couldn't control. There was a feeling stirring in my loins that I had never felt before. It was like my privates were throbbing as loud as the blood rushing through my ears. I didn't know what was happening to me or even how long I'd been there looking at this wasteland. It seemed darker outside now. I looked through all these graphic, savage, lust-filled books. Women as slaves, and not as people so much, as weird dolls to do things to. I got to the last magazine at the bottom of the pile. This magazine was different. It was filled with children, my age, doing these things or having them done to them. Some looked oddly happy. Some looked afraid and crying. A girl, who I thought looked a lot like me, was tied and bound and gagged with black ropes and leather. There were many strong naked men holding her down, with stern and determined faces, and they were writing all over her chest and her belly with markers. They were writing their names and drawing all over her skin! I looked at the child's eyes in the magazine. She looked SO afraid. I was now terrified for this girl in the magazine.

And that's when I heard the crack of a twig snap. Its sound broke the wicked spell. I realized I was terrified for ME now. I became aware that I had not been breathing. I stood up, dumping the magazines off my lap and they scattered all over the pine-needled forest floor. Shaking and hardly in control of my limbs or even my jagged gasps of air, my eyes darted around for the danger that was most certainly coming for me. Then I saw a man. He'd been hiding and watching me. I could not see his face, but I saw the thing I needed to see more than that. He was standing there with a rope and he was coming towards ME. I could see his trouser legs walking directly for me.

I ran like my life depended on it. I darted and bucked and ran like a rabbit. I was going under the pines, like in a hard game of tag. I zigzagged here and there in my strategy to avoid capture until I broke free and hit the road. But I didn't stop there. I kept running. I ran all the way home, not stopping, not looking back. I'd heard the story of Lot's wife. I did not want that man to catch me. I did NOT look back. I did not want to fall down like my sister with the snakes. I did not want to see him gaining on me. I could hear him running behind me for awhile.

My lungs heaving, my throat dry and cracked, my legs aching and heart pounding, I touched the grass of my front lawn. I ran inside and slammed the door and locked it, and I went and hid upstairs in my closet for the rest of the day. I did not eat dinner. I told my mother I was sick. She put me to bed early. I had a terrible nightmare. I dreamed about having large breasts and that I was in Puritan stocks, each one of my small breasts clamped with painful restraints thru the stocks while men took glee in writing their names on them. I knew I was marked. My reality was now knowing that there men who wanted to hurt me like all those other children were hurt.

I woke up terrified in the morning. I remembered all those awful photographs. I remembered the hidden man waiting for me, and knew he was watching my physical reactions to the material that a child should never see, much less be a part of. I felt so dirty and ashamed. I felt that I had SINNED. I felt dirty and bad. I kept telling myself that I did nothing wrong. Maybe I imagined it! Yah, that's it. I'm just a silly girl. It must have been a bad dream, that whole thing under the pines.

So after breakfast and chores I went BACK to that same spot. I knew I shouldn't. I knew it was wrong, but I went back to show myself that there was nothing there. I knew I should not be afraid of my beloved pine trees! I adored that spot with my whole heart! I gathered up my young brave heart and all the courage I could muster and I walked back down the road to the place I was in my dream. With earth-quaking limbs, I walked off the road and turned left and went down into the bank and came up on the entrance to our pine fort. I ducked under the boughs.

And to my disbelief there was that same, damn pile of magazines. But not as I had left them, all splayed all over willy-nilly in my rush to get away. No. They were neat as a pin again, all stacked up straight and golden and mysterious and waiting for me *(or someone else)* to find them and look at them. Straightened all up like in a doctor's office, just like I'd never touched them!

The hunter's trap had been reset. I took off sprinting with that knowledge, I ran back home as fast as my feet would carry me and gathered up my will and, even though I was going to get in trouble, I went and told my mother and father. My mother's complexion turned from a farmer's tan to pale ashen white.

She told me that I was not in trouble. She listened and held me as I cried and cried. My father listened intently and asked me just a simple question or two.

Then he said, "Let's get in the car and you can show me where."

I said, "But I'm afraid, Daddy!"

He said, "Don't be. I will be there. I want to see what you saw."

So I got in the station wagon and we backed out of the driveway. We drove down the road, past the creek, and on the left hand side before Farr's driveway, where the pines were, I told him to stop. I pointed to the spot. I would NOT go back in there. EVER. My father went in. He was in there for several moments. He then came out with the stack of the magazines. He put them in the back end of the car. He drove me to the dump with the magazines on the back of the tailgate. As far away from us as he could get them, and when we got to the dump, Pop got out and threw the magazines into the giant garbage heap. The only thing he said to me about the whole thing was, "They are bad books. Don't go back there again." There was no worry of that. And he let me sit close to him the whole way home to be safe. Unfortunately, there were more horrors to come, but this at least was warm comfort and protection for today.

About that time, the TV started broadcasting the news that a boy was missing. The whole area was turned upside down looking for him. And all I could think of was that it had something to do with Artie Shawcross and the pine trees. Shortly after this the news said that Arthur Shawcross had been arrested for the murders of two children! Ten-year-old Jack Owen Blake had been lured into the woods, raped and killed, and then four months later, Karen Ann Hill on Labor Day suffered the same fate. Karen had been visiting with her mother just a few miles away in Watertown. Jack had been found, dead, naked and with leaves stuffed into his mouth and body.

Artie's mother came over for coffee and cried and cried with my mother in the kitchen. The lawyers had plea bargained with Artie for a lesser sentence if he admitted to the murder of Jack Blake, in order to find out where the child was to be found. Arthur Shawcross would now go to prison *(albeit for a much reduced sentence)* and his parents would withdraw and go into a self-imposed hiding from the press. This would be their last visit out, she said.

I couldn't believe my ears! My intuition had been right. Artie had been so dangerously close. He lured those kids just the same way he tried to lure me in the woods! And they were now dead! They were horribly abused by him before he killed them. He played the game of grass with me and my cat, but he'd stuffed their bodies full of leaves after he killed them! I suddenly felt like he'd been practicing on me, I had been more at risk than I even knew. I was nauseous with the knowing. I SO thanked Jesus and Mary and prayed grateful prayers of thanksgiving for my life. But I was now terrified to the base of my soul. I guessed that I was supposed to be one of those dead kids, but my guardian angel had helped me escape and I had been protected. I had been spared!

I was relieved for myself, yet so sad for my kindred children counterparts who had not been so lucky. My nightmares started again. Mom tried to calm my fears, told me that Artie was in jail and couldn't hurt anyone again. I tried very hard to believe her, but it didn't work. I just didn't feel safe anymore. I was the same age as those same children at the time and I was nearly caught in the same way. I am VERY lucky to be alive. There but for the grace of God, go I.

Arthur Shawcross was tried and convicted and went to jail. That story eventually died down and went away. I tried to go back to feeling safe, but it was way harder than I thought.

Blessed are the Meek

Also living in the area was a family I'll call "The N's." They were an older couple who'd adopted two girls named Barbie and Susie. They lived in a trailer. The father was quite heavy set and didn't talk much and snapped when he did. The mom was quiet but nice. When I stayed for dinner she made mashed potatoes with puddles of real butter. She taught me how to knit and pearl on cold winter days. One time I was invited to stay overnight with the girls. I was about 10 at the time, Barbie 8 and Susie about 5 then.

We had a bath together and then it was time to go to bed. Susie did NOT want to go to bed. I'd never seen a ruckus like that before. The daddy rocked her and put her to bed. I slept next to her in a twin bed. I remember sleeping deeply because I was confused when I woke up in the middle of the night there, sort of disoriented. Something was going on.

The mom and dad were standing by my bed and whispering about me. The conversation went something like this:

Mrs N: "NOT tonight."

Mr N: "It's a good night."

Mrs.N: "She's not ours"

Mr N: (*heavy sigh*) "Well then, wake the little one up."

I didn't know what they were talking about but I felt at risk. Soon I could hear the mother waking up Susie in whispers. Susie started to cry and got up and walked with them down the dark hallway. I laid in bed wondering what was going on. I could hear the rustling of the bedclothes. Once in a while I hear a grunt or a "shush." I was now terrified. What was happening? I gathered up my nerves of steel and curiously tiptoed down the unfamiliar hall. The master bedroom door was ajar. The mom and dad were in the bed with Susie in the middle. She was softly crying and the mom was gently stroking her hair while the dad was doing something that I couldn't see. All I could see was that he was naked and his fat hairy butt was moving back and forth. I remembered with horror the magazines I saw in the woods, and it all came flooding back to me. Heart pounding I went back to bed and covered up just in time to hear footsteps down the hall. They had heard me.

"See? She's asleep. She didn't see. Go back to bed" said Mrs. N to Mr. N.

He was now standing naked next to my bed. His penis

was standing straight up which I saw through the peep in my protective covers.

"You better hope so," said Mr. N, "because if she saw anything, I'll make sure she never sees anything again." I'm sure he said it so I could hear it. I could barely breathe under the blankets.

I debated whether I should get dressed and walk home. But it was late and a long dark road home. If I did leave, they would also know I left and maybe come find me on the way home. I wasn't really sure what would happen if they found me walking home in dark or if I'd ever get home. I thought of Karen Ann Hill. My heart was pounding in my throat as I listened to Susie still crying and Mr. N telling her "What a good girl she was" and "How MUCH he loved her" and "Look at how much she loves her daddy."

I prayed for her a lot as I fell asleep which took a very, very long time. I kept trying to remember the Bible verse that said that "Blessed are the meek" and in my head starting singing over and over "Jesus loves the little children." I tried very hard to believe it, but those words rang very hollow and sounded like a lie to me on that nightmare night. I fell asleep trying to think of Jesus being kind to Susie. That, and I didn't want Mr. N to get me next.

In the morning, Mrs. N made us a big breakfast with Susie's favorite pancakes and real maple syrup and juice and eggs. I didn't say a word but I was cautious and watched everything. So very cautious. The girls and I played Barbie dolls in their room before I went home. In secret whispers I asked Susie what happened. Her eyes got very big like saucers. She looked left and right and in a whisper she told me that her dad did things to her at night sometimes. She said it hurt awful at first and she didn't like it but that she always got presents the next day. She then undressed Barbie and Ken and showed me what they did together. She made the dolls do a lot of different things I'd never even imagined that they could do. She also had a shoelace that she used to tie up the Barbie and Ken dolls together. To me, it felt icky and weird and made me feel a bit sick to my stomach just thinking about all. The world was such a bizzare place. *(I know now that as an adult, doll therapy is often used to bring out experiences like this with traumatized children. I guess the Gods were having me help these girls like this too...even though I was a child at the time.)* Susie and Barbie went on to inform me quietly but firmly "That all daddies did this stuff with their girls." I told them that "My daddy absolutely did NOT do this sort of thing with us. I couldn't even imagine it!"

Susie said, "Well then, your daddy doesn't love you as much as mine does me."

I knew she was very wrong about that.

Now that I am older, I know that Mr. N adopted those girls for a dark purpose. I don't know whatever happened to them. I have always felt responsible in some weird way for being let in on their dirty secret. I was too young for that kind of carnal knowledge and so were they.

I didn't want to go back to their house to play anymore. I'm not sure what I told Mom, but she supported me in my decision and she said the girls were welcome anytime at our house. We always treated them well, even if they did some disturbing things with my Barbies. Sometimes I would open my Barbie case after they'd played with it, and see naked Ken and Barbie tied up with a shoestring. I was immediately embarrassed for the dolls and dressed them as quickly as possible. Those girls still were orphans in my book.

One day, when my mom was driving by the Ns' house there was a black official car there. Mom remarked about it. She murmured to herself, "Hmmm. Social Services is there today." I prayed that Susie and Barbie would tell the man in the black car about the Barbie dolls and also about their own parents. Later, I heard that Mr. N had been sent to prison "for a long time" and "Mrs. N no longer had children and she was alone." I also heard the saying that, "Some people don't deserve children."

There was another farm family in our small town that I'll call "The D's." It was rumored that Mr. D had children by a couple of his daughters. It was common knowledge but the family protected itself and the girls would never testify. One day, when mom was visiting their farm, Mr. D bragged he used a bullwhip on his son Tim. It hung on the wall of the kitchen like a cat of nine tails onboard a slave galley. Mr. D said he often snapped the whip right around his son's neck to "discipline him" right in front of my mother. She was stupefied by his words.

Shortly after that, there was an investigation of Social Services there too. The principal and school nurse called Tim to the Office for questioning. Tim's back revealed whip lacerations and scars. All the kids were questioned. No one would back up the real accusations. Tim swore nothing happened because he knew if he did, his father would truly KILL HIM.

Shortly after that, all four of our family car tires were flattened in the night with each valve stem cut out while it sat silent in our driveway. My mother was also maliciously run off the road by Mr. D, and she damn near crashed the car, but didn't.

I think the final result of all this was that between Artie Shawcross, Mr. Sampson, the N family and the D family, I got a real healthy respect for Sociopaths who can, in reality, live just next door. These people have no conscience, set out to live for themselves, and have no remorse for their actions. I learned that there is a real element of evil that exists. It transcends and invades the safest of havens, and is an element that should be avoided at all cost. I don't know how it is created. I don't know WHY it exists. It just does. God has nothing to do with it, but having faith in something and having people who will listen to you can help.

The real reason that I tell you these awful true stories is so that you may be safe out there. Listen between the lines, to your children and to your children's friends. You should always do something to protect the innocent in this world if you have any possible way to do so. Guard them. Then let it go, be thankful and put it in God's hands. My mother wasn't perfect, and she never gave me the attention I craved, *(which is probably why I seek applause on stage I'm sure)* but Bernie truly was a good person. She meant well, had a good heart and conscience, and she sure was a champion of the meek in my eyes. She did what she could, and it helped.

It's a hard line to walk between loving the world, and being wary of strangers at the same time. But walk it we must. Trust, is a fragile thing, easily broken and never repaired. Live, and Love, my friends, but with "Shields Up."

Be safe and listen with your spider senses.

An Apple a Day

One fine summer day, the birds chatting loudly, sweet grass scenting the open breeze, I did not wake up. Evidently, I was sick. Very sick, burning with a sudden and unruly fever. I don't remember how, but I woke in a sick bed in my mother's downstairs bedroom so that she could care for me in the midst of her workday chores.

I vaguely remember the shock of the "alcohol rubs" that were administered to get the 104 fever down. It was climbing. Alcohol rubs consist of a bowl of rubbing alcohol cooled by ice cubes. Mom called the doctor. She told him my condition.

He said, "Do you have any phenol-barbital on hand?"

Mom: "Yes."

Doctor: Give her seven of them. NOW."

Mom: "Seven? That seems like an awful lot."

Doctor: "It works in these situations."

Mom hung up the phone. She lined up the seven tiny phenol-barbital pills on the counter next to a glass of water. She looked at them for a long time trying to decide what to do.

She was supposed to believe in her family physician's advice. The doctor was God in some ways, back then. You did not go against his advice. But that seemed like an awful big dose for a child. Like an overdose. She prayed. She came to a decision. She broke ONE of the tablets in half and gave it to me. In and out of sleep and consciousness I went. Now when I think back it's like that Pink Floyd song, "Comfortably Numb."

"When I was a child I had a fever

My hands felt just like two balloons….

When I was a child, I caught a fleeting glimpse, out of the corner of my eye…

I turned to look but it was gone, I cannot put my finger on it now…"

It was as it says. I drifted into some really amazing Technicolor fantasy netherworld of Power and Truth. Was it a seizure? Was that the reason for the phenobarbital? Or did it give me one? All I know is that I had an out of body experience. I remember staring at the ceiling tiles. There were so many tiny holes. Then the holes were getting clearer and clearer and closer and closer. That was when I realized that I was floating…hovering above my bed horizontally level with the ceiling and about one foot from it. I marveled at what the inside of the ceiling light looked like. I was being called to fly off and adventure. I wanted to go and see what I could see. It seemed to me that I had gone before somehow and knew where to go next….

But then I glanced back to the bed, and I had the shock of my life. I saw ME on the bed! There was a child, drenched in sweat, tangled in hot sheets, limp and pale and cold to the touch. It scared me so much to see me there that I rushed back to Me. And woke up.

Like Dorothy waking up after visiting the Land of Oz, I heard them say to me, to my groggy:

"You gave us quite a scare."

And like Dorothy, all I could say was: "But, oh the things I saw there!"

Christmas Eve in a Stable

There is magic that happens at the hour of midnight on Christmas Eve in a barn. According to legend, the heavens honor the lowly stable at that hour in remembrance of Christ's birth among the animals. Dorothy and I wanted to watch some magic happen and hear the animals talk. We were allowed to stay up very late on Christmas Eve and put on our barn boots and coats and walked across the road to Dad's barn. Without the sky blanket of clouds to hold in the heat, it was a frigid night. Stars sparkled so brightly out in the country. The deep, navy-blue sky set off the bright stars so clear, cold and crisp. We had flashlights and quietly opened the barn's big double door. It was a beautiful old barn smelling of aged wood, tools, hay, animals and manure.

The first to greet us was a barn owl who sat in its perch in the rafters. Her haunting face circled around. Its startling, shrill cry was like a banshee in the night. Scared the bejesus out of us, even though we sort of remembered from the daytime that it nested there. The owl was an apparition of sudden fright and a warning to watch our step. It flew out the door with a silent surge of wings and was gone as quickly as we were accosted.

We walked past the tractor and stepped on the spongy threshold that lead to the pig pen. The pigs were piled up together, occasionally grunting in their slumber. We stopped and shined the flashlight on them for a moment. We saw a mouse nibbling his way through their trough, eating what little was left from the piggies' earlier feast of slop. We usually fed the pigs in the mornings and took them their water and food. Breakfast for the pigs consisted of leftovers from last nights' dinner and this mornings' breakfast. Toast bits, egg scrapings, coffee grounds and old coffee were put into a galvanized bucket, carried to the pump house and topped off with water to the brim. Add four scoops of grain feed and you have a piggy's breakfast fit for a king! They loved their morning swill. Pigs are very smart. They would get very excited in the morning as soon as the barn door opened. They knew that their breakfast in crib would be delivered soon. They could hardly wait for you to pour it into their trough, and then they would stand with their feet in it and splash around, eating, talking about it with grunts and snorts in a laughing way, while swallowing as much and as fast as they could. They were silent now, at midnight, their bellies full and heating up each-others' bodies so toasty in their straw beds this Christmas Eve.

We pushed on quietly to not disturb any magical happenings and went to the stall where Nanny and Princess lived. Nanny was a lovely bay mare and Princess was a beautiful but obstinate russet Shetland pony. The horses were happy to see us but surprised at this hour. They murmured their greetings in their horsey way and inspected our hands for likely treats. Of course they found them. We had brought a couple of lifted cigarettes (without the filters) and a sliced apple for them which disappeared like magic under their velvet muzzles. We petted them and brushed them lightly with our hands and only spoke a few times to them to soothe them. It was an odd time to be there. The barn was so quiet. The horses were so still.

It was a magical moment. For even though the talking animals never uttered voice to our secret wish request, there was a reverence there in that place that no human could replicate. While the baby Jesus may or may not have been born on this night, the fact remained that it was a goodly place for a birth. It was warm. It was safe. It was alive with hope and comfort and food.

It was also Solstice. Yuletide right here in the barn. One of the longest nights and a cold one, too, and here in the barn, the animals waited for spring in all its green pasture glory. There were no stockings hung here on the barn wall, but fruity promises of clover and cowslips and timothy filled their heads.

Dorothy and I watched the horses breathe in the cold, crisp air and warm it in their chesty lungs and breathe out warm puffs of hot air. The world was a better and bigger place because they were here and that we were here with them. We kissed them on their soft, velour muzzles and turned out the light and let the horses go back to their dreams of sunshine and summer clover. We tiptoed back past the snuzzling pigs and left them to their dreams of found quails' eggs and truffles. We carefully managed our way back past my father's Allis-Chalmers tractor and looked up over the pump house door to the barn owl's nest. She was not back yet from her earlier fright. She was out and about on other mousey errands with silent deadly feathers. I closed the barn door and bolted it.

So, there was magic in the barn that night. The tales were true. The animals did talk but you have to listen with your whole heart.

Catechisms and Schisms

In times of need (whether emotional, mental, physical or spiritual) people have often turned to matters of the soul. My mother and father stayed together, but grew somewhat emotionally apart. Their kids were getting more independent and busy in school. The toddlers were under control. They enjoyed a relatively clean, organized home and farm. That is when my mother turned to her next love-Theology.

I get my love of it and matters of the heart, spirit and all things divine from Mom. Bernie was a wise woman, but only had a high-school education. She graduated from Copenhagen HS in a class of 21 students around 1939. College was not an option for most women back then. Bernice was, however, an avid researcher and detective lady. Given different chances, she was definitely college material. She loved to read, research, ponder, philosophize and write dissertations on her findings.

Mom had converted from the Protestant religion to Roman Catholicism in order to marry my father. Church rules at the time bade her to raise all their children, Catholic. She signed on the dotted line and was happy with it.

Now she had more time to herself and proved that exercise and religion was good for her. Her rheumatoid arthritis was bearable if she took bike rides to church every day. Her soul and her mind cracked open the Bible, the Holy of Holies and she began to absorb enlightenment. In retrospect, she should have probably gone into divinity school. Mom read in the middle of the night when she couldn't sleep. She read in the morning. She started carrying a rosary constantly on her person. She pulled me from public school and sent me off to parochial the next year. I would be in 1st grade there to start.

Life at this point in time for me consisted of parochial

school, *(an hour ride each way every day on the bus),* Theology, religion class, farm chores, at home and more religious training also at home. Mom took direction from the priest and the "Up with People" movement of the 1960s because she wanted to raise her family right. This meant having nightly rosaries with the family. This also meant a considerable amount of time on our knees on the living room rug. Mom would have us gather after dinner dishes and form a circle on the carpet. More than once I heard, "A family that prays together; stays together." We would do a whole rosary every night. Then it was off to bed for me.

She meant well. I know she loved us. Mom really was a loving, brilliant mother, yet she was a stifled woman. She was overworked and frustrated. So in her quest for the key to life, she started doing a lot "compare/analysis" sort of psychology on the Bible contrasted with the Catholic Church dogma. It was then that she peeked behind the curtain and saw conflicts in the church and something just didn't jive in her mind.

Being a good believer, she went to her parish priest to find answers to her unanswered questions by having deep theological conversations with him. When he couldn't answer her questions, then he told her to write to the bishop. When the bishop couldn't answer her questions, she was told to write to the archbishop. Bernie started correlating ideas and inspirations. She wrote and wrote. She typed all day. She typed into the night. Many are the evenings that I wished the incessant sound of the typewriter would just freaking STOP! It was always in the background of my dreams, as was the damn fire department scanner, ever vigilant, ever on the watch for danger and chiming in when something was amiss.

Mom typed in triplicate. She would send a copy to the priest, the bishop or the archbishop and she saved a copy; and the really good ones she also sent to the local newspaper. Her letters often ran in the Editorial section of The Watertown Daily Times. Her fervor did not lessen and quickly she was labeled a "nutcase." I think it was because people couldn't answer her probing questions of dogma and theology.

We went to church some more. I would sit with Dorothy on the wooden pews for what seemed like hours trying to be quiet. We marveled at the architecture, the stained glass and the statues. We sat in empty beautiful churches, while mom grilled the priest or Bishop on theological conundrums that only rabbis would entertain. It was during this time, I got my love of church buildings. I sat in awe of the architecture. I thought about Revelations and wondered about the stone upon which every altar was built, and I wondered what it would reveal if opened. Were there devils in there? Is that where the Lost Souls were kept? If the slab was lifted were the Dead yet to be raised, rise up from within? It scared me to think so. I continued to marvel at the paintings, the stained glass, the smell of candles and frankincense in the censor. I absorbed each and every saint's statue looking much like the Gods of Olympus. They were Gods and Goddesses to me, every last stony figure.

On special days for an outing, we went to "Dalton's Religious Store" and look at all the items there. Inevitably, mom would buy a new "Saint" for the collection at home. This week, it was St. Francis of Assisi. Last week, it was St. Lucy *(my patron saint)*. Next week it would be someone else, like maybe lucky St. Christopher. By this time, Mom had implemented a superbly decorated Catholic altar that any pagan today would've envied

Our home altar had a beautiful, silky, blue satin table cloth on it that my mom had made special. It had lace trim edges. I have no doubt that mom prayed while sewing it. On it, arranged very methodically, were candles, crosses, and in the middle was a gorgeous large statue of Mary.

There was a cushioned kneeling pew just in front of the altar made from a step stool and covered with a carpet square for comfort. Above the altar, there was a bookshelf with many other Saints on Display. Each statue was a patron saint for one thing or another. I'm quite sure my love of Mythology was born here at this mystical place of worship. To this simple farm girl, that altar had all the allure of Lourdes and all the opulence of a Roman cathedral.

Every morning, before breakfast and school, I was told to

kneel before the altar and say my morning prayers to start my day. It was weird, but I sort of liked the ritual and comfort of routine. Let's face it, the world is made up of tiny rituals such as this: Wake up, get up, get dressed, pray, let out the dogs, fix their dishes, smell the coffee brewing, eat your breakfast, let in the dog….in that order. You know, rituals make life orderly, like planting in the spring, harvesting in the fall. Rituals have order, and order brings a sense of comfort. The Catholic Church had order. They burnt Frankincense and Dragon's Blood at Christmas time and Easter time. It triggered an emotional response. The golden censers waft plumes of heady, thick exotic smells. At home and school, I was trained to love God, love order and to do as I was told. Kneel, pray, stand, sit, kneel, confess, pray, obey.

Lather. Rinse. Repeat.

Mary Janes

Today is Ash Wednesday and it got me thinking about ashes to ashes, dust to dust. A time to honor life and death confrontations… and of course, plaids. Plaid parochial school uniforms, to be specific.

When I first attended Parochial school, "Shopping for school clothes" took on a whole different meaning than it does to most kids nowadays. Instead of going out shopping with the student and their wish list of jeans, sneakers, cute tops and such, we went to Watertown and walked into Empsall's fancy department store. We bellied up to the counter and ordered the elements for my Sacred Heart School uniform. On Mom's shopping list for me were:

    Two white long sleeved cotton button shirts
    Two short sleeved cotton button shirts
    School plaid jumper
    School plaid skirt
    Four pair of matching or contrasting knee socks
    New underwear

Six cotton undershirts

Shoes.

Period.

Well, thankfully it was a smart Scottish tartan black watch plaid jumper, and at least the fabric was pleasing to me *(i.e. not scratchy)* at first. *(Later on they changed the uniform to a dress Stuart plaid and it just looked dorky on everyone).* The uniforms were plain old, dark, green, plaid jumpers with a white fabric heart shaped badge embroidered with "Sacred Heart" in red lettering. I admit it was a bit dark and ominous for young children, but the white long-sleeved shirts and choice of forest green or navy blue knee socks helped to brighten it up.

The girls' undershirts were a MUST HAVE, because the nuns said that girls weren't allowed bras until the age of 15. When I was 12, I started growing boobs. But I wasn't allowed to have boobs yet, so no bras were allowed either. The nuns said that it wasn't time. My boobs thought it was time. Never mind if you needed a bra or had boobs blossoming big or small or not. The nuns said that undershirts would be worn until you were 15. There was no debating it. The nuns also informed us that we would be punished if we didn't wear one. We believed them. These nuns would absolutely check you by trying to grab your bra strap in the back and snap it through the jumper before class in the lavatory. The sanctioned administered thought here was that not wearing an undershirt would entice the boys to some sort of animal lust. And, well, if we played with fire, then we would get what we got from the boys and it would surely be a sin and our own fault.

So, I immediately found a boyfriend at Sacred Heart School. Shawn Coughlin. He was a good Irish-Catholic boy. He said he loved me too. We wrote love notes to each other. He would pick me a flower. He was my saving grace. He saw that I was so much more than what the others thought about me. This is my first inkling that romantic love could save you. I have fallen in love several times. Some for the right reasons, some not. But the thing I learned most about infatuation is that it gives you something else to think of, and dream of, rather than your circumstances. It's the meaning of life at the time. It's the twine that can save you from facing an abyss of fear. Blessed diversion. Soul encompassing infatuation would be enough for me, that, and the scratchy scapular with the picture of the handsome bearded kind Jesus. It would be all I needed in life. I just knew it.

Now, if you don't know, a scapular is a necklace in the crudest sense of the word in Catholic form. It's basically a rough square of burlap fabric, sometimes laminated, always itchy. Mine was emblazoned with the visage of a most beatific, kind-faced and handsome Jesus. I was to wear him under my shirt, next to my heart. I was told to love him and love him I did. *(I am sure this is the real reason that many of my boyfriends throughout my life have resembled Jesus in some fashion. Kind, caring, warm and fuzzy Jesus. Unfortunately for me, though, a couple of those boyfriends didn't live up to Jesus' grand reputation.)*

Why did we have to wear a scapular? Well, the answer to that is "Why did St. John the Baptist wear a hair shirt?" *(because he was weird and had some sort a sensory issue?)* NO. He wore it to "Come closer to God through overcoming pain and irritation, of course." Or maybe it was because St. Anthony's Church was in town. Maybe it was because of the Feast of St. Carmel that came up every year there. *(Oh those crazy Carmelites with their bingo and their wheel of fortune to raise money for the church).* Maybe it was just in preparation of wearing a prayer cilice *(an undergarment of burlap or a hair shirt meant to induce pain and discomfort as a sign of repentance and atonement)* later on in life if we decided to go into Opus Dei. Maybe this was the reason that the nuns were so grumpy and mean. Who knows? They told us that wearing a scapular made you a better person and able to withstand the ills that life could throw you, if only you could withstand the inconvenience and rise above the agitation. Also I figure, it was another preparation for future relationship woes.

Here is lesson #1 in Codependency, my friends: "Love is supposed to hurt. Suck it up. Wear it."

Our girlish hair was to be kept "neat and clean and tied into modest pony tails or pigtails." The shoes, however, were a different matter. They were the one article of clothing in our very limited wardrobe that were allowed to show any individuality. You see, by design of the school administration, *(i.e. the parish priest)*, all of the girls in my grade wore the same thing. All of the girls had the same Black Watch plaid jumpers. All of us had to kneel on the floor in front of the nun with the ruler to have their hems measured to be no more than one-inch above the knee. All of us had the same white tailored shirts and matching knee socks *(in either forest green or navy blue)* from Empsall's. The socks were folded at a cuff exactly at the top of the knee. Same, same, same. Everyone knew, however, that the cool girls wore "Mary Janes."

For those of you unfamiliar with this term, "Mary Janes" are black patent leather shiny girls' flats with a strap across the instep. They're adorably cute. They are a bit fancy. But hey, even Shirley Temple wore Mary Janes! I mean, how much more wholesome can you get than Shirley Temple with those dimples?

BONUS: Mary Janes were SHINY. They were nothing like farm shoes! You polished them with a tissue and Vaseline to give them their glossy finish. You could buff them to perfection. In other words, they were the cat's ass of shoes.

I had often told my mom that I desired new Mary Janes with all my heart. Now it was actually time for me to get new shoes as I had outgrown my old shoes! Mom listened and took me to the local shoe store. I was giddy with anticipation! I just knew I was gonna get those elusive shoes! I walked into the store and went straight to the rack with Mary Janes, fondling each and every one. I decided that the black ones (they came in RED too) would be SO wonderful!

Black would go with everything! Yes, I thought red was a bit much and frivolously impractical, but I could see that the black ones were practical for my needs. Yes, the black ones it would be! I would finally be accepted into that stupid towney-girl clique at school.

I went back to sit down next to Mom just as she finished chatting with the shoe clerk. He looked at me examining the shoes, smiled knowingly and nodded and went straight for the back room to get my size. I sat down and eagerly awaited my princess shoes, just like Cinderella in the hearth awaiting the Fairy Godmother's touch of the wand. I could already envision and feel them on my toes! I could see myself twirling in my uniform and doing well in school! These shoes would make me an A student too! And popular! My worries about fitting in were quickly dissolving into shoe box tissue paper.

The sales clerk came out with several boxes in my size. He sat down beside me and with panache; he ceremoniously untied the laces of my shoes. My sensible, old ugly brown shoes were removed and set aside. I hated them for making me feel plain and different from the cool girls in second grade. The clerk could've thrown them in the trash as far as I cared. He set aside these diseased brown things and picked up the pristine, brand new box of shoes. He carefully took off the lid.

Inside were replicas of the same damn sensible shoe!

WHAT??? I looked with disbelief at my mother. Surely there was a mistake??

(BLINK. BLINK. BLINK.)

NO! She took my hands, looked me squarely in the eye and said, "This pair will last longer and you can wear them for lots of things. The other shoes are too fancy for every day. You don't need fancy. You need solid school shoes. You will get fitted for these sensible shoes. Your sister can have your old ones."

To me, hearing this was equal in magnitude to hearing that I had a terminal illness. My heart sank into the bottom of my stocking feet. All the life and all of the air went out of me like a deflated balloon. There would be no Mary Janes. There would be no acceptance into the cool girls table. There would be another pair of plain brown sensible shoes for me *(again)* to clodhopper about in school and be the farmer that I was and always would be.

I don't remember anything else: not the fitting, nor the walk to see how they fit, nor the sound of the cash register, nor the purchase, nor the sullen ride home. To say I rode with tears silently coursing down my cheeks would be an apt picture. I was silent. What could I say? We got home, and I slowly climbed the steps to the house with my stupid bag of leather-smelling, stupid, sensible, brown, new Hush Puppy shoes.

Mom said, "Go put on your new shoes and start breaking them in." I did. Then she saw me still moping and said, "Go outside for God's sake and stop moping." With an afterthought she said, "And DON'T scuff up those shoes."

Well, well, well.

Scuffing up my shoes was the last thing on my mind. Until NOW. I really hated those damn shoes. I went out front to the quiet, country road. I was sullen and walked deliberately. I went to the side of the road where the dirt, ash and gravel was. I thought to myself, looking down at my stupid, stupid, ugly shoes, "I hate you! I hate you, shoes." I was also thinking: "I hate you uniform. I hate you cool girls. I hate you long bus ride. I hate you shoes."

Then, nervously glancing back up at the house *(mostly to make sure Mom wasn't looking and didn't hear what I just said about her too)*, I peeked left and right. Then, when I thought the coast was clear, I began to do what I really, really wanted to do. I ground one heel into the dirty gravel road and ever so directly, brought that heel of my left shoe and placed it on the toe of my brand new right shoe. That clean, leather smelling Hush Puppy shoe that the townie girls are gonna laugh at me about because they are not damn Mary Janes. I started grinding the gravelly dirt and ash and dust from the road onto and deeply INTO the shoes. "I hate you soooo much, shoes." It was my new mantra. I was lost in the trance of my sodden meditation and the creative soiling of my brand new shoes. Grinding soil and dusty gravel aroma filled my nostrils, like a transcendental meditation experience of sorts.

That was until I heard the front door bang open and slam shut behind the locomotive that was now my mother, speeding toward me like a runaway train. I had never in my life seen my mother move so fast, and the vision was terrifying. The look on her face, twisted into a grimace of anger, was out of place on what I knew to be my mother's face. I'd never seen her so angry.

At ME. And she was coming. Oh, God, yah! She was coming for ME.

When I saw her flying towards me, I stopped my mission of ruining my new shoes while immediate self-preservation instinct kicked in. I darted to run to escape, but I was too late. She knocked me down, ripped off the shoe from off my punisher foot and began beating me with it.

(Now that I'm older, I know that she disciplined me with the shoes on which she had just spent good money…probably doing without something else for herself or her family… probably she spanked me for the outrageous Catholic school tuition…she might've flailed me for pushing herself to work so hard and having so goddamn little to call her own in the end…and for the futile goddamn effort and opportunity she was giving this wholly, ungrateful, wasteful child, who looked just like her.)

It was an impetuous, wild debacle taking place on what was once a beautiful, sunny, peaceful lawn. The cicadas lied that autumn was just a couple of weeks away. Mom fabulously lost her temper, and then after a while, she got tired from the effort and was finally spent from the drama and anger. That, and she must have felt that I had learned my lesson. She slowed and stopped flagellating me with the shoe. Mom sat back on her haunches, straightened her apron, firmly handed back the disciplined shoe to me and said, "Put it ON. Keep it ON. And DON'T scuff up your shoes!"

She went back into the kitchen for a much-needed cigarette, a sit-down and cup of coffee to cool off and to catch her breath. I sat outside and pouted and stared at the plain shoes for the rest of the day with the realization that I would be what I was. Plain. And no amount of dressing it up would ever, ever change things. No shiny shoes would ever make it any better.

So it is on this Ash Wednesday, I remember the ashes… and the dust to dust…and that dusty gravel. And those damn sensible shoes. I paid penance that day long ago, wished that I were dead, and I realize now, as I learned then, that it's really all in how you perceive the shoes.

Or how your butt perceived them. *(When I first told my husband later on about this story of my youth, he said, "Wow. You got Hush*

Puppies? I was never allowed to have Hush Puppies. I always wanted a pair.")

As I said, it's all about perception.

Edgar Cayce

Over time, mom climbed through all the chambers of higher learning at the Catholic Church, being led upward from priests to bishops to archbishops of the diocese, I think she even wrote to the pope. They failed to quench her thirst for answers and solve the conflicts she found within the dogma. She went to Bible studies, read, wrote, questioned, and this modest farm woman pondered the meaning of life like some ancient sage or Theologian. Relentlessly, she approached spirituality and religion with the vigor of a woman on spring cleaning day, rigorously citing passages and looking up word in dictionaries, much like changing around the furniture and washing behind the couch. She was THOROUGH. But as any student of philosophy knows, it all leads to more questions.

I was with Mom, by her side on this journey. Old enough to understand some of the quest, I was young enough to be home and involved more than anyone else in the day-to-day. I too, needed comforting after some of the life events I had been trying to forget. I was assimilating life from the parts I was given, as we all are. My mother's life quest became a devout need for making sense out of the Universe. She wanted to understand her sense of spirituality, her husband's religion, her marriage, her life. It was the existential question: "Why am I here? Why do bad things happen to good people?"

Her digging for answers led her to some interesting and bizarre places for information.

At one of the bookshops, in the self help section, Mom discovered the complicated writings of Edgar Cayce. He was called "The Sleeping Prophet," and indeed his work was an amazing phenomenon. He could help anyone with his readings. Basically, he was a God-loving psychic who would go and lie down on his couch, close his eyes; fold his hands over his chest and go into a relaxed state of being. He would then Astro-travel and arrive at the Akashic Records. *(Some philosophers and theologians claim that the Akashic Records are the comprehensive record of Universal knowledge)* Once Edgar Cayce had transported himself through time and space, he would start delivering Universal information, just for that particular person, from the records and *(do what we now call)* "channel."

Bernie read Edgar Cayce's works. He was long dead at this point, yet his books were still popular. His amazing readings had her intrigued. They were curious to me too, but unsettling and complicated. I didn't really get it. What I needed was a feeling of safety. What I got was a whole Universe opened up before me with all its secrets unfolding. Mom did even more reading now because the Church seemed not to give the an-swers to what she needed. She started searching elsewhere, in every bookstore, coffee-shop and sewing circle. And I was along for the ride. For the most part, I was OK with it. I enjoy Theology to this day. I enjoy learning about other religions and the way people find their spirituality in all its forms.

Even more fun for me was that I got to have my mother all to myself and this made me feel special. She would love to have me sing for her on our trips out and about. Getting into the car, I would stand up in the back seat of the Chevy Nomad station wagon, straddling the hump and she would make requests. It was the 60's and Peter, Paul and Mary were a big thing. I had a knack for remembering words to songs and keep a tune. I could belt out "Till there was You" by the Beatles. Mom seemed to enjoy my company and I soaked it up. She played her guitar and sang in the afternoons. I liked that. I wanted to please her and be like her somehow.

One day she asked me to sit down in front of a blank sheet of white paper. She said, "We're going to play a game, you like to draw, right? I want you to take this pencil, close your eyes and don't think of anything, but just let the pencil draw on the paper. When you think it's done, you can open your eyes. It's called automatic writing. But let's pray first." So we prayed.

There was something in the prayer about my pure soul being able to receive the heavenly answers. It was suddenly evident to me that something was going to come through me. I liked to draw. But I'd never done anything like this before. It was gonna be fun! I closed my eyes and started drawing in this otherworldly way. A feeling of my arm stiffening and becoming led by some string became apparent. My pencil seemed to be drawn in several directions. I wondered what it was drawing, but I kept my eyes tight shut and just let my "fingers do the walking" as it were. Something was happening. We did this several times and the drawings that came from it were ethereal indeed. She also had me try some automatic writing, because I was learning my letters. The writings that came out were not spaced but all ran into each other. Kind of like where letters run altogether in Morse code and you have to figure out where the spaces were afterward, to make sense of the information. There was a lot of the word "God" in them, but I didn't really get what they were saying. Mom whisked the drawings away from me soon after I finished with them, and she looked at them over coffee to try to translate them. The writings my pencil had done were kind of rambley, and I suppose she needed time to figure them out.

The last drawing I did spooked her when put alongside the others. I know now that my knowledge of Theology and Dogma was beyond what a seven year old would be. Then one time mom informed me that this would be my last drawing, so we prayed that "God, if there is something you want to tell us, say it now."

I took the pencil as usual, and shut my eyes. The pencil glided in its familiar manner, yet this time it created one drawing in a single line from start to finish. I was never led to lift the point off the paper. I felt the pencil make a perfect circle. The pencil seemed to go all over the page. And then, it was done. The pencil just stopped. I opened my eyes. I saw a single line drawing that any accomplished artist would be proud of. It was a drawing of a Being. It had a single head, broad shoulders and strong arms, a sturdy body with three legs. Set firmly on the ground.

My mother looked at it with a puzzled face and asked me, "What do you think it means?"

I glanced at it and in a voice that was not really mine, said that it was "The Holy Trinity. One Godhead, the Three, the Father, Son and Holy Spirit. It has legs planted firmly in the ground and arms strong enough to carry you. It sees everything. It is omnipotent."

Now, even though I had started catechism, I am quite sure now, that I didn't know the word "Omnipotent" at the time. I saw a look flash across her face that told me that my frank and inspired interpretation freaked her out. She then put away the writings, told me to forget about them and that we were not going to play that game anymore. This was the first inkling I had special talents.

What I learned from this may be what a misunderstood Superhero feels like without his mask. Or maybe what he felt like, after changing back out of the costume in the telephone booth. Empowerment is weird and extremely personal.

The Source

There is a Universal Law. If you ask questions, you will get answers. They may not be the right answers or the answers that you want to hear, but the Law of Attraction states that whatever you dwell on you will receive by manifestation.

Mom wanted answers so much that she brought home another game for us to try. It was a board game receiving quite a hoopla at the time, called Ouija. She brought it out of its box and read the directions. She laid it out on the kitchen table. We placed our fingertips on it "just so" and asked a question. The cursor began to move. I was amazed at how fast it went, and we trailed along behind it. I did not have the capacity to spell that fast. My mom wrote it all down as it happened and started to look a bit worried. I don't think she got the answer that she wanted. No. Not at all. Because after the cursor was done spelling out a long sentence and mom knew what it was, she said, "That's enough of that!" She said a prayer, told me to go wash my hands with hot soapy water while she picked up the brand-new game, walked out to the burning barrel and set it on fire. The brand new game. Weird. I think she did about seven rosaries later on that day, and I wasn't sure why. *(Now as an adult, I believe the Ouija board is not a "game." I feel it's spiritually like leaving your door unlocked in NYC. Anyone is free to walk in. And that's not always a good thing. As a matter of fact, it can be downright dangerous).* Who knew then though? Shortly after this, strange things began happening at our house. Like vampires in stories of old, spirits have to be invited in and, well, without our ultimate knowledge, it seems we'd unknowingly opened the lid on Pandora's Box.

I grew terrified of staying in my room, going in it, playing in it by myself and most definitely sleeping in it. I was convinced that "something" was in the room, although I couldn't see it. I definitely could feel it. Whatever it was, it tended to hide in the closet. I hated going into the closet. That particular closet had fabric curtains and occasionally the curtains would flutter, even though there was no breeze in the room and no window open. It reminded me to be afraid, very afraid. At night after my bedtime story, I said my prayers kneeling on the side of the bed. I would jump in bed, and cover up. My dad would usually tuck me in. All was well, until Pop was gone back downstairs and he shut that damn hall light off.

Then it started….The jiggling of the doorknob. The whispers thru the key hole. The tremulously shaking bed.

I would scream and Daddy would come upstairs. I'd tell him of my fears. He would tell me it was nothing. Then he would dutifully check the closet, check under the bed, and check all around the room. Nothing. I would ask him to read me another story. No, it was my bedtime. He would leave. It all would repeat. It was the scratching at the door, and the demonic whispering of the hateful things in the crack of the door, and the turning of the door knob that scared me the most. I would then gather up all my courage and bolt out of the bed and careen thru the door, rather than be trapped in my room. I would tip toe downstairs and eventually appear downstairs about an hour later and beg to stay up with everyone else. It was the "safety in numbers thing" to me. I did NOT want to be alone up there. No. I had to be escorted back to bed. Sometimes after putting me to bed several times, I would just decide to sleep on the stairs until they all came to bed, rather than face the demon that plagued me in my room, whatever IT was. After many nights of this, the night terrors started. I would awaken screaming. Nightmares hounded me, and no night brought peace

I distinctly remember waking up one night in mid-scream while standing in my room. I was in my nightgown with the overhead light on and my parents and siblings were standing around trying to rouse me from my screaming trance. Everyone was scratching their bewildered heads and looking at me with sleepy faces. Dad resorted to thumping me lightly on the head with a book, which finally broke the spell, and I woke up in mid-scream. I was trapped in the dream world. I could not even awaken from my nightmares. *(Sometimes, even now, though it is rare, I still have a hard time awakening from a nightmare in which I seem to be trapped. When this happens, I have briefed my sleep-mates that if I should have a nightmare, to PLEASE rouse me as I become locked within my dreams and cannot waken myself. I even "know" I'm sleeping at the time, and I can hear my sleeping body trying to scream, but I can't rouse myself to wake. These events are called "Night Terrors.")*

I learned that fear is very malleable. Whether it's experienced from a next-door neighbor who wants to kill you, or if it's come from somewhere ethereal, fear goes bone deep and can last a lifetime if left untreated.

Visits and Visitations

When you immerse yourself in a subject matter, it comes alive. My Mom started having dreams, visions and nightmares. Without a lot of close friends around, she would tell me her dreams in the morning. I have since gotten very good at interpreting dreams. Dreams are one thing. Visitations are another.

Mom once told me she had a visitation from Mary, the Mother of God. What was it? Could it have been a lucid dream or maybe even a spiritual moment? Maybe could it have been some sort of stress-relief valve or schizophrenic vision? Maybe she really did communicate with Mary like those who have experienced something like the Miracle at Lourdes? I don't know. Mom has since passed but at the time she envisioned it. She woke to the distinct smell of roses one night. She got up to see where the strong scent originated. She walked out into the hallway of my Aunt Lucy's house where she was staying then for a bit to help her after Uncle Fritz died.

Mom was greeted by a glowing light of a room lit by some sort heavenly techie and a long processional of saints, all of whom carried roses in their arms as they walked by her. The scent of the flowers was rich and heady. The saints did not particularly note her as they serenely floated past her, but only passed by with calm, angelic sweet faces in the hallway. The last to float past her was Mary, the Mother of God. She carried the biggest bouquet of roses. She wore brilliant white robes and a gorgeous mantle of white. As she passed by my mother, standing quiet and still as the holy parade passed by. Mary smiled a sweet smile at her. Then all the saints and the Holy Mother magically disappeared into the nighttime, and it was dark once again. Yet, the sweet smell of roses remained.

This was a beautiful vision and I remember how vividly she beamed as he described it. She recounted the whole thing which was very real to her. Her face was calm and full of beatific wonder.

Mom also had nightmares. Those she told me about. It seemed that somehow, I had become a sounding board and a counselor at my ripe old age of 7. The nightmare I remember her telling of the most was this:

She was accosted by a demon. He physically took her body and with some sort of comic illusion, stuffed her down into a long-necked bottle. She said it was an excruciating experience. While trapped within this new glass prison, the demon took the bottle and threw it across the room and the bottle hit the wall and smashed into a thousand bits. Mom said she woke up then on the floor across the room, far away from her bed. It was also so vivid to her that when she recounted it to me, she was again seemingly scared for her life… and her soul.

As a child hearing all this, being immersed in all this, I felt akin to it somehow. It made sense to me, all this spiritual desire, these visions and dreams. I mean, at the time there were miracles still happening around the globe with the Lady of Lourdes. There were also sightings of Jesus appearing in snowdrifts on the mountain. These were not Photoshop pictures of miracles and oddities, but real sightings! Miracles were happening. And, by God, they were also happening in our kitchen at the farm-house!

I actually experienced one of these moments one sunny day. We were sitting at the kitchen table, and a circle of light appeared in front of mom and me. I now know it was an Orb, but at the time we both sat in stunned silence as this globe of light floated there. Then, to our wondering wide eyes, it started moving. It floated up towards the molding of the ceiling and then made a path traveling all around our whole long rectangular kitchen and then circled back to settle, once again in front of us, where it hovered and then dropped down into her coffee cup and disappeared. After we regained some normal breathing patterns after observing the ghostly vision, we checked in her cup. We dumped it in the sink and checked. There was nothing in there besides coffee. Bernie was totally convinced it was the Holy Eucharist that we had been visited by. Yes, God's body in a wafer traveling around our kitchen. And, well, I have to agree with her, it really DID look like that! All except for that floating part.

I learned that I would believe what I saw and felt, even if no one else would ever believe me.

The Devil is Left-Handed

Needless to say, the combination of not sleeping at night, and days full of early-morning chores (5:30am) followed by an hour long bus ride to parochial school (Sacred Heart Elementary where I was an "outsider" because I wasn't from the city) made for a much stressed childhood. I was bused in from "the boonies," and ostracized by the city kids for being different. Then I came home from school to my family and all its religious fervor and tried to sleep with the demon in the closet. After almost getting to be a statistic of a serial killer and now this demon in my room...frankly, I didn't like being alone anymore. As a matter of fact, I hated it. All my adult life I have been trying to work out that issue.

Soon I got some more bad news and found out that God did not take kindly to me being Left Handed. The nuns were very clear on this. My left hand was EVIL. I was not to learn how to write with it nor give it any quarter. I was to write with my right hand and my right hand alone. I did not agree with this new law at all because I enjoyed writing with my LEFT hand. Here is where the rebel in me started to raise her wild head.

The nun would slap me and take the pencil out of my left hand or sometimes she would rap my knuckles with the sharp blade side of a ruler, then put the pencil in my RIGHT hand and encourage me to learn my cursive letters with it. Oh, I would try for them, really I would. But it wasn't long before the activity would feel stilted and awkward and the cursive circles would look horrible. So as soon as the nun and her flowing black habit had floated past me, like a judgmental apparition, I would switch the pencil back to my left hand again. I was often caught making marvelous and beautiful circles with my randy left hand. And the punishment was swift. Repeat the spankings and cuffings. Repeat the pencil stuffed back in the right hand.

Oh, I was a willful child. They said I was going to Hell. They made sure I knew it too.

I then decided that if going to Hell meant that the Devil let you write with your left hand, that maybe it was better than getting beaten by nuns and writing with your right hand. I felt like I was already in Hell and no amount of praying could get me out of there.

I hated parochial school. I hated the nuns. I hated my classmates. I hated everything about it except for the library and the sanctuary. I adored the library. Sister Mary Bertha was sweet. If you asked her how to spell a word, she would say, "Go look it up." *(Well, I ask you, how do you look up something you can't spell?)* No matter. The library was quiet and you could do what you wanted and not get slapped by nuns, or pestered by demons, nor chased by killers! And the library was huge and filled with all kinds of things to read and smelled like a safe place in the stacks. The nuns left you alone in there. They wanted you to be quiet. And as long as you were quiet, you could stay in there a long time. I learned to be very quiet. As a matter of fact, I would say I was stealthy.

The church sanctuary was great because it meant that we could get out of class from the evil nuns for awhile and that was a good thing. One teacher, Sister Mary Thomas, was quite a violent person. She would discipline the boys *(who were class clowns)* by picking them up by their hair, shaking them, and sometimes, throwing them against the chalkboard. Sister Mary Thomas would make these adolescent boys cry in front of the girls. She would also make us write things 500 times on a whim. Sister Mary Thomas was a servant of the Lord.

The nuns said that I had to be in a club for some extracurricular activity so I picked chorus. I loved singing and learning new music. It was good to be snugged up safe in the middle of a big group. I liked that. The musical sounds soothed me.

Then the nuns said that I had to choose another group for community service. One that fit my schedule was "The Legion of Mary Club." It was an after-school group that gathered together to pray a novena and then make crafts in between rosaries. We also did newspaper and can drives for the poor. It was a feel-good group and we'd also visit shut-ins and bring them stuff.

It was then that Mary, the Mother of God, told me a great secret. She personally illuminated to me in my prayers that Sister Mary Thomas was not meek and mild and also not her servant. I dared not tell anyone about having a personal relationship with the Mother of God, because, well, who was I, anyway? I was only a disobedient child who wrote with the devil's claw.

Sister Mary Thomas was in charge, and I had better mind her, by God.

I started sleeping on the bus both on the hour ride to and from school. This was good because it made up for my lost sleep time with all that demon-goblin nonsense in my room. Hell, I was not going to let down my guard and actually fall asleep at night and give that thing an opportunity to let it get me. No, sirree.

The nightmares continued. The goblin continued his nighttime terror pace. The nuns did their worst during the day-time. The school kids terrorized me at recess. And still I tried to be a kid.

When left to myself, my creativity knew no bounds. While ostracized at school and made to feel stupid and ugly there, I was the one with the ideas for the games, contests and stories at home with my sister and next door neighbors. I still loved the barn and all the animals, but it was hard for Mom when I was gone during the day.

Bernie was still having problems. Maybe it was the fact that she'd had a total hysterectomy and no one back then believed in hormone replacement therapy. Maybe it was that Mom was just too smart to be stuck out in the country with no one to talk to and no one smart enough to challenge her during the day. Maybe she was indeed, "trapped in the bottle of her life" like her dream.

My Dad was smart but he was gone all day and then came home to work on the farm and yard and garden. He was also a quiet man who listened more than he spoke. And Pop didn't seem to understand Mom and her zealous nature anymore. He and she were drifting apart. He was quiet. She was chatty. There was no big love swoon, only shared years of loyalty and service. There was love, but no passion. There was also honest commitment. Dad said his prayers on his knees, by the side of his bed, every night of his life.

I guess what I learned from all this was that I knew my left-hand was good. I was good. I became ambidextrous as a result. The library was good. The church building was good.

It was the nuns that were freaking crazy.

The Trip to Crazy Land

It wasn't long before Mom realized that the house needed an exorcism. She went to the priest and asked him to come to bless the house. At first, he just gave her a bottle of holy water and told her to anoint the doors upstairs. I suggested that she pay special care to the door to my room. Afterward, I think it just pissed off whatever was in there, because the haunting and nightmares and all the nighttime scares got worse. Mom went back to the priest and asked HIM to come out to bless the house and cast out whatever was there. He did. It did seem calmer, but I was skeptical. Something was still amiss, although it was quieter now.

It wasn't long after that, I came home one day and Mom was packing her suitcase. Were we going on a vacation? No. Dad was taking her -by her request- to the mental hospital in Ogdensburg. Mom told me, coolly, that she was going away and that I would probably never see her again. She was un-emotional, resigned and said goodbye and hugged me stiffly. Her back was straight and she walked proudly to the car. It was the calmest I had ever seen her. She walked to the car with a deliberate manner that reminded me of royalty. All my prayers and pleading tears could not change her decision, and I watched my Dad and Mom drive away in the car. The plan was for mom to sign herself into the mental hospital, and that Dad would do it, if she changed her mind.

Evidently, there was silence in the car for about half the drive there. I don't know what started them talking, but thank GOD, they did. I don't know what happened, or what was discussed. But for whatever reason, Pop turned the car around when he got to the state mental facility and brought Mom home.

In the interim, I was sure I was never going to have a mother again. I thought, first the orphanage... now this!

But hours later, walk back into the house she did. Just like nothing had happened. Like she'd gone on a day trip ride with my dad. The only thing Mom told me about it when she returned was that she had changed her mind. She put on her apron and went in to make dinner. While this comforted me in one way, the lack of discussion about it also confused me to no end. I mean, would she decide differently again in the future?

The following Monday, all the kids in my class treated me so awfully. I didn't know why. Then I was sure that I saw one girl going around whispering to other kids and, well, I thought it was mean. I asked to talk privately to my homeroom teacher nun outside in the hall. Amidst a bunch of honest tears, I told her that the whole class was "against me."

Well, the nun thought that was preposterous! She said, "I'll prove to you that you are wrong, Marilyn. Those children are your friends. Come with me." So, I dried my tears and the nun and I went back into the classroom for her to prove their loyalty to me.

She said, "Class, we are going to play a game, and I need you to separate into two teams. I nominate Marilyn as one team leader and Lynn as the other."

(Lynn was the girl who was doing the whispering earlier.)

(I cringed. Oh God, NO. Really, Sister? This is how you are gonna do it?)

The nun continued, "I'd like you girls to both come up to the front of the class." I gulped and walked up to the front of the class. Sister had us each stand one side or the other of the room.

"Alright now, I'd like each one of you children to come up and stand in line with the Captain of the team of your choosing."

I gulped yet again.

Here it comes, I thought. Yup. The whole class lined up

on Lynn's side.

Not even ONE was on my team! Tears welled up in my eyes but I would NOT cry in front of them. The nun was clearly shocked at the class's display of ostracism and the correct degree to which my intuition proved right. *(In retrospect, I think she meant well but was very misguided and had not though the repercussion.)* She was now confronted with her entire class hating ONE student. What did she do? Did she talk to the class about kindness? Tolerance? Did she talk to me privately? No. She, ah, noted it by doing absolutely...NOTHING.

She let the class fall into the *Lord of the Flies* Rule. All bets were off now and it was ON. I knew I was going to be picked on mercilessly now. She sanctioned it with her avoidance. Sister sent us all back to our seats and we had to open our books. It was never discussed by her. She ignored the obvious. I turned inward, put on a false face front during the day, but really, I was traumatized with being ostracized. I became quiet. As the farm girl in towney-land, I played alone a lot. I read and drew pictures.

My favorite pastime of all was making shadow boxes out of shoe boxes, just like I saw on Captain Kangaroo. He showed me how to make one. You decorate the inside of a shoe box with drawings of windows and furniture and you can even glue fabric curtains on and put in fabric matching rugs and everything! You can make your perfect house! You take the lid and cut a "window" in it on top for sunlight and also one on one narrow side end so that you can peek into it.

I liked that idea. I lived in my cardboard house world. It was safe. This world was of my own making of how I wanted it to be. The family and friends that lived in my shadow boxes were all creative, loving, kind, comforting and happy and best of all, they listened and cared. I guess I knew then, that the roof of my own house and trust had been blown off a long time ago.

The hard lessons to learn here *(which I continue to learn)* are that we can only rely on our own Self. Friends can be brutal and fickle. Neighbors can be unreasonable and deadly. Parents have their own issues and are trying their very best. People in authority sometimes don't know their arse from a hole in the ground.

You have to Self Soothe. Creative expression and nature can comfort you. You can live in your own world and it's OK, cuz they know you and like you there. You are Safe there.

Grease Paint in My Veins

At school, I bonded with one girl. Patty was the fat girl that nobody played with. We were both totally and forever in love with David Cassidy and watched *The Partridge Family* and sang in her bedroom and kissed photos of Keith Partridge. We giggled a lot and had great plans to meet him. I figured the best way to meet him was to become like him, so we should be performers and "Get on the Bus" too *(in some sort of a watered down Ken Kesey trip for kids)*. I signed up for a slot in a talent show production at Sacred Heart. I convinced my friend Patty and my little sister Dorothy to perform with me to a song from Disney's *Jungle Book*. *("To hell with those other kids" I thought. "They have no idea who they are messing with!")*

My dad had given me a record of Disney's greatest hits and I loved the one that Baloo sang called "I wanna be like You." We worked out a skit for the Sacred Heart Elementary talent show, and I practiced the whole thing with my crew! It was a three-minute song from a movie that I had never seen, which now contained organized dance sequences and lip synching to the record.

The big night came and I was biting my fingernails, hoping that Patty wouldn't back out on us. She had an upset stomach. Thankfully, she braved her fears and performance jitters and met us backstage for our show. Dorothy and I both dressed in black sweatshirts and black tights *(years later I would know this garb as "Stage Blacks")*. I thought Patty should be Mowgli, because of her long black hair, and I had her dress as a caveman. I remember the crowd as if it were yesterday. It was set in the gymnasium, all open seating and there was no real "backstage." Patty's father hoisted up our homemade special prop onto the stage *(a refrigerator box decorated to look like a jail cell with bars)* And it was Show Time!

The music started up loud. We acted out the whole song, just the three of us taking parts as Baloo the Bear *(me)*, The Monkey King *(Dorothy)* and Mowgli *(Patty)*. We went out into the spotlights and knees knocking we kicked into our parts. Dorothy and I ran around and danced and sang and mimed fighting over Mowgli in the jail. We rocked my show idea! It was awesome! It was my first time to perform for people other than dragging my reluctant Mom out to the garage for my "play" du jour. Hey! The three of us felt like we were somebody after all! We were STARS!

The kids in my class the following Monday after this Friday night hoopla, told me that I "didn't get it" and "that you obviously had never seen the movie." *(Which was true. We didn't go to the movies. But I didn't care what the hell they thought of me. I had read the BOOK and I felt it was MY skit. A conceptual artist had been born.)*

The lesson for me here was that I did- and still do- have great, fabulous ideas, as do YOU.

Don't let anyone rain on your parade just because they are not motivated to do their own creating. YOU DO IT ANYWAY. .

Focused Energy

One day I stumbled upon a new lifetime love: a shelf of library books at the school called "Folk Tales." Russian and German stories like Baba Yaga, The Snow Queen, Rumplestiltskin and more! I read and read and read. My room was too terrifying to sleep in and gave me the willies so Mom let me move into the other bedroom upstairs. My new room seemed safer. It was brighter. It was mine. I didn't like the closet in that room though, because the goblin *(or demon or whatever it was)* quickly learned that I'd changed rooms and soon found me there. This time though, there was no lock on my new room door. The demon would just menace me, from the door, and from under the bed or by the side of the bed.

One night I was so scared, blankets pulled over my head tightly, that I prayed to my guardian angel that the catechism book so firmly said I had. I immediately became aware of a PRESENCE. I peeked open one eye. The room was filled with brilliant white light. I hadn't turned a light on, and it was dark just a moment ago. I looked over by the dreaded closet, and there was something I dared not believe was true. An ANGEL.

An HONEST TO GOD ANGEL!

He wore brilliant white clothing, with shining silver armor, sword, shield, and was handsome as all get out. I instinctively knew he was "guarding me." He took my breath away, he was so beautiful! He filled me with courage and with pride and with joy. I also immediately became aware of other feelings. I felt "not worthy" and terribly afraid in my "human unworthiness" that the nuns had previously instructed me about my baser nature. I remembered in my Bible that

"Ye shall not look upon the face of God and live." I then became afraid of this beautiful being protecting me. I shut my eyes and thought something like: "I can't see you. You are too terribly beautiful for me. Thank you for coming. Be with me, I need you, stay with me, but don't show yourself to me."

I opened my eyes and the Angel was gone. I missed him immediately and regret to this day that indoctrinated response I issued that night. The good thing was that the nightmares stopped after that. Just stopped. The door knob turning and the whispering thru the keyhole stopped. And I also began to have some magical powers after that. I know you are going to think I'm delusional when I tell you this. But there were no movies back then about what happened next. I was not influenced by TV *(not that we were able to even watch TV much back then, nor was there anything on programming that even came close to influence me)*, nor had I read any books or heard anything like what happened next.

I remember sitting on my bed one bright summer day and was looking at my dresser top, the dresser with my new embroidered dresser scarf that I had recently made. It had on it the usual things: brush, comb, jewelry box, and also a plastic figurine of Mary the Mother of God in an arched little trellis alcove. The trellis was pink and the statue of Mary resided within it. You could open the doors of the trellised alcove and see her. You could close the doors again and keep her safe. The little plastic unit was closed at that moment. I don't know why, but I sat there and thought to myself, "I'd like those doors to be open so that Mary can come out and be my friend."

Just then, the doors of the little plastic figurine began to open! BY THEMSELVES!

Slowly, slowly, before my young untrained and focused watchful eyes, my thoughts made those doors OPEN ON THEIR OWN. That couldn't have been me that did that! I did NOT know anything about telekinesis as a child. So I thought, well, to prove I didn't just do that, I'll try to raise that cup of pencils on the dresser. Yah, that's what I'll do. I focused on the cup on my dresser and tried to lift it with my mind. The cup rose and levitated in front of my very eyes!

Shocked at the magic happening in front of me, it was punctuated by the voice of my sister downstairs calling me for dinner. The cup fell. The pencils splayed all over the floor. I ran downstairs. I was pleased, but also shocked and scared by the power I had just witnessed. My own focused power.

I put the knowledge of my power away and tried not to do it anymore. I knew I couldn't control it and the frequent warnings of my mother and the nuns' voices in my head that said: "Satan loves to get a hold of beautiful young girls like you. They are what he likes the best. He likes to control them and it helps him do his bidding." So I hid my power away to be safe. I told NO ONE. Would they believe me that Angels exist and that I knew it to be a fact? I wanted to be safe so Satan wouldn't find out about it and use me. This power has come and gone intermittently in my life, untrained, raw and fleeting to this day.

If only I had not turned my back on it as well. It was ignorance and fear. I guess I felt I didn't need to be any more of a freak of nature than I already was.

The nuns were awful, my classmates were horrid. My mother was distant. My father was quiet. My siblings were not around or were too young to relate to me. So my parents did what they could to change my focus and make me happy. They got me a pony. Distraction can be a good thing.

A Pony For You

Like most young girls, I wanted a horse. I had gone to the New York State Fair with my parents one summer and spent a lot of time at the Coliseum watching all the horse competitions. There were both English style and Western style riding there. I was mesmerized! I was inspired! I was hooked. I picked up all the literature I could find on horses. I was totally infatuated with them and wanted to learn everything about them. I researched and narrowed the breeds down to single choice. A Palomino was the perfect horse for me. Pintos were just wild and Arabians were too exotic. I lived and breathed getting a Palomino horse. I talked about them all the time. I gobbled up books, pictures, dolls, anything, everything, and all about them. Their blonde manes and tails. So beautiful. *(This would be the formula way of how I obsess on many infatuations throughout life.)* So to make my dream come true, my mom and dad got me a pony. A pony. The thought was nice and all, and I loved them and appreciated the thought for the gift. And please don't think me too snobbish or ungrateful. But it was a pony. A pony! A pony is NOT a horse.

Oh, she was a pretty little Shetland roan, and she was a size that I could manage. But a pony is NOT the same as a horse. No freaking way. Not in size, not in prestige, and certainly not in temperament. I had to be happy about the pony for the sake of my parents love for me and this was quite a gift, but deep inside, I still wanted a horse. A HORSE. My parents figured that I was young and little, and if I could take care of a pony, it would be good for me, and a good start in horsemanship. I could work my way up to a horse. I'm sure there were the financial constraints to think of as well. So I set out to love her with all my heart. But I had been dreaming of something bigger than me. Some power animal with whom I could bond. A sweet friendly soul and kindred spirit that I could ride like the wind on! ESCAPE! A vision of freedom and power!

The pony we acquired would not gallop. No, nay, never. Trotting was her speed, no matter how much you tried to persuade her. I endeavored to be a "good steward" of my newfound pony and take care of her, just as if she was a horse. After all, a pony was like a small horse, right? Wrong. Mom and dad had bought her from our neighbors down the road. The pony already had a name. Her name was Princess. She was well named.

Aside from the two strikes against her of her breed and her name, Princess was a pretty little thing, and I really tried to love her. I got up every morning, and went outside to feed and water her and give her treats. During hot weather, my folks bought me some stuff to put on a cloth and rub around her face to keep the flies off. She hated it, but I always hated to see the flies gather around her eyes, licking her eyes like some cow in India. She was now officially my "4-H project." I got more books, this time on training horses *(and PONIES)* and learned how best to lunge her before I rode her. When she chose to be ridden, it certainly was a joy. I pictured myself as some sort of Princess too. Trotting through the pasture my hair flying behind me, I pictured myself approaching a castle and being a fair maiden. It was also about this precise time that my faithful steed would decide to do a dead stop. Ass over teakettle forward I tumbled while she snipped clover. It was like some sort of Looney Tunes Yosemite Sam and Camel moment.

Now, let me tell you a bit about Princess. She was raised for about 12 years before we got her and had spent her life thus far as a "pasture pony." Basically, she was a pretty lawn decoration to admire. Her former daily routine consisted of coming up to the fence, getting treats, getting petted and then going back to an uninterrupted schedule of grazing. She was rarely ridden and she was not at all trained. No, because that was going to be MY job now. Princess was as close to an asshole that an animal could get. Lunging her consisted of me, her on her harness and a long leash called a "lunge line" and a tickler to inspire her with. Yah, that and a lot of begging and cajoling. She just wasn't interested. Tapping her with the tickler didn't even phase her. She did not want to work because she was a PRINCESS, after all. She wanted to be left alone in her throne room and let the servants wait on her with sugar, carrots and apples. She lived to be petted and adored. And rightly so, for wasn't she a princess after all?

After school, I got out the tack, got her out of her pen, put on her bit and bridle. Putting a bridle on an unruly pony was harder than putting a dress on a cat. She would use her weight and power to side swipe me, knock me over, pin me to the side of the pen, to do whatever she could to persuade me to let her be. Instead, I attempted to saddle her, brushing her first, to get a pleasant experience going for her, and throw her off the trail that we were going to go for a ride. Then when she was nicely brushed, I'd throw the blanket on her, and talk to her in soothing tones about what fun we'd have. It was now saddle time. Her western saddle was hand-tooled leather and lovely with flowers and leaves! I put it on her and she would try to wiggle it off while I tried to cinch the saddle strap. The little trickster would actually puff herself up and bloat her belly out and distend it ON PURPOSE so that the saddle would slip off when ridden. When I finally got it on, I would put my left foot in the stirrup and swing up and over to get on. Yessiree, just like a cowgirl! I was going to finally get to feel the wind blowing through my hair as me and my trusty steed went on adventures! This is when Princess would wheel her head around and bite me.

"Ha ha! You missed me, you little vixen!" I said with a jaunty air and we'd set off! Just me on my gallant pony steed in the buckskins of my mind on our quest for adventure! Like

Cisco Kid! Like Roy Rogers and Dale Evans! That was when she'd buck me off again.

"Oh, it's gonna be like THIS, is it?" I'd say from the dirt when my Scottish heritage would kick in. I would pick myself up, gather the reins, slap this little backbiting demon pony with the whip once for a warning, and I'd tell her we were going for a ride, and then I'd get back on. You HAVE to get back on the horse that bucks you off. You HAVE to show them they will not win. You are boss. Not them. You have to win-win-win at this game or they will be the bane of your existence. Lather. Rinse. REPEAT.

I worked with her for a couple of years and I really started to find reasons to not ride her. She was training me now I guess. I grew to hate her. Sad to say, but I learned to hate a pretty little Shetland pony.

Princess also had a habit of bolting over the fence and trotting herself back home to her old pasture and barn. Here is where they would happily greet her at her old home sweet home, with sugar, and then call us and tell us that she was there again and could we please come get her? Dad and I would get in the station wagon and drive down the road, and fetch our wandering equine traveler back home. I would trot her horsey ass back to the house while dad followed in the car behind.

Once she chomped a giant chunk out of my abdomen the size of a quarter. My parents thought I was learning fortitude. I however, was learning survival of the fittest. Man over beast... or Girl against Nag. It was then I decided I didn't like ponies or horses anymore for that matter. Hell no. I decided that I didn't like them much at ALL.

My parents, seeing that my change of heart *("we knew you'd outgrow this horse kick you were on, honey")* and the fact that hay and straw were now selling for the price of gold, a Spartan winter loomed large, ...my folks decided to part with our dear old Princess. So she was going to be someone else's Princess. My horse phase was now officially over.

They put an ad in the paper and found a great home for her. Princess was sold to a great farm, with other horses to play with, a big barn, with nice people to train her. A perfect life was given to her on her royal silver platter, yet again.

One thing I did learn from this pony was that leopards don't change their spots. Stupid, demanding, spoiled creatures will always be so, no matter how hard you try to get them to change. I also learned that karma is a bitch.

Did Princess learn anything? No, she dreamed of greener pastures! She dreamed of sugar way back home! She did not want to integrate at her new environment either. Princess scaled her tower and jumped the fence again, and tried to go back home to her sugar castle pasture down the road, as always before. But the Princess ran into a deadly evil along the way and got hit by a car.

Thus ends my Princess tale.

But They Are Sweet And Kinda Crunchy

It was about this time that I realized that I couldn't see well, or at least my third-grade nun teacher realized it. I keep asking her what she was writing on the board. She said, "Stop it and read it for yourself." I then told her that couldn't see the words on the chalk board. So Sister told me to pull my desk up as far as I needed to in order to see it properly. I pulled my desk right up flush to the chalk tray and said, "This is perfect!"

"You need glasses" was her epiphany. So Mom took me to the Eye Doctor. During the intake, as I was sitting in the fancy mechanized chair, the Eye Doctor asked me the usual questions about sight, floaters, distance vision, up close vision and the like.

Then as he was going down his checklist he asked, "I'm sure you haven't, but I'll ask it anyway; have you ever eaten paint chips?" He was ready to check it off as a "No" until I said, "Yah, all the time."

I thought my Mom was gonna keel over. "WHAT??" she exclaimed. "You can't be serious."

I informed her with the following: "Yes, they are all over

my bedroom window, and they are kinda fun to peel up, kinda like peeling a sunburn or popping tar bubbles on the road. They taste sweet and are sorta crunchy. We don't ever have anything sweet and crunchy in the house to eat." The Eye Doctor looked askance at my worried Mom. Then they both turned and looked at me funny. I didn't know why...I told them the truth. Mom scraped and painted my bedroom windows that day when we got home. No more sweet and crunchy chips and I got my first pair of Ugly Cat's Eye glasses that week. That'll teach me to tell the truth....

Saint Bashing

The first time I got married I was 7 when I had my First Communion. No really. Symbolically, the Priest told me that this ritual was equivalent to me marrying Jesus. I got the awesome white lace dress, the white shoes, a gold cross necklace; I even got a Bridal veil in the form of a beautiful white mantilla! It was awesome. I liked Jesus.

Mom had been going along all this time to the Immaculate Conception Catholic Church and Mass in Brownville, as much as possible, doing her daily Bible readings and study, making margins notes as she went. Then one day, when I was 11, she stumbled on this verse of the Second Commandment reads: "Thou shalt not make unto thee any graven image, or any likeness of anything that is in heaven above, or that is in the earth beneath, or that is in the water under the earth: Thou shalt not bow down thyself to them, nor serve them: for I the Lord thy God am a jealous God, visiting the iniquity of the fathers upon the children unto the third and fourth generation of them that hate me; And showing mercy unto thousands of them that love me, and keep my commandments." (Exodus 20:4-6)

Well something was bothering Mom and got her thinking, she had an altar, didn't she? Didn't she bow down to Mary there? Weren't all those acquired statues of Saints that she prayed to, twice a day...Weren't THEY "graven images?"

Mom prayed about it. She'd spent a LOT of good money on those statues. She prayed to them daily.

I, particularly, was fond of Jesus *(he was nice all the time and so handsome with his long hair, beard and kind face.* I also admired St. Francis of Assisi *(he was so kind and protected children and animals)*, and my namesake, St. Lucy. Then there was Mary, the Mother of God, she was so pretty with her veil. I didn't mind kneeling down before breakfast anymore and saying my quick prayers to them. It was routine. It was familiar. But now, my mother's conscience was being needled by GOD.

When I came home from parochial school one afternoon, I walked into a surreal scene. My mother was smashing all the Saints! One by one, she took them and smashed them on the floor. Bits and parts and ceramic chunks flew everywhere! Nooo! I begged her to spare Jesus! He was my buddy! It was like He was being crucified all over again! "MOM! Please DON'T break them!! Not St. Francis I like him! He's nice to animals!!" PLEASE! He protects ME, mom!

She was adamant, "Oh NO, they don't! They are FALSE GODS. We won't have any FALSE GODS in this house!" And she proceeded to sweep up all the broken bodies, dismembered heads, ceramic dust into the dust pan, took them out to the burning barrel and set fire to our faith. She watched over the barrel until it went out. No more Mary! No more St. Lucy! No more St. Francis and the sheep! The last to go was the "Child of Prague." Wise baby Jesus standing beatifically in his ermine robe and crown. NO MORE JESUS GOD? I didn't know WHAT to think! Who was I supposed to pray to now?? I felt like I was a widow and I was only 11. Oh, yah, God is in HEAVEN, he didn't have a face, or a shape. I didn't have the kind Jesus to look at and love anymore either. The vengeful God she was smashing all these statues, for didn't have a form or a shape.

"And we aren't going to that idolatrous whore of a church anymore either!" She said with finality *(having just recently finished the book of Revelations, she was brimming with adjectives straight from the Bible).* She told me she planned on letting me finish out my sixth-grade year at Sacred Heart Parochial School, but then she planned on enrolling me back in our home district in public school. She didn't write a check for tuition that following year and instead filled out the forms for General Brown public school.

But I didn't know any kids in my home school. My father was pissed as hell, to say the least. In the past he had listened to her rant and rave on her point of view. He knew how much we'd all been through, praying, the fanaticism, the rosaries, and the money she'd spent on the statues on his one income. It was AWFUL the way that they were fighting and screaming about religion.

Our daily routine was gone, no more ritual Sundays, my faith and everything I believed in was smashed and burning in the barrel, and now, it seemed, I didn't even have Mary or Jesus on my side either. "Why Mom, why?" was all I could ask. "Because the church sold us a bill of goods, and the Saints are all false Gods," she said.

I was now paddling up shit creek without my crucifix.

Searching for Jesus

While I missed the grandiose Church buildings, the echo in the chambers, the Saints, Jesus and Mary, the candles, the ritual, the drama of Good Friday with all the Gothic cloths on the statues, the God given wine and wafers, the frankincense and myrrh and dragon blood incense. I was NOT going to miss the woolen uniforms, the hateful children, the constant scratch of the scapular, the nuns, their punishments, the putdowns, the rulers. No, Siree, I wasn't going to miss a LOT of it. Public school was a bit scary to think about, but exciting too. I was going into seventh grade, when all the middle school kids came together at once into one high school. It was a way better time to do it than just being a single new kid coming into a brand new school.

I was so looking forward to the next September and wearing REAL school clothes for the first time, going school clothes shopping, having new friends close to home and a short bus ride. Things were looking up! Mom pulled herself, me and Dorothy out of the membership of the Catholic Church (and my father's faith), against Dad's wishes. Bernie decided to go back to her own Protestant roots and so, we went on a Spiritual Quest with her. We went church shopping for the next five years. Pick a Christian religion. Any denomination. We probably checked it out. OK, well, a lot of them anyways.

First, Mom had friends at the Baptist Church so we started there. Egad, what a wild opposite pendulum swing from Catholicism that was! The Baptists were friendly, I'll give you that. They had suppers, basketball games, outreaches, missionary nights, get-togethers, Sunday school, morning Sunday worship, evening Sunday worship, youth group with basketball on Tuesdays, Adult Bible study Wednesdays. Basically, you went in to church on early Sunday morning for the mandatory Sunday school and you got out on Thursday night. It seemed that we were there ALL the time.

I liked Sunday school. They used a different Bible than the Catholic Bible. I was able to pick out a "Good News for Modern Man" Bible, with cool line drawings in it. While my Sunday school teacher preferred me to bring in my King James Version *(as it was deemed the TRUE Word of God rather than the Bible I liked)*, I personally preferred the Good News one. I was a hippy Bible freak now. We memorized Bible verses weekly. I like to study and read, so it was OK. I especially liked the parables as they reminded me of folklore and fairytales from other countries.

I made a terrific drawing of Daniel in the lions' den and was so excited to show my Sunday school teacher my awesome extra credit drawing! She looked at it uninterestedly and dismissed me with a "We aren't studying Daniel today, please put it away" without seeing it. I felt slapped as if by a nun. That sort of flew in the face of the "joy" passages they made me memorize. Hmmmm. There also seemed to be a lot of fear in this place about Revelations and a vengeful retribution God. If you were "saved," however, then he was your best bud.

There were other things, too, that I wasn't thrilled about. Like the fact that you weren't allowed to play cards or dance. I mean, really? Not even Old Maid or Crazy 8s? What about all those Psalms about King David and his joyful music and dancing? I wondered how they could cherry pick stuff out like that. Also, over time, I noticed that the same people kept coming up to be "saved" every week. Then I wondered, "If Salvation was "once and for all" then why the weekly redo?" Good point.

One Sunday I was sitting in the pew with my sister and my mother, and to be perfectly honest, I wasn't paying attention. I was bored and I had tuned out. It all sounded like the same sermon every week of which the outline was: "Jesus loves you. Jesus hates sinners. You are a Sinner. Come down and be saved. We'll heal you down here with the laying on of hands. Come be healed." As I said, I wasn't very engaged at the moment. My mind had wandered, and I was playing with the pencils or drawing most likely. All of a sudden, my mother got up out of the seat. I noticed and perked up and whispered to my glassy-eyed sister, "Hey! Mom's leaving!" I grab Dorothy's hand and we both get up too. We thought, "YAY! Finally! We are outta here!"

But then, instead of going to the back of the church and out to the happy parking lot to get into our get-away car and get the hell outta there, like I thought, Mom made a bee line right down front and center of the church!

Halfway there, I realize that Dorothy and I are now on our way to the <u>front of the church to be SAVED.</u> Good Lord. There was no one but the preacher down front and he was now deliriously happy to see us coming at his invitation! Actually, he was GIDDY with it! He shouted, "PRAISE God! A whole FAMILY being saved at once!" He wiped the sweat from his brow with a big man's handkerchief. "Praise JESUS!" He beamed. The congregation clapped! There were hoots, hollers, and conversations in tongues.

Let me tell you, what I really *wanted* to tell this guy was, "Hey, don't put the kettle on! Me and my sister were just following our mother out of here and we can't wait to leave and shake the dust off our feet." But that wouldn't sound very nice *(even if it WAS Biblical)* and probably not at all "Christian," *(except for when St. Paul said it)*. And so, we were technically "saved" that day. And baptized. With all our clothes on. In front of God and everybody. Good grief.

Then came the rounds of Wednesday-night prayer meetings, these meetings were "Optional" but really mandatory. Oh, and lest I forget, there were the festive, End-of-the-World films like one called, "A Thief in the Night" subtitled: "I Wish We'd All Been Ready." Death, destruction, fear and the always festive subject of Armageddon, you know, The RAPTURE? Yah, just what Marilyn needed. More fear about shit that was gonna get me and end my life. I sat in the back of the station wagon on the way home, hearing the conversations after one such meeting. I remember physically trembling and shaking in terror after one of these prayer meetings. Of course they all chalked it up to "The Spirit moving and shaking within you."

But I thought of it differently. I thought they were all a bunch of crazy idiots to focus on all negativity and punishment. As I sat in the car, I quietly tried to get a handle on all that had been given to me to sort out, while watching the trees and cars go by. I looked out at the black night sky, searching the stars for answers.

In my heart of hearts, I still believed in a warm, loving God, (even though, the one we were being taught about at the moment was fierce, terrible and vengeful.) Yah, the one the Baptists preached about was one mean mother fucker that you wouldn't want to mess with, much less get close to.

The stars seemed cold and distant in the stark November sky. I knew my happy, kind, loving, bearded, hippy Jesus from my Good News Bible was still out there, somewhere. I knew it deep down in my heart.

Now that I'm a grown woman, I still love Jesus. I am programmed to be almost instantly in love with any guy who looks and acts like him. It's the total package of real commitment love wrapped up in magic, sprinkled with a flavor of the Underdog Social Outcast thing, with a touch of Hippy

Love that is really appealing to me. I'm sure it all goes back to the Catholic and the Baptist input in my life. That…and Jesus is just so irresistibly furry and handsome.

Wade in the Water

"Wade in the water
Children wade, in the water
God's gonna trouble the water…"

The first time I was baptized I was an infant in the Catholic Church. Which was fine, but now Mom was suspicious of everything that the Church had told her, so she wasn't sure if it really "counted" in heaven.

Next, Mom decided to take our Eternal Salvation into her own hands, for our health and edification and she baptized me and my sister Dorothy in the bathtub. But not feeling right about that either, *(being as how it wasn't like John the Baptist out in public in a real body of water, or by a preacher)* we evidently, were not officially set yet with a place at heaven's banquet table.

So, we then got baptized for the third time at the Baptist Church *(as previously described).* But when Mom left the Baptist Church, I guess that particular baptism didn't count either, for she was still bent on getting the job done right.

Our family often visited our grandparents at their camp at Chase's Lake. It was a beautiful mineral lake and the water was rust red from the iron deposits. A clearer, more pure and healthy lake there never was. Mom had decided that this was going to be the best place for Baptism. You have to imagine an ordinary summer day now, families and children splashing, playing, cooking out hot dogs and playing catch on the beach. Mom waded into the water with her housedress on and everyone was looking at me and Dorothy and she baptized us right there in front of God and everyone. She then waded back to the beach to sit with her mother and discuss spiritual things and eat chips.

I, however, heartily agree with my younger sister, Dorothy,

that "the last baptism was the BEST 'cuz we got to go swimming right after."

A Vacation to Remember

Early one hot summer morning Mom packed me, Dorothy, Dad and a pile of picnic stuff into the car for a day trip. She gave Dad the directions. It was to be a vacation we'd never forget! She packed a cooler filled with rolls, sausage and peppers, onions, beer and sodas along with a Coleman stove. Bathing suits and towels were also packed, in case we found a place to swim along the way.

Where were we going? It was to be a surprise! Dorothy and I were giddy with anticipation! Was it Santa's Workshop? Or maybe Enchanted Forest in the Adirondacks? Oh, we hoped so! Mom warned us that it was a long way and we had several stops to make, so we settled into the hot back seat with coloring books and cards. Dad didn't seem all that excited, but he dutifully drove on.

I think if we had driven straight to our destination, it would not have been such a long trip. How'ere, Mom used this opportunity to stop along the way and visit a couple of rectories of Catholic churches and meet the local priests that she'd been writing to. So, we waited for her in the car while she had her momentary touch with Greatness.

After waving good bye to a couple of new priest acquaintances and their modest quiet house keepers, we were back on the road again. We were still in anticipation of the ultimate journey's end until we pulled into the parking lot. After six hours in the car for a three-hour trip, we had arrived! But where were we? We got out and curiously looked around.

Surprise! We were at The Shrine of Our Lady of Martyrs in Auriesville, New York! Mom said we were in for a treat! We were here to learn all we could about the Native American martyr, Kateri Tekakwitha. There were also many other martyrs to pray for, so we best get busy, because that's not nearly enough time to experience this kind of fun. We only had four hours left till the place closed for the day!

Ode to Joy.

Here is where the story of the 17th century Mohawk village and the Jesuit priests who evangelized them were set in historic concrete and wood for all eternity. And it felt like eternity to me. Evidently, these priests tried converting the wild and savage Mohawks and were thusly tortured and murdered for it. We saw the chapel, the shrine itself and the ravine where the bones of a martyr lay in an unmarked grave. We had to say a prayer *(much like at the Stations of the Cross)*, at every painting of each of the North American Martyrs. Boy, howdy, we were having fun now.

Personally, after looking around, I thought to myself, that the Indian way of life was pretty unique and interesting and they must have just been protecting themselves from having to say rosaries all my life...I mean...THEIR life. What's not to like about living in the woods and running and playing with half-naked Indian children? Why would I want to cover up on this hot day with wool robes and crosses and kneel when I could climb trees myself?

I sort of took the Indians' side in all this. I felt like killing someone too. Here we were, inside a musty chapel on an amazing, hot, summer day! We were looking down into a lovely wild ravine and instead of being happy to be out in the woods, I was feeling horrid. Like somebody died. OK, like a whole bunch of somebodies died. I mean, what could two young adolescent girls wish for more than this for a summer vacation?

We got holy water as a blessing. The only thing I wanted *(besides not being there at all, and instead to be in a body of water swimming and splashing)* was something, anything, from the gift shop. I picked out a St. Kateri prayer card and relic. She looked like a beautiful Indian Princess and there was a bit of forest wood attached to it. I wonder if she touched it. We are talking amusement park city wild fun here, minus the fun, with the addition of scourges.

When we were finally allowed to escape- after the appropriate candles were lit and prayers were said- we said a reverent goodbye to the chapel priest *(our third Holy Man we met that day)*. We set off again for some kind of relief from our martyrdom adventure.

Pop mutinied and parked the car at the first rest stop with a beach he could find and dropped the tailgate of the station wagon. Done. He pumped up the Coleman stove and Mom got out a frying pan. She loaded Italian sausages, fresh cut onions and peppers into the pan. I got out the rolls and Dorothy set the picnic table with paper plates. Cold root beers, Mom's potato salad and potato chips were inhaled with great abandon. The wafting smell of this decadent delight in the fresh country air was indeed a treat, and the other folks in the parking lot marveled at the smell too, as they ate their dry, peanut butter sandwiches. Pop cracked a deserved cold beer for his driving efforts.

Today's peek into the harsh reality of our state's history and Indian legend was very different than was this moment, sitting here, all together in the sunshine.

We all sat in shirt sleeves and felt the summer breeze. As my sister and I put on our bathing suits in the back seat of the car, I guess I was glad after all. It WAS grand to be alive and about to swim in fresh water and play in Mother Nature like a wild Indian child.

And I, too, thanked God that I was not a Jesuit priest.

Christians in Jewish Clothing

We went along with the whole Baptist thing, hoping like crazy that my Mom's infatuation with it would dim. It did. It was because they sort of got on her case about her smoking cigarettes and occasionally having a glass of beer. Mom worked hard. She got up early and she worked until she went to bed. She believed in God and most of what they were peddling. However, she wasn't going to give up smoking or having the occasional break of a single beer with her husband sometimes when he came home from work. It was the only social time they had to-gether. She was on my side about the dancing and card-playing too. She and Dad liked to play gin rummy sometimes with their friends on a Saturday night. Company would come over, and Mom and Dad and their friends would have a beer and they'd get out the stinky Limberger cheese, *(which is, of course, 'Farmer-Brie')* and pepperoni and crackers and play Gin Rummy. And it was all good in my mom's eyes, and well, she thought it was good in God's eyes too. So, after being lectured by The Baptists about her social drinking, dancing and cards, well, we didn't go back to the Baptist church anymore.

And I rejoiced.

Onward.

The next church on our visitor schedule was the Seventh Day Adventist Church. They seemed cool to me, kind of like a bunch of hippy Jesus freaks…at first. Mostly, I thought they were Jewish. I mean, really. Except for the part about Jesus be-ing the Savior, they celebrated the "Sabbath" like the Jews on Friday night and all day and night Saturday. They followed Leviticus to the letter regarding food, drink and whether or not to sleep with your wife when she's menstruating. Maybe she should "go away to a nearby lodge and spend the seven days in cleansing" as the Bible said. They followed the Bible, literally. And they were health nuts to boot. Exactly like Euell Gibbons at the time. This group was totally vegetarian, and very much into food, culture and the possibilities of the Bible meal plan. Mom felt responsible to Dad and his diet, and well, we were Carnivores. They were awfully strict when it came to almost everything. Like I said, from the observance of the Sabbath on Friday night, to the strict dietary laws….it was like living with a Sadducee.

And bonus, if we didn't go here, Mom wouldn't have to quit smoking cigarettes, give up the single glass of beer ei-ther…and now….drinking COFFEE was also forbidden here. We visited there a few times, but it became evident that this was NOT the church for us.

Also, they believed that the dead in the afterlife have no

Consciousness. None. Nothing. Nada.

OK, not what we believed. But as long as we're here, we might as well try the potluck.

It was my first taste of vegetarian fare, (Seitan, Tamari and sprouts.) And bonus, they wore Birkenstocks here, didn't bathe or shave much. The bohemian in me liked that.

A few of the guys looked like Jesus too.

I really started to like this cherry-picking.

Holy Rollers

Well, after the 7th Day Adventist visit and near-miss membership there, another new church beckoned to Mom. It was the Assembly of God Pentecostal Church. This church's service was much like a scene from the movie *The Blues Brothers* when James Brown leads a service that sets everyone's feet dancing and jumping. While the movie showed some gyrations and dancing, this Assembly of God church shined in their receiving of the Holy Spirit in the form of tongues rather than dancing, because, basically, we were a bunch of white folks who had no gift for movement. While the Spirit did sometimes move a person to convulsions, they never really got to dancing like in black churches. I would have really liked that. Unlike the Baptists, Holy Rollers LOVE to dance!

If you don't know what this phenomenon of "speaking in tongues" is all about, I'll tell you: it's from the New Testament scripture that says the Spirit of God came down in the form of tongues of fire, right after Jesus rose from the dead. It seems the doors of heaven opened so that the Spirit could come down to man, and then it came to rest over each of the apostles heads there and each in turn started speaking in foreign languages in "other tongues," and while they did not know the language, they each in turn could understand it, especially if they had been given the gift of interpretation." I'm paraphrasing, but that's basically the jist.

So, there I was, going to yet another new church, and I

didn't know anybody. Again. But at least it wasn't the Baptist church, nor was it the 7th Day Adventist or the Catholic Church, so I hoped for the best.

I walked in and everyone there, at first, looked like a normal person.

Then the music started it was sort of a loosely constructed jam session with the musicians getting into a groove. OK, so it wasn't my favorite music, but everyone seemed to be enjoying it.

People started to sway. It started getting warmer. Warm, like really warm, like you need to take off your sweater now, sort of warm. Women started using fans. People started murmuring low, a soft and sweet, "Thank you, Jesus, oh thank you Father" sort of commenting and talking to themselves while rocking back and forth. The murmuring went along with the music for a bit, sometimes growing louder and acting like a wave of sound. "Oh precious Jesus, thank you, Lord" the man next to you is whispering a bit louder. The whole congregation murmured similar sounding prayers to themselves, and it started to build in urgency and volume. Then out of the blue, a voice with the cadence and rhythm of a story teller cut above all the others in some sort of gibberish that I'd never heard before. The speech had intonation, tempo with some sort of meaning wrapped up in the nonsensical blather of something that sounded like a cross between French and Chinese…and pig Latin. The congregation welcomed this outburst as a gift from Heaven. That's what it was to them. The Spirit had ARRIVED.

A crescendo of gratitude welled up, and then an answering call followed from others who were also receiving the gift of tongues. It reverberated like an echo thru the tropical sanctuary. Soon, everyone was standing, arms up and outstretched, rocking back and forth, and talking either to themselves in an out-loud prayer to God, speaking in some fantastical language. The musicians in a groove trance were still playing on and on and on, while jamming the same riff over and over.

About this time, just as you hope that it's time for it all to end; the ushers come out with baskets for the offertory portion. The preacher then said that the experience they were receiving from God is now related directly in proportion to how well they are blessed by God, and that in turn is somehow related to their wallet and purse. People entranced, start putting in wads of money and checks. The ushers pick up the baskets of over-flowing money. The people keep praising God, caught in some sort of a transcendental trance, and just when you think it will never ever end, it stops.

It just stops.

People are sweating, some are having convulsions on the floor and there is a circle of men all around them, laying on hands, storming heaven for that individual. There is a general calling out of demons from that particularly afflicted person, who then dramatically convulses a bit more. There are tears, sweat and the occasional outburst of yelling or jumping. The congregation then left the church building, spent, wiped out and yet somehow refreshed and cleansed from this cathartic communal orgasm.

Later on, when I was a bit older, I would use sex & drugs & Rock' n 'Roll to replicate this very same effect.

He's Not the Kind You Have to Wind Up

Well, after the excitement of the Pentecostal Church, we were all ready for something a bit calmer, quieter, somber and closer to home. So we visited the Presbyterian Church in the village nearby. What can I say about it? Well, it was a lot quieter and the benches were hard. That's about it. We didn't get much of a spiritual tug or awakening there but after the excitement of the Holy Roller church, that was perfectly OK. Maybe I was getting jaded, but it was now pretty pale and bland in comparison. We were still hungry for something else.

We then tried the only church left in town that we hadn't tried yet, the Episcopal Church. *(Like Mae West would say: "When deciding between two evils, I like to try the one I haven't tried yet").* Here we settled in and got comfy for several years. It was "Catholic-Lite" to me.

It had all the ritual, candles, format, pews and kneelers of the Catholic religion, except it was a lot more "user friendly." Priests could marry in this denomination. Over time, they even were cool enough to let women, gays and lesbians into their pulpits. It was "cathedral-like" in the architecture. It didn't have a lot of spiritual shakeups or whirling dervishes or unachievable personal deprivations *(except at Lent, and even then deprivation is a personal choice and not mandated by God).*

I was now in seventh grade. My previous years at parochial school had not prepared me for public school society. I was a very good student at Catholic school mostly because I had been slapped with a ruler *(edge blade down)* if I wasn't a good student there. It wasn't so much motivation for good grades as avoidance of pain that motivated me. Those nuns knew their way around a ruler, I can tell you. And let's face it; pain is good preparation for your adolescent years.

When I was 11, I smoked my first cigarette on the railroad tracks with my new friend, Tammy, when she stole one of her mother's Old Gold cigarettes. We lit it up on the railroad track behind Genner & Brennan's grocery store. She said through the cloud of blue curling wisp, "You'll cough a lot at first. But you get better at it if you practice." I put myself to the task with vigor and practiced seriously. When my mom found out about me smoking, she said, "I'm not going to be a hypocrite and tell you not to, while I sit here and smoke myself." So she allowed me to smoke at home, without much ado, and then bought my cigarettes and I started smoking with her like two old friends.

I did well at academics, and pretty well with the other kids. I started going to "Episcopal Youth Retreats" on occasional weekends. My church hopping adventures during previous years, made me somewhat of an adept young sage at those events. I remember being in a small group of teenagers, and the hippy movement was pretty strong then. Some of the group leaders at the retreats were trying to be cool and with it and all that. Yah, they wore tie dye and bell bottoms and beads.

At the beginning of this one particular small group session, the group leader guy says, "We are going to do an exercise. All I ask is that you be silent, aware and participate." Then he took out an apple, looked at it INTENTLY and showed it around the circle. He polishes it. He regards it again. He takes a bite out of the apple and then, calmly delivers it to the person next to him. That person, in turn, takes the apple and looks at it INTENTLY and takes a bite and passes it on to the next person and so on till it goes all around the circle and back to the presenter. He then is quiet for about a minute and then says, sort of hippy philosopher all like, "So…what do you think it means??" *(And he drew out the word "means," like "meeeeans").* No one said anything. I thought snarkily to myself, "Oh come ON. Really? NO ONE?" So I raised my hand meekly and he let me speak.

With the voice of some divinity school student, I said, "It is obviously communion being shared by us all, with the apple being Jesus' body offered up for us to share. The apple also represents us conquering sin, the symbol from Adam and Eve. The skin, His body, the juice, His blood."

The presenter looked at me in disbelief. *(Blink, blink, blink.)* He said after a pause: "Well, that was quick. You just said in two sentences what we were all supposed to discuss for, like, the next forty-five minutes. *(Heavy sigh)* Now, what do we do for the rest of our session?" I suggested Jethro Tull and we had a much more interesting conversation about music, spirituality and teenage faith. We marveled at the deep lyrics of Tull in "My God" and the hypocrisy of organized religion. I believed, as did Ian Anderson, that God was within us. I also came to the conclusion that I didn't have to go to a church anymore to find my spirit. As a matter of fact, I realized that I didn't like getting dragged to church, and I wanted to have my OWN spirituality now. I knew that the Spirit lived inside me. After all, I had my own Guardian Angel with me, didn't I?

At another Episcopal Youth Retreat, I got my first back rubs, learned how to French kiss, sang some hippy Jesus music, shared Led Zeppelin lyrics with some new kids, watched a family perform like "The Partridges," and worried about some weird teenager having convulsions and hallucinations because he dropped untimely acid at the church retreat while he was away from home late that weekend. Yah, it was a trip, a real getaway weekend of church fun.

Back at home, the Episcopal priest had his own problems. His wife was ignored and neglected by her husband. He was obviously an alcoholic. *(Let's face it, wine before breakfast for morning communion every day can probably turn a lot of goodly priests into more than social drinkers).* They had a couple of teenage boys, Pete and Ben, who were about my age. They were wild and unchecked. Ben sang loudly out of tune for all to hear and was never deterred by anyone's objections. Pete, his older brother would sit and rock back and forth in his chair with his long hair hanging down while he tranced to the music. Guess which one was my boyfriend?

Yah, Pete was once caught inside the bottom of my sleeping bag while I was in it by my friend's mother, when we were camping out in their backyard. I think I was 14. We hadn't done much of anything. Yet.

I learned about rock 'n roll music *(Zappa/Queen/Johnny Winter/Pink Floyd)* and other things with the PKs *(Preacher's Kids).* I became greatly philosophical with these guys and we spoke at lengths on theology, religion, spirituality, and the Occult *(which, I learned was just a right wing word for Spiritual matters which a lot of people don't want to understand).*

What else did I learn from these preacher's kids? Important things like: I learned how to break up a lid of weed responsibly and fairly amongst four friends, how to roll a proper joint, how to makes roach clips out of bobby pins and alligator clips, how to make a pipe if you didn't have one from a toilet paper roll or an apple, how to do a bong, how to build a bong in art class, how to chug a beer and how to do shots of whiskey and a proper tequila shot. I learned most of the lyrics of any album I liked, and learned to sing over the top of those with out of pitch voices. God wanted me to experience all things. I learned how to dry hump till it made the fellow and me crazy. I also puked my guts out learning the hard way running with the big dogs. Got the T-shirt, and puked on that too. It was sort of a secular slide from there.

I kept my Guardian Angel very busy after that.

Sex & Drugs & Rock 'n Roll

After a whole young lifetime that infringed on my personal space, comfort zone, psyche, trust and soul, well, I decided to express myself. I was about fifteen when I learned how to play guitar. Mom played an old Gibson copy called a "Kalamazoo." It was a pretty guitar and had a tortoise shell finish. It also had action on it so high that you could nearly pass an upright dime through between the strings and the fret board. I asked mom to teach me. She said she didn't have time, but I was welcome to use her guitar. She tuned it, gave me some Mel Bay guitar books and a pick and said, "Call me if you run into problems." *(This was also the way she taught me how to use her sewing machine when I was nine).*

The first problem, of course, was that the Mel Bay books were for right-handers. But no worries, right? The nuns had already made me ambidextrous, so I started playing guitar right-handed, even though I was left-handed. Problem solved. If you didn't know where I was, you could always find me with the guitar in my room, reading, writing, and singing to records. I had quite a collection of music, "for a girl." My guitar became my boyfriend. It had a personality that I imbued with strength, courage, expression, freedom and safety. I even named it Leon *(for Leon Russell and Leon Redbone.)* I learned the trick of how to sing and play at the same time. I realized that I could make other people happy, and grab some much-needed attention at parties. I was getting to be one of the "cool kids." *(At least in my mind, and that, to me was really all that mattered).*

When I was 15 I went on an overnight far away *(75 miles)* and went to stay at a friend's house in Liverpool so I could go to the Aerosmith concert. Unfortunately, after I got to her house, word came that our tickets to the concert were being refunded because the drummer's house had burned down and they canceled the gig last minute. I didn't realize that instead of a planned rock concert I would end up meeting my future husband instead.

Dave Underwood, at the time, looked like just like my long-haired skinny Jesus. He was passive, kind, funny and musical and starved for love and lust. He was my everything. We were both smitten. We wrote fantasy love letters back and forth across the miles between us. I decided when to become a woman with him and my days of dry humping thankfully were over forever when I was 16. Not being a virgin anymore was a gift I gave to myself. We spent every weekend we could at each others' houses, and in each others' beds.

He and I went through a lot. The distance of living 75 miles apart, while in high school is quite an impediment. Our family life was way different too. Also, Dave's best friend, Ted interfered in our relationship a lot. Ted encouraged Dave to pull out my chair from under me as I was sitting down at a Halloween party. I was dressed as Janis Joplin and I fell on my previously broken tailbone. More than my pride was hurt that night. Ted convinced Dave to "play the field" and break up with me when Dave graduated from high school, so that Dave could go to Europe and "bum around" for awhile unhindered. Well, needless to say, I was heartbroken.

One day I got a phone call from my next door neighbor, Pete. He said he wanted hang out with me on the hill by my house, and could I come meet him? He had a surprise for me. He sounded unusually perky. Too oddly nice sounding, for he was usually sullen. OK, well, I wasn't doing much. Dad was out in his garden like he always was. There was no one to talk with. I was kinda bored and lonely. I would've really rather stay home, but instead, I walked up into the field that overlooked my house. I should've listened to my intuition.

Pete had a small campfire going, there was a cooler, a blanket spread and he was sitting waiting for me. He acted more friendly on the phone than he did when I got there. "Want a beer?" he said as he popped open a can. "I guess. What's up?" I asked him. "He didn't say much, but seemed preoccupied. He wasn't chatty. Finally I said, "Well, look man, if you aren't gonna talk to me after I walked all the way here, then I'm outta here." He then quietly told he liked me for a long time now, and wanted to date me as he tended and poked and prodded a small campfire. I told him that I was flattered but not interested in him as a boyfriend. That's when Pete tipped his hand and pulled out a shotgun. I said, "What's that for? You going hunting?" He said, "NO. Take off your clothes." You have GOT to be kidding me. "What? Come ON Pete. You don't really want to do this. This is not how "romance" is supposed to go. What would your good Catholic mother think of you doing this?"

"I said take your clothes off" and threatened me by cocking it and pointing it at me point blank. The day was so lovely. I could hear birds chirping. He said he would have me and I could either go along with it nicely, or he'd rape me anyway or kill me and fuck my dead body. I really thought he was bluffing and shitting around. That's when this high school classmate stood up and I could see he had a hard-on making a big tent in his pants. Really? How can this scene make you horny? I knew that he knew his way around a gun, most of the kids did as we lived in the country and the boys were hunters from an early age. I never thought that I was gonna be the prey.

I heard rustling from the bushes. There was someone hiding in the bushes, watching the whole thing from the sidelines! What the Christ. Someone was watching and getting off on this scene, I thought. "You are jacking off to this? What a twisted fuck you two assholes are," I said to them both. I had a very good idea that the accomplice in the bushes was his inseparable best friend, Tim. These guys were guys I'd watched a few movies with. Had a few beers with on nights and chatted long into the evening. They were kinda weird, but really, they were teenage boys. They were all weird, in my opinion.

I should've (*and nearly did*) turn around and walk straight back down the hill. If I did, I'd risk getting plugged in the back. Paraplegic. The ironic thing was that, from here, I could actually see my house and its safety from this budding crime scene. I wondered in a flash:

Would Dad just hear a gunshot and just figure someone was hunting?

Would Mom hear about it on the scanner?

What would Pete and Tim do with my body?

I wondered. I wouldn't put anything past these guys. They lived on farms. They knew about lye. We all had pigs. Tim had bragged he was responsible for all the bomb threats at the HS recently. I felt cornered and trapped. Trapped by people who were definitely unbalanced. It wasn't a game of braggadocio with them anymore. I could see that now. They really WERE as weird as they had joked they were. Ah.

I stalled, coddled, coaxed and tried to bargain a reprieve. I reasoned. I reminded. Cajoled. No such luck. So finally I succumbed to the demand, resigned myself and said "fuck you assholes" and laid down on the blanket so carefully prepared for this act of dominance. When Pete dropped his pants, I saw that he actually had a rubber already ON his pencil dick. The fucker actually had prepared for this when he called me! It was all premeditated, including the friendly phone call. He was waiting for me the WHOLE TIME with a condom on. I was livid. The whole act with him flailing around thankfully took all of about a minute. Thankfully, he was a come-too-quick-champion. Yet he did what he set out to do. He had me whether I wanted him or not, and Tim freaking WATCHED and backed him up. I didn't know which one was worse. I swore that I'd never trust again after this. I wouldn't look at him. Not that he'd ever look me in the eye again after that.

I pulled up my unsanctified jeans *(conveniently without any semen trail to take to the police as he prepared for that with a condom)* turned around and was walking the trail back down the hill to my house. When I heard some talking, I looked back and saw Tim come out of the bushes to stand by Pete. The last thing I heard as I left, added a stabbing insult to my injury with this from Pete: "Hey! The gun wasn't even LOADED!" I heard them both laughing their asses off.

Embarrassed, mortified and stinging from inhuman dealing and female violation, with every step home, I silently cursed them to the deepest and lowest ninth level of Dante's Ninth Hell *(which is conveniently and appropriately reserved for Betrayers.)* I hoped they would find the justice that I beseeched from Heaven. Please God, make it so. I couldn't wish it to happen to more deserving people, the fuckers. The real reason I tell you this story, isn't to garner sympathy or for any pity. Rather the reason I mention it, as at one point, I didn't know if I was going to be able emotionally put this story in this book or not. I told a girlfriend who was interested in my writing progress so far, and I mentioned my dilemma about whether I should include the rape.

Tragically she said, "Yah, well, we all have one of those stories."

Really? Then it hit me that unfortunately, rape is such a common occurrence to women as a population. And I thought, what a truly fucked up world we live in where "we all have a rape story" is almost a universal thing. In our country alone, in the United States, about one in every four women have reported being raped. That's ONE IN FOUR. But that's not the big news! The big news is that 60% are never reported. And 40% of women are raped by acquaintances. I also wanted to include this story, because I was just at a movie marathon with some girlfriends this weekend. There was a rape scene in the movie. My friend started spontaneously crying next to me when the character in the movie said that she "didn't want to report the rape. I can't. I just can't." I figure there must've been an untold story in this friend's life, as well.

Many women don't report it. How can we? We become a pariah if we do. We had nothing to do with the violence, yet we are blamed for it, somehow. The worst remorse I have in my life is agreeing to not turn in someone who raped someone dear to me, on the promise she made me give to her after she was brutalized. She feared for her life. I will always, always regret that promise. The fucker should've gone to jail. Maybe even had his dick chopped off. Instead, women internalize it. We rationalize it. We accept the blame for it. We carry a lot of guilt. We try to put up a brave face. We instead learn to medicate our fears, betrayals and anger with food, drugs, alcohol or bad relationships which mimic the boundary abuse.

I personally buried myself in my room, isolated myself for months on end with my music, my guitar and my artwork. I wrote and cried a LOT. Then, my heart scarred over, I dried my tears. I did some soul work, and I forgave…

But I never forgot.

And just in time too. Soon, high-school parties and cliques opened up to me with my voice and my guitar, as I regained my sassy attitude. I played solo at the General Brown HS talent show when I was seventeen. I still have the program of that night. Most of the kids in school didn't know that I even played guitar till this "coming out" moment. I walked out on stage, with my feathered Farrah Fawcett bangs and sat down alone on the very large and scary stage. It was my first time in front of a really big audience. The lights were really blinding. I played "House of the Rising Sun" and Neil Young's "Down by the River". By myself, out there on the stage boards, I sang about addiction and killing your lover, right there in front of God and everyone. My parents were in the crowd out there somewhere. I dedicated my timeslot to my mother that night. Aside from my choice of music, she was pleased, I think. I was very aware that I was not in control of my sweaty palms, earth-quaking limbs and nervous knocking knees. Somehow, I got through it. There was applause. I didn't win (*there was a garage band that rocked the last slot. Oh isn't there always?*). I did prove to myself that I had balls, courage and the gift of voice and music to give to anyone in hearing range.

Janis Joplin was my role model. She was deep-hearted yet tough as nails. She and I had so many things in common! She had been an outcast in her home life in Port Arthur, Texas. She had a lust for life, had some rough knocks, and still she wanted to live and experience love and life.

She experimented with sex and drugs and rock & roll and well, if it was good enough for her, it was good enough for me. So after the Talent Show, I followed in Janis's footsteps. I slipped my collar and went to a bar, got drunk, washed down a couple of speedy white crosses and picked up a likely handsome Jesus-looking, but dangerous stranger and fucked him silly. I faced my fear head on. I figured that You can't take from me if I offer it to you. You can't fuck me over, if I want to fuck you first. I didn't sleep for two days when I got home. Later I found out that this particular guy was a very bad man. A jailbird with a bad past. Shit. I didn't know that at the time. But then again, I wasn't looking. I was leaping.

(Here's another Life Lesson I learned late in life: Guys who look like Jesus should come with some sort of paperwork in advance of you fucking them. Why isn't there such a thing? Hell, I could've used it for a few more likely guys in my past. You don't know what they don't tell you…and in that instance, they can still fuck you over by keeping info to themselves.)

I continued drinking and drugging my way through high school. It was the Janis Way and I was a devoted follower in the ways of The Rose. And I rose above it all.

I'm full of silliness and surprises! After one night's carousing, I sashayed into a room of drunken sleeping teenage revelers in the wee hours of a morning, wearing only an apron. I held a wooden spoon and woke the guys and told them that breakfast was ready and that I had made pancakes. I walked back to the kitchen, away from my friends, who then were drowsily waking up their hung over brains, not sure if they just saw a naked young Goddess in an apron. When they all came to the kitchen I was fully dressed and pancakes were waiting with coffee. They were never sure if they really saw me, or if it was some sort of a weird mutual fantasy dream.

One day, after a particularly good batch of weed was consumed in secret in mass quantity; I stood up from the kitchen table and walked to the living room to lie down. At least that was my intention. Because I was also a practical joker, both my mom and my sister thought I was pulling their leg and was gonna "fake" a last minute turn quick at the end. No such luck. Evidently, I blacked out WHILE continuing to walk and proceeded to walk straight into the wall and smack dab crashed into the fish aquarium. I woke up on the floor, soaked with a fish flopping around by my head.

Shortly after several of these recurring blackouts, fainting spells and resulting migraines I was hospitalized and tested extensively and diagnosed with Petit Mal Epilepsy. I was treated with Dilantin and Philantin, respectively. Petit Mal is known as "absence seizures" which features sudden lapses of consciousness, and evidently, I'd been having them for several years and the zoning out I'd been doing was actually a real disorder. Everyone had just thought I was keeping to myself or being stuck up. I wasn't actually "there" at the time. While it's a milder form, it can still be dangerous, depending on what you are doing when you black out. Unfortunately, those particular medications have side effects of depression and adds an increased risk of suicide thinking. Oh boy howdy, did it. I tried slicing my wrists once, tried overdosing on my medications, and even considered drowning myself in the bathtub, but thankfully thought better of it. After awhile and some research, I realized it was the <u>medication</u> that was making me feel so badly, and not my inner sweet self.

Later on in life, I realized that I felt like the girl in the story *The Red Shoes*. I had been denied being me, acknowledged, and was not only emotionally and soul-starved. But I was young. So in order to get through my high school years, I did what some do. I was miserable and medicated myself with alcohol and drugs to pick me up, barely avoided being pregnant, hung out with friends (some good, some bad.) I marinated in music, art, writing, alcohol, weed and amyl nitrate. I was encouraged by friends to try huffing, but after doing it several times, I told them, "No thanks. I have enough headaches and altered consciousness already from the Epilepsy. I'm all good with that shit." You get what you pay for, I guess.

My creative side was prolific, producing countless paintings, drawings and stories. I found popularity mostly because I was a bit whacked and unpredictable. I told my sister that my goals were easily attainable such as: "I just wanted to grow my toenails long enough to click when I walked barefoot." I smoked cigarettes in the boy's bathroom in high school. I never really got in any serious academic trouble as I'm kind of a nerd, but a nerd who was always walking on the teetery edge of life. I hadn't learned to value myself…yet. During all this, I found that love and lust give the same feeling but are only wrapped up differently…

and I liked both.

Traveling Companions

I graduated from General Brown High School with a good grade point average and Regents diploma. But I had a lot of health issues during my senior year. *(All four wisdom teeth out at once, tonsillectomy and adenoids surgery, pilonidal cyst, ingrown Japanese foot warts, Shingles…all proof of the anger I had but was turning inward and manifesting on myself).*

Finally, I got through all that shite and on Christmas Day in 1978, when Dave called from Texas and apologized and told me he couldn't live without me, and invited me to come down to live with him and Ada and Ted….well, I packed immediately. I convinced my parents that it was time for me to go. I emptied my pittance of a bank account that had $250 in it and bought a one way bus ticket to Texas.

Mom was not pleased that I was leaving, and she told me so by claiming the soon to be empty room and painting what was my former bedroom as I was packing to leave. She took me to the bus station early one January morning in 1979. I had a duffel bag and $130. She told me to call home collect at every bus-stop layover. I promised I would, and with tears from Mom and my little sister Dorothy, and with echoing smiles and tears from me; I left home and lit out for independence.

I'd done a lot of Greyhound traveling back and forth before from Watertown to Syracuse New York during my teenage relationship with Dave. But that was less than a hundred miles one way to his house from my parents' home. A fifteen hundred mile cross country trip on a one-way ticket with not enough money to buy another trip back is a different animal altogether.

The myriad of travelers included business people going from point A to point B, also the partiers who convinced the driver to stop at a convenience store to get beers, but then the driver wouldn't let them carry it on. This pissed them off royally so they smoked joints inside the Greyhound instead. That turned into a boon for me. The bus driver stopped the bus and came back a few times bitching, but he could never quite determine the actual culprits, so he gave up after awhile and just kept driving while we just kept smoking.

I had left home with long hair washed and braided for the three-day trip. I had covered my braids with a bandana for the winter ride to dry. When I got to Texas I intended on brushing it out to hopefully appear to be a beauty queen to my long lost love's delight. Then there was my interesting short layover in Tulsa, Oklahoma at 3 am one bleary morning. Walking into the large bus depot ladies room, I saw my first homeless people ever. They had come in to get warm and sleep inside on this 15 degree bitter cold night. One lady was sleeping in one of the stalls. I know she was sleeping because of the snoring. Another woman was stretched out on the "purse rail" under the mirrors. I had no idea someone could do that kind of perching while sleeping. I washed my hands, checked my braids, and glanced at the bird woman stretched out on the narrow metal ledge. Noting it, I said, "Great balance" and walked out to get onboard my next steed to my promised land.

While standing in line to board on this frosty dark morning, a lady behind me said "Nice hair" to my braids. I groggily said "thanks" to the oddly dressed traveler. I looked down and realized that she had her socks on OVER her shoes. "Ah" I thought. "Hey, want to get on ahead of me?" I asked her. Oh yes she did and as I boarded she asked me to sit with her as I had expected. I walked right by her spinning eyes and sat down with a handsome young black man in the back instead. He looked like the safer choice for a seat mate. His name was Mike. He was really quite nice. I soon was introduced to "the little guy who lived on Mike's shoulder. His name was "Charlie," said Mike with a truthful face, and I came to learn that Charlie was an asshole. I never did see Charlie, myself, but Charlie proved to be full of antics and was constantly pulling jokes and making Mike laugh to himself. He was definitely the better choice for seat partner entertainment value.

While on a layover waiting in the bus depot in beautiful San Antonio, I met two guys there. They had been cruising the bus depot "for something to do" and introduced themselves to me as "Spike," a tall, thin black guy and "Kung Fu" who was a short, feisty, obviously very inebriated proud Mexican fellow. We talked. They thought I was beautiful and amazing. I thought they were very interesting and loved to listen to their drawl and talked about the differences in where we were from. I stashed my duffle bag into a bus depot locker and walked across the street from the bus station to get a beer with them at a bar. I was eighteen and it was legal then. I knew absolutely no one in this town and all my belongings were safe in some hide-away. *(If ever there was a mark...I was it that day. I knew it. I didn't care. I went anyway. I felt aware of the situation at least.)*

Being outrageously confident, stupid with a splash of Super Hero, this young woman from New York told these stranger guys that she was going cross-country and that she only had $125 on her person and all to her name in the whole world with which to start her new life with, <u>BUT she was gonna buy them EACH a Lone Star beer anyways cuz they were cool.</u>

Well, they couldn't fucking believe it. In the land of the south, this was unheard of! I told them that the Civil War was over and they thought so too, but there was a whole 'nuther feelin' from the guys with the rebel flags and gun racks on their trucks. I was flabbergasted that there was still so much prejudice. I was very green.

We played pool and then they bought ME a beer. REPEAT. These two young, strong, misfits told me they lived in what was a southern culture of old prejudice. They were dumbstruck and astounded that some cool white chick from New York would not only spend time with them and trust them but even buy THEM a beer with the only money she had! To reward my bravery, they took me under their wing like a long lost sister. I had body guards now. The bartender just shook his head disgustedly. We left and Spike and Kung Fu showed me San Antonio only as two street rats could. So far away from the raging blizzard in New York, we walked along in our shirtsleeves down the beautiful river walk in the twilight January night of San Antonio. Spike pulled out a harmonica and started playing while I vamped the blues under a bridge as the boats went leisurely by. This idyllic, perfect blues scene was punctuated occasionally by Kung Fu puking his guts out in a bush. If ever there was a Janis Moment, this was freaking IT for me. I was in Free Girl heaven. Four hours later, they got me back to the bus on time for my departure, unmolested, with a happy adventure under my belt, and safe and sound from my Guardian Hell's Angels, they gave me hugs and a kiss to have a good life. These two strangers became my friends that day. I don't know whatever happened to these sweet street rats, but I do hope good things followed them for showing their kindness to me.

That moment proved to me that some people that are seemingly bad, aren't. I already knew that some people that are seemingly good...aren't always what they seem either. Life can be a bizarre illusion. My faith in the human race got a wee bump up for the better that day.

I now had just $100 bucks left to my name *(thanks to the shared beers)*.

I was 18 years old, free, independent, 1,500 miles from home and the world was wide open for me. My brushed out hair looked great and I wasn't even concerned that I hadn't a clue to where I was going or what was to happen next.

Yellow Rose of Texas

I may not have been scared of getting off the Greyhound in Richman, Texas, but my bus driver sure was. It was 11:30 p.m. and the bus station was pitch black and closed for the evening when he pulled his trusty steed into the parking lot to drop me at my final destination

As I stood by the side of the bus, the driver handed me my duffle bag from the baggage compartment and said: "I don't know you, but, sister can I give you some free advice?"

"Sure."

"When I leave, I want you to immediately call a taxi and then go wait in the dark till the cab gets here. OK? Promise me?!"

"Uh, ok." I thought the advice was a bit cryptic and unnecessarily creepy but thanked him for the ride and the bus pulled away.

And then I knew why: The bus had left me, a northern unattached teenage girl, alone, in the dark, 2,000 fucking miles away from anyone that I knew, in a state known for rednecks, posses and tragedy, and the bus station was closed. It was black as pitch except for the bright light beaming a cone of white light down onto the telephone booth. I went to the deserted phone under the only street light, opened the worn yellow pages, called a cab, told them where I was, and that I was going to wait in the dark to be safe. Then I hung up, gathered up my few belongings in the whole world, waited sitting on the curb, in the dark and prayed that I was all alone for now.

My nerves were on high alert and my intuition scanned the horizon and surveyed any movement all around me. It was quiet. It was barren. A hot rod went blowing past with the music blaring, and I was glad they kept going and didn't know that I was there alone in the dark. I was also so very glad there were no other beings or creatures around me. Visions of Spanish ethereal beings from Carlos Castaneda hovered in my memory. Were there any "Allies" here? I hoped so. I went and stood against the building and tried to camouflage myself as part of the wall. I became as invisible as I could for what seemed like an hour. It had really only been about twenty minutes when a taxicab pulled in. THANK THE GODS. I was ever so grateful to see someone come to rescue me! I only had an address on a crumpled letter from Dave that I cherished. He was currently living with a couple of friends of ours, and I had the address and a promise of shelter. They had no phone. I dearly hoped the cabbie could find it in the dark. The cab driver and I drove around for an hour. It seems that Rosenberg, Texas was set up in "grids" or blocks. If we crossed from one block to another, it would cost a whole lot more money. Fortunately, the driver was up for a midnight adventure and we finally found the place. I had him wait, until someone came to the door, to make sure I had the right place. For fucks sake, I didn't want to get dropped off somewhere in Bumfuck, Texas and be left there without a trace. This was obviously not a "nice part of town." There were some Mexican low riders out and about and people on the streets talking and yelling. They may have been as nice as Kung Fu, but I didn't know for sure. I went up to this strange dark house, which the cab driver thought was the number I had on the address. It didn't look promising. After knocking and waiting for what seemed forever, a familiar face came in view! Dave opened the door, and I was "home!"

Jesus rescued me once again! After living on a bus for almost four days, *(and with now just $80 to my name)*, I was relieved to say the least! I waved a goodbye to the cab driver and dove into my new independent life on my own…in a galaxy very, very far from home.

Nudists in the Making

Life in rural small town Texas was a trip. The place where Dave, Ada and Ted were staying in when I arrived was the most bizarre thing I'd ever seen. It was a small one level southern house up on blocks, like many down there. Yet the landlord decided he wanted to "rent out rooms." So with plywood and

2 x 4s he carved the house into separate dwelling spaces. There was neither refrigerator nor kitchen sink. No problem! We had a cooler, didn't we? We had a shower stall. We had a toilet. Ok, no door…but we had each other. We washed dishes in the shower. This probably would have gone on for a lot longer, except we also shared the "kitchen" *(if you could call it that w/o a sink or fridge)* and we also shared the bathroom with another boarder who was a stranger. Well, not for long. It got weird. We were all just divided by a piece of thin plywood.

One night while Dave was at work, I was watching TV. The windows were open to let in the February breeze. I didn't think anything of it, and decided to change my clothes. I took off my jeans and shirt and as I was pulling off my bra, I heard something that made me freeze.

"Mmm, mmm, mmm," said a man's voice as clear as day. It wasn't our roommate. I didn't know WHO it was. I dropped to the floor. With heart pounding in my throat, I realized there was an intruder just two feet away from undressed me leering at me through a simple screen window! But then I took a different perspective. *(Oh, STUPID, STUPID Merlyn! Changing your clothes with no drapes or shades drawn! You fucking idiot. You aren't in Kansas anymore.)* I stayed on the floor, dragging myself under the bed and stayed there for about a half hour. Whoever he was went away. THANK GOD. I became VERY aware that I was not living in the boonies anymore and couldn't behave as if I was. I learned instant street savvy.

Ted was blatant about not liking me. He was best friends with Dave until I came round. I was Yoko Ono to his Beatles mind. It wasn't pretty. One day, I was trying to learn "Suite: Judy Blue Eyes" by Crosby, Stills, Nash and Young on my guitar with the new songbook that Dave got me as a present. Ted burst into my room and physically stopped my hand strumming on the strings and yelled at me in my face: "STOP singing and playing. GIVE IT UP. You suck!!" Horrified, I put that song away and haven't touched that particular piece of music since that day. But, being a willful woman, I didn't stop playing or singing. You know what? "FUCK HIM with a big stick." I would take my guitar to the park and do yoga and play my guitar on a blanket in the sun. I persevered. I kept playing music. I kept practicing.

Shortly after this, we got tired of the cramped quarters and showering and washing dishes at the same time and moved into a house with "just us." That was me and Dave as one couple, and the little family of Ada, her toddler Chelsea, and Ted.

It was SO hot in Texas in the summer! We lived about 30 miles from Galveston as the crow flies, and it was humid as hell. It was like getting hit with a hot, wet washcloth when you walked outside. Exiting an air-conditioned cooler right into a sauna! But at least now we had our own place. We still didn't have a fridge though. So it was decided *(or rather bossy alpha Ted decided)* that Dave and I would be the ones who would go out and get a used fridge for the house. Dave knew a place he'd seen and wanted to try that place first. It was a scrapper's delight. Cheap used appliances, cars, motorcycles and bikes did abound there at "Old Blue's Appliance and Used Car Lot."

We looked through rows and rows of dubious choices of refrigerators. One was a rusty old rounded-edge fridge with a little metal ice box inside. It was totally oxidized all over. That was its color-REAL RUST. And then we met "Old Blue." He had on a baseball cap that had an emblazoned John Deere symbol on it and he was walking up to us carrying a Lone Star beer at 10 a.m. on this fine morning. He cleared his voice with a spit of tobacco and said, "Howdy! That 'chere icebox can't be beat! Works like a sonafabitch. You can take it for $35. I'll even guarantee it works for you for a month o' Sundays. *(snap)* Want a beer?" We did. Seeing as how we were broke and coerced into buying a fucking fridge. We bought it. Yes it was fugly. But you know what? It DID work like a sonafabitch. It was great! Alpha Ted was way less than pleased and bitched about it forever. The only thing you needed to do, was about twice a summer you had to "defrost" it by getting a hammer and a chisel and chip off the glacier of ice that would swallow the icebox and also the kitchen floor into a frozen winter wasteland. We didn't mind. Well, Dave, Ada and I didn't mind anyways. I bought it just to say "Fuck you, Ted! Oh, and by the way, here's your fridge." Suite Judy Blue Eyes, MY ASS!

The neighbors at our new house were interesting. On one side was a Mexican family, people who were quiet, kind and unassuming. They grew a garden with cactus that they would harvest and fry up daily. On the other side was a strange white family. This unit consisted of an old man who had a "bed warmer" Spanish girl who cooked for him and... We never learned her name, cuz that's how he introduced her to us. She smiled a weird smile. She was not to go outside and waited hand and foot on this ugly, mean spirited old man who treated her like crap. I think she was probably an illegal alien and was just happy to live here. The other family member was a kid about our age named "Boo Boo." No shit. That was his name. We saw the birth certificate with that name on it! He was the son of the old man. He was allowed to live with the old man but not in the house. He built a plywood shed and lived in it as his home in the backyard. We'd talk and share joints through the chain link fence. He was a good kid, dropped out of school and was looking for a job but he didn't really want one. He was happy to live in the shed on scraps the old man threw him. Strange people. Strange times.

Come to think of it, we were strange too. It was too hot for us as "Nawtheners." We were all friends and yet individual couples, it was the '70s, and we were all pretty much a bunch of hippies. Ada, my mentor, was about seven years older than me and a strict vegetarian. This was extremely cool in my eyes, however unattainable by me, a farm girl carnivore. I admired her and wanted to emulate her. Ada always smelled of patchouli. I adopted the scent as my own. Bit by bit, we became more and more different from the rest of people. Cooking vegetarian *(in BBQ land),* playing music at all hours of the day and night *(and it wasn't country for the most part),* trying to acclimate to the heat, we started going around the house with fewer and fewer clothes. It wasn't long before we were all nonchalantly sitting around buck-ass naked and watching *Saturday Night Live* on the TV which we rented once a week for that singular purpose.

One morning I emerged from my bedroom and Ada was painting the molding of the living room to work the upgrade off the rent. It was about 100 degrees already at 9 a.m. She had her hair all piled up on top of her head. No shoes, no clothes on…except for a bra. "I need support" she said sheepishly with a grin and kept painting.

We didn't have a pot to piss in. We got our furniture from the Salvation Army. I nailed stacked cardboard boxes to the wall open end out, so that we could have "shelves." We cooked vegetarian and drank a lot of Pearl and Lone Star beer, and smoked a lot of weed and were perfectly happy. We also didn't bother to invest money in curtains. The old man now sat on his porch facing our house. We were cheap entertainment. Hmmmm. Maybe I should've called this story, "Voyeurs in the Making" instead.

Sheik Yer Booty

Life was fun in Texas. We ate a lot of vegetarian cooking as well as good old BBQ, felt independent, basked in sunshine, banged around sultry evenings in a Karmann Ghia. We also had an impressive 8-track tape collection in the car. One of my favorites at this time was Frank Zappa's latest record, *Sheik Yer Booty*. He was dressed on the cover of the album as a sheik. Pretty hot, and I've always loved Zappa's guitar playing and way-out-there fun music. It was 1979 and the Iranian hostages and the gas pump shortages were recent news. Zappa's songs can be contagious. He tried something new in this one and it was much akin to what later on would be called "rap." The whole album was loaded with bass riff and catchy phrases. One of our favorites was the chant "Rammit, rammit, rammit…. rammit up yer poop shoot, la, la, la, la..." Ada and I were addicted to this silly song. We blared it from the car windows in the driveway. Well, when you are in a hood, you have to do something badass. Even if it was just silly humor, it was a fun song. Not sure what the neighbors thought, though.

I got a job working at a "Captain D's" Seafood restaurant. I was hired as a waitress by "Ed." His real name was Emad. He was Iranian. I learned the cash register and was good with people, so I got quickly promoted to Hostess, then to Dining Room Supervisor. Oooh wee. Ed told me one day that one of his friends from overseas had been "watching me." He really liked me. He wanted to meet me. This guy was shrouded in mystery as "He was of noble birth" and "Already had three wives at home" and "He was looking for number four and had cast his 'eye' upon me." *(WTF?)* So Ed informed me about all of this with great panache. Truly, I had noticed. It's kinda hard to miss some Jesus-looking guy who comes in well-dressed suit sharp to a fast food joint and sits in the lobby with his two "bodyguards." When I had nicely but repeatedly asked if I seat them, one of the bodyguards would speak for the quiet Sudan guy, and say, "Thank you, but no. He is just observing." Ed also asked me, privately, if I was interested in going out on a date with this sheik dude. He also immediately asked *(a bit too quickly in my honest opinion)* this unnerving question: "Also, ah, do you bruise easily, by chance?"

What kind of fucking question is THAT? Ah, YAH. I DO bruise easily. Is this a "sorting out question" for His Highness? Does he like it, or No? Good God. My answer? "Um, NO, Ed. I am not interested in dating a moneyed mystery foreigner who may marry me, treat me, use me, abuse me and strand me out on a road somewhere in Bumfuck, Texas. Thanks, but I'm all good." After my rebuff the sheik dude never appeared on the doorstep of that Captain D's again. It seems there were no 'hush puppies' there for him.

Lesson learned here and MASTERED: Beware a quiet, Jesus looking guy with money, body guards, three wives and a penchant for bruises. Yah, it's a big tip-off.

Born to be Wild

That, of course, led to the next belief that only Jesus-looking guys WITHOUT money were still on the roster! But hey, lucky for me, there are still so many of THEM from which to choose.

I got a bicycle in Texas to bang around on. It was an old balloon-tire Schwinn. Big old balloon tires were awful in hilly upstate New York. But here in flat Texas they were a great ride! So soft and comfy! My new ride was blue, and I got a really big old cushy seat for comfort. I also bought a wire basket for the front and wire saddle baskets for over the rear wheel. This way I could live "green" and ride to get my groceries and to the library. I loved that bike. It was a good, honest quiet life with a little herb thrown in. I was 18 and like the song, everything "was Alright now."

One hot Texas evening I was riding my bike and I heard a motorcycle. It wasn't going very fast, but whoever was riding it was just tooling around, up one street and down the other, burning time. Then I saw him go past. My heart stopped. I swear to God it was one of the long-haired bearded guys from my favorite mega band driving it! We were IN TEXAS for fuck's sake. I also knew which one of them it was. I was SURE of it. I had all their albums. I KNEW what he looked like. I'd drooled over him before. It was the spring of 1979 and I knew the band had just come off of extensive touring and was currently on an extended hiatus.

Then I realized, I was only about 40 miles from Houston. I was in an outlying village, in Rosenberg, Texas! The band had to be home off tour and had time to just be cruising around! This rock legend was just being a "regular guy" out and about in his neck of the woods. Oh my God!

Of course, I chased him on my bicycle. "Waitin' for the Bus" became an instant ear worm just then. I started humming the chorus, "Have Mercy…been waitin' for the bus all day…"

I lost sight of him. Finally, I gave up the chase (*bicycles don't go as fast as motorcycles, unfortunately for me*). I gave up and decided to go to the store before I rode home. And THERE, there was the Harley. It was parked right in front of the mom-and-pop corner store. He must be inside. I was in luck! I propped my bike against the store and bravely strode in. Me in shorts and a halter and sandals and long blonde hair. I saw him in one of the aisles. He was wearing jeans and a t-shirt and his long hair and beard. It was an UBER MUSIC JESUS sighting!

"Hi" I managed to say in his presence. I dared not utter that I knew it was HIM or say his name and break the magic spell. "Hi back" he said and grinned a dusty smile.

"Nice bike." *(conversation opener)*

"Want a ride?" he countered. *(Conversation continuer and a bit of a dare…)*

"Really?"

"Sure."

Oh HELL, YES! Before I knew it, I was leaving my propped Schwinn there against some store and sidling up behind a Rock Idol of mine, on his Harley and riding out into the desert on a wild rock' n' roll night! I couldn't fucking believe it! My arms were wound around his waist. Our hair flying and feeling the hot summer night now cooling as we drove for miles out into the sweet desert air. It was dark now. As we rode, his songs ran through my mind. I reached down while he was driving and let my hands slid along his strong thighs. My fingers lingered tantalizingly around his zipper. I felt that he liked what I was doing. It was immediately apparent with the growing wood that sprang to life. What was I doing?? Oh my God, I don't know, but it was thrilling! I was connecting to a Rock n'Roll GOD. Pretty soon, he pulled the bike over at a crossroads. There was no one around. He swung around on the bike and kissed me. We French kissed forever. He said, "You're sweet. You want to drive?"

"ME? I don't know how."

"That's OK. I'll drive it. You can sit up front and steer it. I got your back." So we switched places. I had my sweaty palms now grasping the handlebars of a big fucking Harley with him riding behind me. He now encircled MY waist with his hands as I drove. It was AMAZING. The night air! The stars. That machine in my hands! The landscape was so FLAT. I could see the curve OF THE WORLD. There was the thrilling hum and exquisite buzz of the motor right beneath my legs. The vibrations gave me very sexy ideas while it purred...so did I. His hands started roaming around and exploring my body as I kept my hands tightly on the handle bars. It was up to me driving this thing. He felt my breasts and was gentle and sweet and caressed me really lovingly. After awhile he slipped his hand up my shorts. He found me to be quite wet and excited. It was the night. The bike. The spontaneity. It was MAGIC for fuck's sake!

I'll admit, there was a moment when an awful thought or two crossed my mind. The fact that he could be a mean man to me, and that I'd already had enough meanness in my life. The fact that I had the power in my hands, right now, to hard crank turn this bike handles sideways. It would send us flying through the dark night sky and catapult us to our deaths or start us on impaired lives of quadriplegic existence. It wouldn't take much. Only a quick jerk of my hands to the left or right. I had the power of over us both of life or death in my hands at that very moment. I lingered on that thought. But instead I held on and steered straight as an arrow down that long flat road.

His hands were making me even wetter. He was so snuggly. He was like a furry big bear man who was cuddling me safe. I never came out and asked him his name. I didn't want to break the spell. I psychically knew his name. He was safe with me by not telling me who he was. We both knew the situation. I was his date for the evening. I found him to be the sweetest man. So sexy. So strong. So wild and yet so tame.

Those delicious sensations! The warm Texas summer night wind, the feel of the Harley under my ass, my fists clenching the handlebar grips of this monstrous machine, the roaming hands of a rock God, our hair whipping about our faces in the wind....I was overwhelmed. It started as a sweet thought, that ran up my belly to my smile and ran right back down between my legs to the tips of my toes. I came hard while steering that bike. He let me finish and slowed the bike down to a stop. He kissed me again. He asked nothing from me. I murmured my sincerest thanks. He brushed the hair out of my eyes and hugged me sweetly. We changed places on the bike and he drove me right back to the mom-and-pop grocery and my patiently waiting bicycle. I thanked him for the ride and the lovely night's adventure. He kissed me goodbye. I told him that I would never forget this and that he was the sweetest man.

He waved goodbye and smiling a wicked sweet smile, as he drew in the lusty scent of me lingering on his fingertips. I waved back and smiled a thankful smile. I never saw him again. It was what Erica Jong had written about in her book, *"Fear of Flying"* when she described a moment such as this as a "Zipless Fuck." It was magical, unencumbered, spontaneous and sexual, and yes, a moment rarer than spotting a unicorn. I loved that music even more after that. Score 50 points for Sweet Jesus.

Have mercy.

Health Kick

I adored Ada. She was so beautiful to me and as close to a hippy that I'd ever been around. She was a total vegetarian, into non-violence and the environment, had a perfect body that tanned easily and had long, kinky hair. She had a penchant for cooking organically and eating raw foods. I could never understand why she was with Ted, who seemed be a total redneck hunter from the backwoods of the north, who had heartily adopted Texan ways and assimilated quickly. She was the doe to his hunter instinct. Yet, physically, they had the hots for each other and were a couple and we were all friends (*well, friends-ish for me and Ted…*)

I decided to break some of my farm-girl eating habits and my cigarette smoking addiction because of her good influence. I was now 18 years old and had been officially smoking since I was 11. I was now up to a carton of Newport Menthol 100s a week. It had been that way for a couple of years. There was what seemed like a fat lady on my chest at night. I had an ashtray on the side of the bed. It was the first and last thing I did every day and it was killing me.

So, I started my "toxic purge" by going on a 5-day yoga fast. The plan I found in some hippy book was to enjoy just a cup of juice for breakfast and another cup at night. It was intense. I stopped smoking, did an hour of yoga and went swimming for an hour in the sunshine before riding my bike every evening. To keep my hands busy from not smoking, Dave & I made a lot of wind chimes, and I learned macramé and cooked big dinners for everyone, but I would not sample a bite. I dropped 15 pounds in five days. I felt awesome.

After almost a week of this kind of regime, Ada and I rode our bikes down to "Ed's" coffee shop one morning. Ed served up good strong Joe in china cups and saucers. We sat on soda fountain spinning stools and gazed out over the counter of cherry cokes to a big bay window and watched the train go by. I loved that. I had three cups of black coffee and chatted. I then rode home on my bike. And then? I got earthquake tremors. I realized that in my purged clean slate of a body that coffee is a big time DRUG. I had the shits and couldn't get off the pot. I was sure getting a good cleaning out finally! Both Dave and Ada came into the bathroom while I sat there purging my brains out, and they begged and pleaded for me to break my fast. I finally did agree that my body was "done" with the fast. That night I started back eating with raw veggies.

I know how to do fasts much better now. But the good thing was that the purge cemented my desire to quit smoking cigarettes and I never went back to them. Oh, I tried a cigarette 3 weeks after that while at a bar having a beer. I bummed a cig from someone. It was my brand. It was HORRID. I never went back to smoking...tobacco.

Growing Into It

Fast forward a bit with me now....give a nod to many rock concerts that we saw in Houston's Astrodome...Jethro Tull *(Ian in his leggings and Gilded Butterfly codpiece),* "Yes" *(in the round on their revolving stage with us in Row 2)*....past more fights with Ted being a cock. Even a knockdown drag out row with him and my now hero, Dave.

Dave and I bonded in a big hippy way.

We were 2,000 miles from our homes and families and relying on each other. We were making it happen. We were also homesick and decided that we really didn't want to live in the Land of Rednecks and humongous palmetto bugs *(read "Super Cockroaches").* We had hunkered down through hurricanes that could rip your roof off and had had enough of sweat, posturing racism rants, and being blue in a red state.

So, we quit our jobs, gave away or sold items that what we weren't gonna travel with. We pulled all of our stuff out of our cardboard box makeshift shelves and packed our wee little sports car with everything we owned. There wasn't a lot. No furniture. Just some clothes, a couple of guitars, $500 total to our name, plus a pup tent and camping gear, a Coleman stove and some damn good muesli. We set off for the long trip back to New York. What couldn't fit inside the car was strapped on top of our Karmann Ghia.

Coming back home from yellow burnt grass, dried in the hot Texas sun, to settle in gorgeous Upstate New York in July was a thing of beauty to experience. Summer was now an exquisite pleasure with leafy trees, miles of GREEN and the flush of color!

We took up transition residence on the screened-in porch of Dave's childhood home. It was now apparent that the last tenant had cats as pets *(read: FLEA INFESTATION).* We would awaken in the night, itchy with bites and swore that we could hear the fleas pinging toward us to bite the shit out of us. We could hear the faint clicking sound of the fleas bouncing toward us on the hard wood floor to find us like a heat-seeking missile on a target in the dark from across the room.

This propelled us for getting an apartment of OUR OWN. It was bliss. We developed a new relationship with my parents who were now both retired and getting back into their music.

Bernie and Earl were a duo called "Golden Country" now that the kids were grown and he was retired. They played at retirement homes for seniors and were involved with "The Black River Valley Fiddlers Association." Mom and Pop were starting to enjoy their time together. Sometimes, I would drive the hour and half and join them on weekends and went to events with them. I played my biggest on stage gig yet at the Clayton Arena with my Mom and Dad and that fiddle group. I think I had to pee 15 times before I went on, I was so scared! But my parents were there, so proud of me and backing me up. It was awesome.

Pop liked to square dance. Mom did not. So sometimes, Mom would have me accompany Pop to the dances. Pop's diabetes was a constant, so he would need a chaperone and a ride home after a couple of beers. No, he shouldn't drink. But drink he did. And we had a blast. I remember driving us home, with Pop still whistling in the car to the tunes he'd just cut a rug to. Going fishing and dancing and drinking and playing with my Pop is a memory that I delight in to this day.

What with life being good, and Dave and I were now settled somewhat and family life was promising. I did the unthinkable. I proposed marriage to Dave in bed after a particularly good romp. Dave was 19 years old, six-feet tall, skinny as a bone, had the cutest happy trail from his chest belly hair to his nethers, was into playing his guitar, drawing, writing poetry and making things with his hands, living off the land…and BONUS! He looked and acted like Jesus. How could I possibly resist him?

Float past him easily accepting my proposal. We got married three weeks later, at Mom and Pop's farmhouse. In the living room.

With friends and family hastily called together for a make-shift-bring-a-dish wedding. They all assumed I was pregnant. I wasn't. I didn't want kids. I was just an impetuous Gemini. We'd been together since I was 15 really. We were married on a cold and sleet-grey day in March 1980. I had not yet turned 20. The wind blew sharp and bitter and the rain sleeted on the windows outside on our wedding day. Yet daffodils bloomed on the table with their sign of hope of spring to come. It was an intimate gathering in my parents' living room and we were married by a Justice of the Peace. I'll never forget his name. Coleman Hinckley married us in my family's farmhouse; and right after that ceremony, Coleman's wife picked him up right away so they could go grocery shopping. *(How's that for a magical day of your wedding?)*

I had been ill all week before with bronchitis and still was barking sick. The family doctor gave me his cure all for everything, a shot of penicillin, for my wedding present the day before the ceremony. *(Dr. Ronson prescribed Penicillin for EVERYTHING Always. Even going for a checkup, I could feel my palms starting to sweat the anticipation of a shot).* Ah, love!

After our party was over, Dave and I got into our little car and tried to make it to "The Arsenal Street Motel" *(a wedding gift from my parents).* But first we had to pull over and try to dislodge the shoe and cans that someone had tied with fecking <u>bailing twine</u> *(Read: Kryptonite)* onto our axle before it wound around it. Dave slid under our micro car, laid under it on the sleety-wet road, in his suit jacket and attempted to cut the bailing twine with the only thing sharp he could find in the car which was... his disposable razor. He was not successful in cutting the twine much but it was successful in giving us both a heaping dose of marriage reality from the get-go!

The Hat Man

I was now a young married woman at the ripe old age of 19, and Dave was an aged 20. Surely, I wouldn't advise kids to get married that young now, but it was right for us at that time. I learned that life is best when you can lean on each other.

We had nothing but love though, and I mean that truly. We were piss poor broke, on Food Stamps and HEAP. We lived on my Mom's canned tomatoes for a whole month once. We had no phone, no money, and one unreliable car. Dave got a job working out of town during the week and I stayed in the apartment and tried to keep busy and make a home for when he was with me on weekends. These were some of my loneliest times.

I worked at fast food joints during the week, while Dave worked at the other end of the state. We said our goodbyes at four a.m. on Monday mornings and I didn't hear from him again *(without a phone)* until he walked back in the door at six p.m. on a Friday night. It was damn hard.

Yet with a little help from my friends and my own will-power, I got out and got around. I walked or bicycled wherever I needed to go. I was relying on myself, my intuition and my savvy.

I remember getting my hair cut at my friend Debbie Slade's shop, "The Hair Machine," when out of the blue, I started shaking violently. Tremors like a seizure went through my whole body! I was vibrating so much so that we stopped the haircut. I immediately called my Mom from Debbie's phone to tell her what was going on. I needed comfort and information! Was it the Petit Mal epilepsy rearing its ugly head again? She said, "Oh, honey, what time was it that you were having these tremors?" I said, "Just about a half hour ago at 12:15 p.m. I was in the chair here getting a trim." She said, "Well, are you sitting down? I just got word from your Gramma, Grandpa James just died….it was at 12:15pm. He just slumped over into his soup and died mid-sentence. I bet you are feeling his fear of death and of his uncertain eternity."

Grandpa was crotchety that was for sure. He didn't believe in Spirituality, that much was certain. This is when I knew for sure that my psychic gifts of my youth were still with me, but I wasn't at all sure that it was a good thing.

Dave and I were enjoying living in our own cute little space. Our apartment was upstairs in an old rambley house, 1940s decor. The old couple who owned it were nice enough. Although when we originally viewed the empty "for rent" apartment, we got the strict warning to always use our entrance as there was only one way out. I thought this was against the law for housing? The old landlady said, "If there was ever an emergency, you could use the door to our side of the house that's in this hallway here on your side. It'll be locked on your side only. But really, use it only in a dire need or if there was a fire."

No worries. It was a privacy issue. That was fine by me too, so we signed the lease and moved in. We were happy there.

The day after my experience at the hair salon when Grandpa died, I had an interview for a job. I got ready and walked down the flight of stairs to go outside. I turned the door knob to open the outside door, and it turned but wouldn't open the door. The door knob just continually spinned round and round and wouldn't ever catch.

I'm a smart girl. I could figure this out. I quickly went back upstairs to find a screwdriver, but unfortunately, Dave had taken all his tools with him on his week away, and the one remaining was too small. I tried using various knives, nails, even the proverbial hairpin. Nothing. I couldn't remove that damn door knob! So, without a phone, not many other options, and a husband four hours drive away, I did what anyone would do. I went downstairs and pounded on the door and hoped that the landlords would hear me and let me out!

The landlady heard something, and she went to her door, but when she saw no one there on the porch, she shut her door again! I pounded on the walls, beat on the door, yelled, screamed and cried to no avail! They were old and deaf and could not figure out what was happening and thought I was having a dance lesson or something.

I went upstairs and decided to use the door to their side of the house. It was the "forbidden door" that was never to be used unless it was an emergency. Well, I deemed it a definite emergency! I moved all the stuff blocking the shared door and unlocked it from my side and opened it up.

The abyss had been breached. There was a dismal and dusty hallway and the light streamed in a way that I had never seen before. I quickly found the path to the unused stairs that led down to their garage. I tried to go outside through their garage, but they had it locked up tighter than a drum. They were indeed a paranoid old couple. So, then I knocked on their kitchen door, which was inside of their locked garage. Saying that they were surprised to see me there, within their locked garage was, indeed, an understatement. I told them my story and my imprisonment in my own home. The old lady said she thought she heard something quite awhile ago, but couldn't figure out what was going on. To calm my nerves, she gave me a cup of Comfrey tea. The landlord promised to fix my doorknob, which surprisingly enough, opened easily from the porch outside, but was stripped and would just spin round and round from the inside. Weird.

I got to my job interview late, but at least I wasn't trapped anymore! I was relieved. I went back home to my cat and my quiet apartment with the nice, new functional front door knob.

That night, as I went to sleep, safe and sound in my locked apartment, I was visited by something terrifying. In the middle of the night I awoke to the feeling that someone was in my room. It was quiet and there was no reason to assume that anyone had broken in. But there WAS a terrible feeling of dread. A heavy, stifling feeling like evil was in my room. My cat, Sha-Sha, growled. He never growled. I squinted and quietly looked around in the moonlight.

Yes. Someone was standing at the foot of my bed. He was a dark figure in a long black trench coat and he wore a black 1930s fedora hat. I could not see his face in the shadows. He was a stranger of demonic visitation. He seemed to be clean-shaven and short-haired, but his presence gave off such negativity that I screamed. Then he disappeared and was gone. Just like that.

My heart was pounding in my throat. I turned on the light. All was well. The locks were still locked. Nothing was amiss. My cat was worried. I tried to calm myself and managed to pray my way back to sleep. Without a phone, without the comfort of my loving husband who was far away, I felt I was not safe anymore. It must've been a dream. A terrible nightmare of a dream.

The next night, the visitor who I thought of as "The Hat Man" came again. This time as I was comfortably sleeping, I became aware that The Hat Man was back in my room again and closer to me than before. Without opening my eyes, I knew what I would see if I dared to open my eyes. I could feel, without looking, that he was merely inches from my face. His dark face was grinning madly at me. I could imagine his leering toothy smile so close to my cheeks. His eyes stared into my brain…into my soul. His breath was upon me. I was TERRIFIED to the depths of my very being. Evil emanated off this shadowy figure of the night. I could detect his dark malevolent spirit through my closed eyelids. He was daring me to open my eyes. I knew that if I opened my eyes, I would die! He would capture my very soul.

Instead, I closed my eyes tighter than ever and clenched my fists. I screamed NO! Go away! in my mind. I even prayed that my husband would save me. But my strong husband was not there. I was alone. After what seemed like forever, of constant prayers and pleading, I felt the malignant ethereal presence dissolve and I tentatively opened my eyes.

The Hat Man was gone. Then I started to wonder: Had the Hat Man come in to my apartment through the "Prohibited Doorway?" Was it was because I was all alone all the time and unprotected and felt vulnerable? Was it because my crusty old Grandpa James had just died and was floundering and afraid in another dimension and I received the psychic shock waves? Was "The Hat Man" the embodiment of Mr. Death? Was it simply the visitation of a staved lost soul? Was I having some sort of sleep paralysis? I have been known to get "caught in my dreams" and need my bed mate to wake me from dreams I sometimes could not easily escape. Was it the dark part of my psyche fucking with me or telling me that I should change something in my life? I don't know the answer.

It was not until I started writing this story, and got it finally out of my conscious memory here to you, that I decided to do a little research on it. I went to Google and typed in "Demon with a black Fedora" just for giggles *(you should too)*. I was flabbergasted! I read MANY stories about this shadow figure. He exists!! And YES, his name is "The Hat Man!!" *(Who knew?)*

What I envisioned IS the same vision this demon shape appears to countless people round the world as. They all say the same for his description. Dark man. Evil presence. Dark trench coat. Black fedora or black hat. I had become one of many people that have had a visitation from this awful apparition!

Evidently, this is a demon that appears to people in this same way. By the bed. In their sleep. He is said to be a Sleep Demon. He exists to brings FEAR. He feeds off fear. He is a dream demon and breeds the fear that he feeds off of. When I researched it, there are more questions than answers to this demon. What I do know from reading many articles long after the fact is that The Hat Man is a truly odd and frightening experience for MANY people out there. Interestingly enough, I also read that the only way to rid yourself of The Hat Man is to tell him "NO! Be gone!" and to pray. Pray to whatever God you respect. Thankfully, I did that instinctively. Maybe it was just a warning to connect to my faith and soul. Maybe the Universe was telling me that being empty inside, would give fear a foothold. It would be there waiting and anxious to fill the void. And maybe that's why my grumpy Grandpa may have been afraid at the time of his death…and maybe, just maybe, I had just been given a timely karmic heads up to straighten myself the fuck up.

Mommy Merlyn

One night, after I was exceptionally hormonal and PMS'ing, ranting, shitfaced on beer and sitting on the roof of our house arguing; Dave talked me into getting pregnant. I don't know HOW that conversation went, or why he wanted to have kids with a mad woman, but there was something said about "You just need to settle down honey, a baby will help you. You'll be a great mother" and a "Please come in off the roof" sort of cajoling. Well, he had me convinced to get off my high horse *(or roof)*. While I could've gotten angrier, I remembered seeing some high-strung female animals on the farm and sure enough, a litter DID help some of the more neurotic ones calm down. I had no direction. Fuck it. I'd try anything.

So, I cleaned my act up, stopped drinking and smoking pot, started getting my faith and prayers polished back off and pretty soon, there I was, going off the Pill and planning how to get preggers instead of avoiding it like the plague, I courted it. I got pregnant right away and carried the baby fine. Jesse was born in 1986, and she was the best thing that ever happened to me up to that moment. I wouldn't change a thing. I stopped going out and made a real effort to be a good wife, mother and homemaker. No one had heard of Martha Stewart yet. They didn't need her. Because I WAS her.

I was a mommy now, and a damn good one! My new baby girl, Jesse, was an absolute angel and a brilliant child if there ever was one. I was complete. I made a complete turn around and was now considered upstanding! I read my Bible backwards and forwards five consecutive times. I could quote Scripture. I baked bread, and put everyone on a whole foods and organic lifestyle. It was like I was a Seventh Day Adventist from my childhood.

I made presents and cards and we lived on Dave's one income. If I had the garb I could've been Mennonite. Jesse was the best thing for me. I don't know what I'd be like today without her. We were now a family. I loved it, and she was perfect.

Then my whole life was changed again. About two years later, I found myself pregnant again even though I was NOT planning on it. I gave birth to another baby girl. My dear Shawna Rose was born.

I thought she looked "different" in the delivery room and said so. The nurses whisked her away saying "her Apgar scores are low and we want to incubate her and pink her up a bit." At least that's what they told me. In the recovery room, while I was reveling in the after moments of the delivery, two serious doctors came into my room. Without any transition or setup they bluntly said: "We suppose you know that we think she has Down's Syndrome."

Well, Fuck NO, I didn't "suppose" I knew that at all! These

two doctors laid out the news to us, full bore, with full orchestration and then at the end they asked us this: "So...will you be taking the baby home? Or leaving it here?"

Dave and I were flabbergasted. Not only had we just had our bubble burst but now they were insinuating that we'd abandon our child, just because she "wasn't perfect but retarded." For Gods' sake, it was 1988 in America not the Middle Ages! Anger mixed with devastation and sprinkled with indignation is a salty dish indeed. "<u>OF COURSE we are taking her home!</u>" was what my husband and I blurted out in unison. We were a family. No matter WHAT.

At first I didn't believe the prognosis. I figured the doctors were wrong. They HAD to be. But soon, after blood tests and research I had to concede to their assessment. Shawna Rose Underwood had Down's Syndrome. And bonus! She had two heart murmurs at birth and was having heart failure. My own doctor did do a kindness to me though. He suggested that I get a private room and have the baby "room in" with me. It was a gift to not have to see a roommate mother with her perfect baby next to me at the time.

I learned be her advocate right away when this happened: In the middle of the night, I stirred from my exhausted hospital sleep and found a strange nurse quietly doing something to the baby. Groggy with sleep, I asked, "What are you doing?" To which the stranger nurse replied, "Just changing her bracelet. You go back to sleep" and she covered me back up and patted me. The synapses in my brain were confused and shook off sleep. "Her bracelet should match mine." I sat up and the nurse took off. I called the nurse's station and inquired as to WHY her bracelet was getting changed. A different nurse told me that "NO. Her bracelet should match YOURS." And we both looked at the baby's bracelet which was now missing. Someone had tried to steal my baby! God knows why. It was a Catholic hospital and all I can think of was that some zealot tried to take her and delete her from society for me because I would NOT put her up for adoption. BASTARDS! I bonded with my new baby like a fierce mother lion and I imagined that

Jesus and I rocked her to sleep that night in the hospital. Yes, handsome Jesus was with me again in my mind and holding this sweet little baby girl. Never again would I doubt my charge to be her protector. She was safe with me. Dave and I promised each other that we would do our very best by her and Jesse. No Matter WHAT.

We bundled up our beautiful, pink baby girl and went home to discover what real life meant to our new family. Downs did not run in either of our families. There was no rhyme or reason for the birth defect. I was young. So was Dave. The only thing I can think of was that it was a chemical environmental issue involved. Thinking back to the day I got pregnant, (we had been faithfully using birth control), I had done two things. I had sprinkled a hazardous flea powder in the house and I had also hand sprinkled the lawn with fertilizer, without gloves for both items. It wasn't until after Shawna was born, did I realize that poison is poison.

The doctor explained it as at the moment of conception, one chromosome just "gets sticky" and decides to go in the opposite direction than it normally would've and that's probably what happened and it was just "a bit of bad luck." It wasn't a "Perfect Barbie Cookie Cutter" Life anymore…but a life with a fierce new reality of heart murmurs, disabilities, adjustments and acceptance, and hopefully, tolerance from others. I went home to our house on the river and laid Shawna in her beautiful bassinet in her new nursery. She was home and safe. Funny thing, though, the very next day a pair of cardinals started making a nest in the pine tree that brushed against the nursery window!

I called Mom and told her what was happening, and she said, "Oh, Marilyn, that's your Gramma! You know she always loved cardinals. She is sending you a message that she is watching over you and that precious new baby with the appearance of those birds." I knew it was true, too. And in the following weeks, I watched that pair of birds set a nest and raise three babies just as we were raising a new special baby, all the while believing that Shawna had a guardian angel watching over her.

Cardinals symbolize Hope, Love, Cheer, Pride and Renewal. Thanks, Gramma for this baby bassinette blessing.

At about three weeks of age, Shawna had a "psychological evaluation" done for her acceptance into school. *(Can you imagine that? A "psychological evaluation for a three-WEEK-old?)* It is now a documented fact that children with disabilities function much better and make more solid progress if they are put into Early Education. Shawna started receiving Early Intervention and Early Education when she was one MONTH old. Teachers, speech therapists, occupational therapists all came to our door several times a week. I did my best to give both my girls and my dear husband whatever was needed to make them happy and healthy and smart.

Shawna started going to school at 3 years old. People think it's hard putting a 5-year-old on a school bus? How about also strapping a 3-year-old toddler, who doesn't have words yet, into a car seat on a transport and sending her to school for therapy and instruction? Tough doesn't begin to cut it.

My girls never went to daycare. I was a stay at home mom and we lived on Dave's one income, and that's the way we wanted it. Dave and I bought a house and set about making it our home. I scrubbed, polished, painted, baked and scrimped. I clipped coupons, made all our food, walked the kids in strollers every day. I got involved in volunteering at their schools and at the local library. I was a room mother at school, became a totally God-fearing, Sunday school teacher who could quote Scripture. I loved Jesus then with my whole heart and soul. I was saved. I was also a fun Camp Fire Leader with my kids. They were in 4-H too. I put in a garden and canned veggies. I made all our gifts. I gave the kids art lessons and took them on field trips. I home-schooled them sort of, in my way in addition to their school attendance. We had lots of fun! We finger-painted and did science projects. The girls grew up with a stay-at-home mother who played guitar and sang during their nap times and baked.

Endings & Beginnings

Those years with my little girls were a whirl. Shawna required a lot of attention, instruction and care. I also felt that Jesse, now "the big sister" but still a child, needed extra to balance out the attention her little sister had to have.

When Jesse was about 7, she too, was diagnosed with a possibly debilitating issue. She had pretty severe Scoliosis *(a 46/48 degree S curve)* and went through the process of trying to deal with the unwieldy structural handicap before her bones hardened and she was hindered for life. There were many hard shell propylene braces made for her periodically to wear and for us to enforce the wearing of. Every time Jesse grew a bit, we'd take her to the orthopedists and they'd stretch her out on some sort of a rack contraption table, balance her on it and wrap her in bindings and plaster of Paris and make a form for a new brace. We did this for about five years. It was hell keeping her in this awful torturous device. I felt so bad for Jesse. She was so vibrant, so carefree, such a tomboy and now here she was in this restrictive cage, which she had to wear for twenty hours a day! She would often unzip the Velcro which held it onto to her torso and slip out of it in the middle of the night. We had to do the awful mean thing and make her keep it on during this time of growth, and I admit a few nights we duck-taped it on her to keep her in it. It was only to be for a short while in the grand scheme of her life...while her bones were soft to keep the correct shape. Still it was a nightmare for her...and for us putting her through the constructive repair process. I give Jesse a lot of credit and kudos. She is a true trouper and a hearty soul.

I also realized that through all this upheaval, I needed to get out of the house a bit and do something just for ME. I was going bat shit crazy stuck out in a rural village, being a full-time mother, doing therapy on the kids and being Suzy Cream cheese homemaker. So, I started going to college at 32 years of age *(and eventually graduated with a 3.9 GPA)*.

My awesome Pop, Earl, had been fighting a lifelong battle with Type I insulin dependent diabetes at about this time. What a horrible fucking disease that is. His kidneys finally shut down and he went on dialysis every other day. He was in the hospital when Mom decided it was time to burn the barn down. She had been trying to convince Dad for years that the barn was unsafe. He didn't agree. Most of the family didn't agree either. It was an old barn, yes. But it was still pretty sound for the most part. OK, so it was falling down in parts. We were all fond of it and what it stood for. Mom, however, also wanted to see down the road and the barn sort of obliterated the view. As she sat at the kitchen table with her coffee, she looked down the road and would have to imagine the vista, what with the barn in the way. But while Pop was in the hospital of January 1995, Mom called her friends in the Fire Department and set it up with them to come and do a controlled burn. She didn't think they'd do it so quickly on the next nice day for it. Dad was not present to see it happen, thank God. It was a truly tragic sight. To me, Dad was his barn. The barn was Dad. I, unfortunately had to be the one to tell him when I went to see him the hospital after the whole thing was cold ash. I said, "Pop, I don't know how to tell you this….but it's about the barn…."

He said, "So she's done it then?"

"I'm afraid so. I'm so sorry, Dad. I really wish she hadn't."

"Me too." He said with a sigh and was visibly crestfallen. It was like the song "My Grandfathers' Clock." He now felt that he was done. It seemed to be a sign to him. A couple of weeks later, he told Mom, "I'm just so tired. I don't think I can keep hanging on." So Mom held his hand, told him she loved him and said, "You can go if you need to. We'll be ok. You did your best." He looked at her sort of relieved and just sort of decided to let go. He died the next day. Pop never did talk much. Yet he said so much with his silence. I felt his death like the passing of great patriarch. I was lost. But I still had a family to lead.

Adding to the major stress of losing one of my parents, I felt the big responsibility of raising two children with different disabilities. Then David came home dismal that week and told me he lost his job due to downsizing. Then his severance paychecks bounced. My dear kitty "Mitty Woo" had to also get put down due to a debilitating skin disease and illness…ALL IN THIS SAME FREAKING WEEK. Come on, God. Really? NOW? Nice timing. But wait, there's more. Dave then took a job in a factory close to home in the interim, and developed carpal tunnel syndrome *(instantly aggravating 15 years of being a computer draftsman)* and then he had to have immediate surgery "on both hands at once." He was then helpless and needing me too for about two months solid. I had to do everything. Helping him to bathe, get dressed, and potty and to take care of the kids, the house. Now I was Cinderella.

It wasn't long after this that Dave and I started fighting. A LOT. In retrospect, it was par for the course, and totally understandable under the stress that we were under. I thought we needed to fix our marriage. I had heard that a date night and a little "R & R" time could help stressed couples. I encouraged Dave to go out with me and get a drink and start our music back up and play at open mics. He tried it a couple times just to please me, but he was not really interested anymore. He said he was a "musician, not a performer." He was just too painfully shy and decided that he really didn't like being onstage. He was also jealous when I went out to play by myself. And by God, I wasn't staying home every night of the week after I had been home all day, every day, with the girls.

To make a long story short: Dave left New York and flew to Hawaii to live… and I went onstage. When he left, *(which is what he felt he needed to do to find his new path),* I felt stranded with the mortgage, the girls, no job, no money and no paperwork filed on either child support or marriage. It wasn't long but eventually our marriage went to divorce court. We still loved each other, but we couldn't take the stress that life had handed us. We accepted the fact that we had grown, but we had grown apart. But hey, we had really tried to make it work. And 17 years was a damn good try.

God Is Deaf

OK, well maybe God wasn't deaf, but it sure fecking felt like it. I had been a good Sunday school teacher and Christian. I had called and called out to God but there was no answer. I was now raising two handicapped small girls alone, no job, no finished degree, no work history and no money. Mate non-existent. Dave had credit. He was escaping from the pain and our breakup. I know that now, and I didn't blame him. I wished I could've too. I had been a stay-at-home mom for years, and didn't get that luxury. I kept on keeping on. Kids on early school buses. Working several jobs. Trying to pay the mortgage. No breaks. No escape.

I drank a lot. I cried more. I learned how to read Tarot from a Gypsy. I was searching for answers and I got them. I cleaned houses for a job while the kids were in school. I busted my ass. At one point, I had six jobs a week! There were the three separate houses to clean every week, plus the job of housekeeping at The Sherwood Inn, and the job I did housekeeping at another motel, and add on top an evening job at the college as admin assistant. I learned new music and played at night. I dreamed I worked as a musician and had a job at the Renaissance Faire. There would be long-haired guys there who would listen to me sing. I just knew it.

I tried to control the only thing I could in life. ME. I weighed and measured every morsel of food I ate. I dropped 60 pounds and RAN, RAN, RAN. I was running nine minute miles. I was desperate to run from a failed marriage and trying to advance towards a new life. You CAN change your life. Just kick it in the ass until it gets going! Throw yourself at it noon, day and night. And in the meantime, just believe in yourself. BELIEVE in better times. It WILL come. Things WILL get better. You just have to kick it. And if it doesn't get better? <u>Kick it harder</u>.

How I Met Your Stepfather

I had first met Wayne in my college English class back when I was still married. I was trying to get out of the house for my sanity's sake at the time and get some "grown-up" challenge instead of reading kids board books out loud at home.

This gorgeous long-haired guy walked in to my English class, a week late. I thought he was lost and should be in a Tel Com or Art course instead. As he talked to the teacher and explained his lateness for starting, the teacher said, "Go have a seat."

This handsome silver-haired roadie dressed in stage blacks was coming over to sit down in the chair right by me. After shuffling around in his stuff, he turned to me and I looked into the deepest sky blue eyes and he asked, "Do you have an extra piece of paper?"

Our eyes met and I knew I was in trouble right then. He too, was smitten. He needed help with Shakespeare and Greek Tragedy, and well, I had tri-colored markers and knew it backwards and forwards. We met for tutoring sessions in the student lounge. I tried to lure him to my house while Dave was at work. But when Wayne called my house, and a man answered, he realized that I was married and hung up. Wayne asked me the next time at class, and I told him yes but we were having trouble. It mattered not. He would not meet me. I could no longer tempt his company. Damn it. He, however, did not quit thinking about me, but went home to cold showers for about two years wishing things were different as well.

One day, about five years later, as I was leaving class after a final on a beautiful May Day, I ran into Wayne in the parking lot of college. He was standing talking to one of the guys who worked in Tel Com Department there. But when Wayne saw me, he immediately forgot himself and the fellow next to him in mid-conversation. At one point I told Wayne, "I don't know if you heard or not, but David and I separated." No, he did not hear that before. He waited for all of about 10 seconds and asked, "Want to go for coffee?"

I did. He had "some service calls to make on his job" but I was "welcome to ride along." I jumped into his old grey Chevy van. It was filled to the brim with gear and fast-food containers. I pushed stuff off the passenger seat and moved items from the floor in front of it and sat down. *(In retrospect, I should've taken this as a lifestyle choice of his, but only chalked it up to "bachelor living").*

I put my soon to be un-sandaled feet up on the dash as we rode around. He took me to Nine Mile Point. You know, the nuclear power plant? A strange but interesting first date where we talked non-stop the whole afternoon. We saw the tall ships in Lake Ontario in Oswego on the way. Bought a couple of quarts of beer and went home to drink them together at my house before my girls came home from school. When he first kissed me (he'd wanted to do that for years) he nearly crushed me with his overeager bear hug. We started to date, he spent the night one weekend when the girls were at their dad's. I still wasn't sure about him so I kept one eye on him all night, in between the lovemaking.

Come to find out, he was a musician but had put his guitar on the shelf many years earlier. His first wife had told him she didn't like his music at all and to put it away. When he met me, he dusted off his picking guitar fingers and started playing music again. Wayne was a genius, electrical wizard of recycled gear, made things with his hands, was a roadie for rock'n'roll bands and owned his own stage, sound and lighting business. Yes, he was an odd bird. He was eccentric, non-violent, horny as hell and he had long grey hair and a beard. He did not look like Jesus. He looked like Zeus! *(I guess I was trying to branch out of my regular "type" mode here).* Wayne didn't mind that I had kids. As a matter of fact, he wanted to be a parent. He was a great dad but wasn't allowed access to his son after his divorce. My girls would be the opportunity he wanted to get to be a dad. He was a fair man. He had all kinds of knowledge about gigs, rock'n'roll folklore, and brushes with personalities and great-ness. We were both hooked. We rocked each other's world.

Dave and I remained friends because of our dear girls. It wasn't easy at first, but both the guys I married in my life have been far and above the best and kindest men. Dave and I were officially divorced in December 1997. Dave has truly always been the best dad to my girls. He and I just couldn't live together anymore.

That same Christmas, I came down with a high fever and strep throat. While I burned up on the couch, nearly comatose while the antibiotics kicked in, both Wayne and Dave entertained the girls, got pizza and were not only civil, but FAMILY. They took care of me and the girls and became friends. Indeed, these were two men who really loved me and my girls for real. Our first divorced Christmas was spent all together as family, (and we usually share it somehow to this day.)

Jump ahead to Wayne proposing to me that following February, right after a romp on my living-room carpet. We had just been playing music all evening and singing and we were both pretty tipsy. Of course, I accepted. He really didn't need to impress me but he did again right after this moment.

July 1998, Wayne's business, *Harrison Audio & Stage*, was chosen as the Sound Contractor for the 150th Anniversary of the First Women's Rights Convention in Seneca Falls, NY. The guest speaker at several locations was going to be the First Lady, Hillary Clinton. It was all very hush-hush. For a month before the event there were intense security clearances and secret time schedules and arrivals and destinations. Wayne was up late most of those nights concocting wiring harnesses, panels and checking gear to make sure all was top-notch for the occasion.

On the day of the events, I said, "I wish I could meet her. You are so lucky!" He said, "Well, come to the museum today with the girls, and I'll get you in." Really? COOL! So, I got the girls, myself all dolled up in our best summer dresses and invited my next door neighbor and her two girls to come for the ride to Waterloo, NY. Hopefully we'd get a glimpse of the First Lady! I really admired her very much. So independent, solid and fair.

We got to the museum and found the event was going to be outside at the McClintock House. This is where the convention was planned 150 years ago with Susan B. Anthony, Elizabeth

Stanton and Lucretia Mott among others. Upon arriving, we saw a roped-off area with lines of white chairs for where the V.I.P.s were to sit close to the podium where the First Lady would be speaking, only inches away. There was definitely a hustle and bustle going on.

Wayne saw us, came over, kissed me and said, "Well, I've just met my hit man."

"What?"

"One of the Presidential Staff Bodyguards just introduced himself to me as my gunman. Just to let me know that he's got a bead on me the whole entire time, should something go awry and I turn into a terrorist. He's packing heat. Lots of it."

"Oh my! Now I'm scared."

Wayne said, "Don't be. It's the usual. Remember, I've done this work before. I met Hillary at a gig in Times Square years ago, she's a cool lady, a real person. And actually, as far as my gunman goes, he's got a good sense of humor and is nice. It's just his job. He's already checked over all my equipment and the podium three times."

Well, that put a different spin on things, now didn't it? I looked around at the rooftops to check for snipers and drew the girls closer just to be safe. It was a beautiful, sunny day and one where I really didn't need to worry. Wayne left us and went up to finish setting the microphone on the podium and adjust the height of it to match Mrs. Clinton needs.

Wayne came back to our little excited group, standing just outside the rope limits. We were waiting with anticipation! He said to me, "But why are you standing out here? I got you seats."

"Seats?" Oh my God. He got us seats. He turned me over to an usher.

"Right this way, Mrs. Fuller." *(Mrs. Fuller? We weren't married yet. That's next month! But OK…)* I followed the usher in, and my girls and neighbors followed behind me. I figured how wonderful! We were "inside the rope limits!! Woooot!" But the usher didn't take us to the back row where I figured our assigned seats were. Nor did she take us to the middle section of the small seating area. She took us TO THE FRONT ROW. Oh my God. The front row! And on the seats? There they were, with paper name tags with all our names on them. "They know our names?" I asked Wayne with definite disbelief in my voice.

He replied, "They know everything. It's their job."

So, I sat myself down, on a chair with my name on it, right straight front and center of Hillary Clinton! I couldn't believe it. She was right there, only a yard or two away from me and my children.

"Ippon!" *(the Judo term for 'perfect throw")* I said to Wayne as he walked by. "You win. I'm thoroughly impressed with my husband-to-be."

"I thought you might like this," and he handed me a red carnation to boot. "And a flower too? I think I've died and gone to heaven."

"Don't be too impressed with the flower. I took it from one of the arrangements on stage for you." *(Yah, that's about right. Later on, in years to come, this kind and silly hard-working roadie would also bring me discarded graduation flower sprays from stages at colleges so that I would get flowers from him. I usually take the monster flower arrangements apart and make about five arrangements from them for the house. "No sense in them going to waste" he'd say. I am just happy he doesn't work at a funeral home).*

But I can't stop the story there. Hillary came out and gave a very uplifting speech about Women's Rights and I was so honored to be listening to her with my own girls; Jesse who was then about 12 and Shawna who was 10, and Barney. *(Shawna brought her Barney doll with her. He went everywhere with her at that time, tucked under her arm.)* I didn't think life could get any sweeter at that moment. My husband-to-be, was an important person in my life, and in also in the business of life, here now happening in history. My girls and friends were with me to share this important moment, just before we married and to give me the shot in the arm about women, and our Power in this world. We are not to forget it. I gathered a lot of wisdom and courage from Hillary's speech that hot sunny day. Then Mrs. Clintons' speech was over. And an usher came up to us and told us if we wanted to meet Hillary in person to line right up. I was one of the first ones in line. OH MY GOD. Floored again!

So, the girls and I were right there to shake the First Lady's hand too. When Shawna approached Mrs. Clinton, it was awesome. Hilary took several moments to speak with her in particular. Shawna of course, had no idea of who she was meeting. Just a nice lady who shook her hand and talked to her like a person. Shawna had her Barney doll wedged up under her own armpit while she shook Mrs. Clinton's hand with her other hand. "I like Barney too" said the President's Wife who was also a mommy. And they both had a nice wee conversation, with Shawna speaking what she could manage, as her speech was not that easily understood. I was flabbergasted and left that event walking on air. It was just so out-of-this-world extraordinary the way it all set up! About three weeks later, I got a large manila envelope from The White House.

"THE WHITE HOUSE? What could they be sending me??" I opened it and in it were several 8 x 10 colored glossy pictures of Jesse, Shawna *(& Barney under one arm)* visiting with Hillary Clinton! "How did they know who they were? How did they know where to send it?" I asked incredulously.

"They know everything," repeated my very wise and handsome fiancée.

About a month later, on August 28, 1998 *(8/28/98 an auspicious day with an easy-to-remember date for us)* we got married. I had the florist make me a bouquet that "smelled" amazing, because I figure ALL flowers are beautiful. It was magnificent and it decorated our headboard after the wedding for the next two days with the most luscious flower scent. The day was gorgeous. The bed and breakfast was divine. This was the day that Harry and I r-u-n-n-o-f-t to get married. We put our instruments, luggage and flowers in my car and headed for the Bed &Breakfast in Little Falls, NY. We met The Justice of the Peace and the new life ahead of us with eyes wide open. I buckled my seatbelt, started the engine and I looked at my husband to be off to tie the knot, smiled and said, "Well… I hope this works out."

He said, "Yah, me too, honey."

We stayed in bed most of the weekend, except for an underground honeymoon to Howe Caverns and took a ride on a boat on an underground river. It was truly a unique start to our marriage. We've been doing unusual things ever since.

We had our reception at our house a week later. Harry had set up a stage complete with rig and sound and lights. My Mom came and she even took the stage as she'd done so many times before. But this time it was without Dad. Our musician friends were asked one by one, by her to accompany her. Mom put on her Martin guitar. She always wore it low slung. She was Queen of Country Music. When she was ready, she said, "Hit it boys!" And all the guys looked at her and each other without a clue. They'd just met her and she'd forgotten to tell them what song and what key. But they soon figured that bit out and it was lovely to hear her sing again. At my wedding.

Later on in the evening, when all the guests had departed and a lot of the summer party had been picked up, a microburst storm blew through our area. We awoke the next day to no power. And paper plates spread over the next door neighbor's yard. As a matter of fact, our town, and county and we found out later, much of New York State was without power. It was the great microburst storm of 1998. It seems our party was epic.

Harry rose to the occasion with his generator and solar lights and thank the Gods we still had enough potato salad and wedding cake to live off of for about a week. I realized then that I'd picked a real survivor in Wayne. As a husband, I knew he would take care of me and my girls. He's messy, but at least he wouldn't let us starve. We'd find a way to not only survive, but we'd thrive. I just knew it. Being in power outages, just at the beginning of your relationship, you find you ramble late into the evening over camp fires. We'd done a lot of deep conversations and we'd talked a lot previously about our lives, our hopes, our dreams, our weaknesses, our needs. We had made a promise to each other that we would try our best to stay together. No matter what. No matter if we even had an itch for someone else *(which had been problematic for both of us with former relationships, the want to stray)* but instead that we would both take it in stride and give each other some space and time. We would allow each other some freedom to be our own individual selves. We were married, but we were not dead, for God's sake. There would be no "affairs" because we would each be aware of it, IF there was someone else. Should the time come and we wanted someone in our life to add, that the other spouse would have to approve of them. There would be no tearing us apart as a married couple. We were here to stay. We had fallen prey to others before and it had cost us relationships. Infidelity was not going to be part of our contract together. We were aware of our sexuality and needed some security and had to address it. We were committed to one another and no dalliance was going to affect us. IF and when the opportunity ever to arise that we should want to be with someone else, we promised each other that would cross that bridge when the time came and just be honest about it.

Over the years, a couple of people came into our lives and went. We tried hard to make it work with them. Some worked well, some, well, not so nice. Yet, we grew. Our marriage held. Wayne and I felt that we are grown ups and individuals, not just a married couple. We knew that love is a grand thing and is not narrowed by society's views of what love SHOULD be. Love cannot be corralled into a single serving box. By allowing each other some freedom to explore, we have held true to each other. We are friends first. We know where our bread is buttered, shall we say. It hasn't all been beer & skittles, but it's been pretty fabulous all in all.

Wayne has been such a helpmate to me with raising my two girls into being the wonderful young ladies they are. He has been a strong, kind and fair influence on them. He also helped me get through another dramatic event, which was the loss of my mother:

A lifetime of smoking cigarettes finally caught up to Bernie, when she got sick with emphysema. It was awful to watch her go through so much pain. She had seven lung collapses all told. She actually quit smoking after the third one. It's tragic to watch someone you love have a cigarette right after a breathing treatment. Damn you addictive cigarettes. I helped as much as I could, and advised her best I could, but fifty years of her stubborn smoking was just too much damage to fix.

One night, my sister Dorothy and I were helping Mom get into bed just before she died in April of the year 2000. She still had her bawdy sense of humor though. We got her on and off the potty. We dressed her in her jammies. When she handed us her eyeglasses she said "Here's my eyes." Then she handed us her hearing aid, "Here's my ears." Then she took out her teeth and handed them over to be placed in the cup and said, "And here's my choppers. Getting old is SICK, isn't it?" Well, we all couldn't help but bust a gut and laugh over it. We just loved her for it. It was soon after this that Mom lost her battle to breathe.

As a testimony to love, forgiveness and acceptance my husband Wayne and my first husband David were both pallbearers at mom's funeral. As a gift to me, and to a very great and musical lady, Bernie Brown, they showed how to be loving human beings when they agreed to carry her casket as brothers to each other …and as her sons. Dave and I have remained good friends and we are there for each other at holidays and times of need and support. We still love each other and always will.

But the worst was not over. When I got home from the funeral, my dearest pet cat of all time, Sha-Sha, who was the love life of my kitty world, was found dead. He was 13 and had just up and died. Again, God? Why NOW? What are the fucking odds on this? Jesus! Both my cats had died on the same time frame as my parents. I was doubly grieved both times, with no furry meow to share it with. I had always considered them a comfort to my soul, in happy times and in bad. Yes, my cats have had a tear bath from me. But not now. They, too, were taken from me at the same time of my utmost grief.

Life has to go on and you have to have something to live for.

Wayne and I decided to carry on in Mom and Pop's musical footsteps and keep singing and keep getting out performing as a musical duo, and we continue to try to keep the old music *(like Mom and Pop loved)* going forward. And while I've sang at funeral before for friends, I wouldn't sing at either of my parents' funerals. I just couldn't.

I had no heart to sing with. I was mute.

Merry Meet

"Merlyn" is my nickname from high school. I originally got named it during my teenage phase of Arthurian legend fascination. You can even see it under my senior picture in the yearbook.

"Wayne" became "Harry" for his stage name because "Harrison" is his middle name. Merlyn and Harry are our true heart names and a new musical duo named *Merry Mischief* was born. Neither Wayne nor I can remember how we came up with that name for the life of us. But I'm sure it was in some epiphany some night. Or maybe it was some vague memory of a line in Shakespeare that lingered there from English class when we first met. Anyways, the name fit and stuck from the first utterance of the sound of it.

And it felt fine indeed. The harmonies that come when we sing together are really amazing. Life was making some sense again, even if my mate was a hoarder, he was still pretty awesome.

Fairy Godmothers & Amniotic Fluid

Wayne decided that today was the day that he would spend working on the hot tub while I worked on other things. I promised myself I would sew, write and do some things for Me today, regardless of what anybody else was doing.

The hot tub has been a bit of a nightmare since we acquired it as the result of a horse trade. It's very old Jacuzzi model for which we can't get schematics or even a simple manual, nor can we get it running. It had then been in process since the previous summer.

After waiting on then giving up on – Jacuzzi for critical information, Wayne *(read: Mr. Engineer)* finally bypassed them and went to a good local spa and pool store and started talking electronics with the owner. The owner was smitten with Wayne and shared their mutual love of chatting about mechanical doo-dads. Wayne could probably be hired anytime by this guy for working on spas and pool, IF Wayne wanted to do such things for someone else *(which he doesn't)*.

So now, Wayne has been retrofitting and reconfiguring this whole tub. It's an engineer's nightmare and dream come true. I don't feel the same and have often referred to the spa as "that Albatross in the backyard."

As I sat humming to myself whilst sewing...Wayne came bursting in from the deck at one point shouting, "Honey? I fixed it! It's running!" So, the next few hours were spent with him giving me blow by blow updates on the temperature of the spa. "It's at 65 degrees now!" Later, "It's at 70 degrees now!" And even later, "Hey, it's at 85 degrees now! It won't be long! I figure by maybe 8 o'clock we can try it out!" *(It was like contractions, I mused to myself..."pant, pant, pant...just remember to breathe! They're coming faster now, two minutes apart! Wont' be long now, honey!")* When it got to 95 degrees, I seriously started wondering where our bathing suits were and got excited myself. Is it really possible that this old broken down albatross may actually fly? Were we really, really, finally going to be the proud owners of a real, working hot tub?

The two of us slipped giddy like into 103 degree water. I have to tell you, it *was* a dream come true. Like a Fairy Godmother gift! It was more than awesome. It was like a hot spring in the woods. It was like a rocking chair in your mommy's lap. It was better than cookies and milk. It was primal. It was amniotic fluid.

Garbage Day—May 20, 2006

"And on the seventh day of creation, God looked around and saw that it was good. And rested." But the rest of us had to throw out the fecking garbage.

It was spring clean-up day again here in Jordan. Wayne makes his living from cast-off gear, creativity and when combined with an engineer's mind, he can make something wonderful out of nothing. Which is all well and good...but there's a lot of clutter that can go with that magic. I had been encouraging him to "let go" of some of the treasures (like styrofoam and plastic bottles), he was complying...a bit. I was giddy with anticipation. I had finally convinced him of the benefit of filling a trailer to go! Woot!

Wayne and I got up at the crack of dawn *(5:30 a.m.)* to finish loading said trailer with last minute junk, got into the van and parked as close to first-in-line as possible for spring clean-up day. We sit, second in line. It was 6 a.m. We off and on chat groggily with our coffee and wait for the hurling to begin. We thought it started at 7 a.m. Come to find out we will have to wait even longer, because it really doesn't begin till 8 a.m. *(insert the blame game here for misinterpreting information)*. But then we spied a man come to start opening up the line, a wee bit early at 7:15 a.m. because there is a substantial waiting line of 20 trucks, cars and trailers behind us out to the road. We just needed to buy our garbage sticker. But seeing as how we did not have one, we were told to pull off to the side, so that others who "do have a sticker" can now get ahead of us. Shit. So much for getting up early and being first in line!

Bonus! It started raining. While we were impatiently waiting for the garbage hurling to begin, the conversation between us started turning sour. It was too damn early and we were grumpy with a lot of repressed inner garbage ourselves. And we were carrying more than just the crap on the trailer behind us. It was kind of like garbage day inside the vehicle too. We watched others go ahead of us. Our talk scratched the surface, peeled a crusty edge up, turned bitter, and we started picking at it. The true savage digging in began. We quickly slid down the garbage shoot of conversation and got down to unearth the soft, pink underbelly. Pretty soon the dialogue between us sank to the likes of: "Your mother", and "get a real job" and "never liked your kid anyway" which were being dumped out and flung by both of us, in heaps and piles. Wayne pulled evasive tactics to leave the ensuing war. He abruptly left and slammed the van door to go talk so nicely and sweetly *(and blatantly)* to a total stranger, as though he was a nice man…

So I in turn dumped his full travel coffee mug out the window when he wasn't looking. Ah, romance.

A lady came mercifully to our van window and finally sold us a sticker to throw away our garbage. We got out and used our energy for a more positive purpose. We hurled the junk out with great abandon onto the mountain of trash that was already there before us.

After all was done and thrown onto the heap, we drove quietly away. We both felt somehow relieved and clean on one hand, like the now-empty trailer behind us and also as tired and filthy as our jeans were from flinging the emotional trash. We go to have breakfast together at 7:45 a.m. feeling like we had already put in a full day, which we had.

Later when we were home soaking our bones in the new hot tub, our icy stares and cold-shoulder dispositions melted into guilty smirks from both of us. A truce was struck. I realized that sometimes it's good to get rid of all that crap you carry, inside and out. Bonus: It makes your heart feel like the smell of Pine Sol, and then there's room for more love.

The Blue & the Grey

Harry and I were now out and about playing music professionally. We specialized in historical re-enactment events and played music guerilla-theater style right in the trenches with appropriately chosen music to match. With the type of old traditional music we played, our outgoing personalities and my penchant for costuming, it was a perfect fit. We were "Theatrical Musicians."

The gig for this particular day was to play as wandering minstrels at a Civil War re-enactment and encampment. We dressed ourselves in civilian Civil War-era garb, strapped on guitars, drum and threw in our basket of CDs and headed to Peterboro to its 15th annual skirmish.

If you have never been to a historical re-enactment event, I will tell you that your mind can come to life in such magical time-traveling places. Whether it is a Civil War gathering, pirate feast or Renaissance faire, it is a treat to bend time and place and everyone, from patrons to actors, plays with it.

We started this day by being the music for an old-time cakewalk *(Read: "Musical Chairs" for costumed patrons with homemade cakes as prizes).* After the game was done, we sashayed about the grounds and serenaded ladies in Scarlett O'Hara dresses. We played nursery rhymes and children's songs for little schoolboys dressed in Confederate and Union uniforms. Generals attired in both fancy blues and grey tapped their leathered boots whilst we crooned songs of wartime and tunes of home. We met one dapper General who asked us to play a song. When pressed for his actual heritage, he gave us the knowledge that he was born here in the North, even though his Confederate character was from Louisiana, while his own family came from Scotland. So I decided to launch into "Flower of Scotland," a beautiful song from the land of pipe and drum. Almost immediately, this strong and sturdy General then welled up with tears when we sang the lyrics, "Flower of Scotland." I must say, it was a most endearing, yet interesting sight to see a tough old Northern man dressed as a southern Confederate general weep openly from hearing a Scottish fight song against the English. Some things are timeless links, aye?

After a festive day of cannon fire, gunpowder and rifle skirmishes dressed up with petticoat ruffles and downing sausage sandwiches, we headed home, a bit richer in purse as well as spirit, and no worse for the wear. We are grateful for the history lessons we gave and received. It's good to remember how savage war was... and is. I mean, to realize first hand, how terribly devastating, how loud a cannon can actually be, and how savage a bayonet is in the hands of a stalwart young man, is sobering knowledge indeed. The songs we sang about "Johnny" coming home were especially poignant with the current knowledge that our "Johnnies" are still in Iraq. Those age old lyrics that remind us that more often than not, Johnny may not even come home at all. And if he does come home, it is often with damaged heart, mind, body and spirit. All the "Johnnies" over the centuries usually arrive home with their fatal memories, frequently missing limbs, damaged hearts and souls and crippled minds. How could they not? War is hell and not to be romanticized. These are just a few thoughts about why historical re-enactments are more than just entertainment to me. They are necessary to our culture and our joint memory as humans.

The White

We drive on home to do an actor's quick change, pick up daughter Jesse and go meet youngest daughter Shawna and my first husband, Dave, at the church for Shawna's evening High School Graduation Baccalaureate service.

It occurs to me then after our day's events at the previous Civil War Re-enactment *(where families were torn apart and brother fought brother)* that our family has indeed recovered from the seeming war that was our divorce. As my first husband Dave, and my current husband Wayne and I all sit in the pew together, we have put our differences behind us and can get back to being a family again. Our cannon fire, thankfully, has ceased and we now all sit in silence, peace and prayer. It is a day of graduation and completion, indeed. Not just Shawna's, but ours as well. It is perfect symbolism.

Shawna will be graduating with her class of typical peers. Shawna has been anything but typical. With the Downs Syndrome that she's carried, she has worked just as hard as all the other students of her same age *(I think maybe even harder)* to get to this point in her life. She will be graduating with her classmates and peers. She has paid her dues.

The graduates-to-be filed into the church, the girls in white caps and gowns, the boys in blue. Then it was time for the senior choir to get up to sing for the gathered community. Out of the blue and unannounced, Shawna gets up along with some of the other seniors and goes up to join the choir. *(By the way, Ah…Shawna isn't currently IN this choir- but used to be- a few years ago? Details…details.)* The choir director and participants were all very gracious and adapted to the extra curve ball *(Note to self: I now have renewed hope for this particular batch of flexible and inclusive graduates)* and Shawna is nestled in to stand front and center and sing with them. She did pretty good lip synching too. We were all so amused and proud of her *(now that's ballsy!)*. After the service, the future citizens of the world all promenaded out to the lawn of the church to have their pictures taken in their cap and gowns and to hobnob and schmooze and chat with everyone in their fancy graduation attire. We, the parents, were also very proud of ourselves and each other in raising this special child.

Bernice practicing with her band "The Cowgirls." 1939?

The Browns. Rick, Gary, Chris, Adele, Earl, Bernice and Marilyn.

Earl Brown Air Force. WWII.

Marilyn, 2 years.

Bernice gives new baby Marilyn bath in handy roasting pan.

A Mary shrine from Dad's
personal photos from
overseas 1944.

Marilyn's First Communion.
Immaculate Heart Conception
Church, Brownville NY. Father
Ruddy. 1968.

Sacred Heart
School Uniform.
1966.

Watertown Daily Times
38   Watertown, N. Y.
      Thurs., Sept. 7, 1972

Body, Believed Jack Blake, 10, Found in Woods; Police Will Test Blood-Stained Trousers

Local Paragraphs

Masonic Bowling League
will meet at the Watertown
Bowl Sunday at 8 p.m. Persons interested in forming a
co-ed league are asked to attend.

The Delta Alpha class of
Hope Presbyterian Church
will meet at 3:30 p.m. Friday
in the North Watertown Cem-
etery to attend the funeral of
Mrs. Anna Gould.

Miss Gail E. Mattraw,
daughter of Mr. and Mrs.
Gordon Mattraw, 908 Franklin
St., has returned to Brock-
port State University College
where she is a senior, major

The Jefferson County Sheriff's Department is trying to
link the disappearance of
Jack O. Blake, 522 Water St.,
a badly decomposed body believed to be the missing ten-
year-old boy, and a pair of
blood-stained trousers with
Arthur J. Shawcross.

Shawcross, 27, is the al-
leged killer of little eight-
year old Karen Ann Hill,
whose body was discovered
late Saturday under the Pearl
Street bridge.

The Blake boy, who turned
up missing last May 7, has
been the subject of extensive
searches.

On Wednesday the sher-
iff's department began
searching the heavily wooded
triangle of land adjacent to
routes 31, 37, and 12.

On the second search a
body, thought to be that of
young Blake was turned up
and clothing found near the
partially covered skeleton
was identified by Mrs. Allen
Blake as that worn by her son
the day he disappeared.

Jack O. Blake

The Long Search For Boy

Highlights in the long
search for ten-year-old Jack
O. Blake, 525 Water St., who
had been missing since May 7
— four months ago today —
follow:

May 8— Mrs. Mary Blake,
his mother, reported to city
police that the boy has disappeared; that she last saw him
at 2 p.m. Sunday when he
went to play at the Clover-
dale Apartments playground;
that he may be hiding in
Pools Woods, north of the
apartments; and that he was
reported seen with a man
who guided him into the
woods.

May 10— City police inten-
sify search, aided by volunteers, following sharp criti-

Air Service Not Likely

Murder in our area. Jack Blake 1972.

170

Texas. Health Kick. 1978.

Dad's Barn.

David Underwood. 17 years old.

Marilyn & Dave's Karmann Ghia trip from Texas to NY. 1979.

My very own little family. Dave, Jesse, Shawna and Marilyn. 1988.

Dave and Marilyn's Wedding Day in Mom & Dad's living room. March 29, 1980.

Wayne Harrison Fuller at our wedding party. August 1998.

Marilyn and Wayne Wedding Day. 8/28/98 Little Falls, NY.

Hillary Clinton shakes Shawna's hand with Jesse in middle. Women's Nation Rights Convention. July 1998.

Shawna is a Special Olympics champion swimmer.

Merlyn 2013.

Merlyn. MC of Traditional Stage and Performer, Irish Festival, Syracuse NY. 2012.

Slainte! Merlyn Fort Myers Medieval Faire. 2013.

Harry & Merlyn. Merry Mischief Pirate Show. Cortland NY 2010.

Merry Mischief Minstrels. 2013.

Merry Mischief Wedding Minstrels. 2011.

The Red

As we joined the crowd outside, Jesse and I come to the horrid conclusion that Shawna must have *(gasp!)* just started her monthly period. It is now quite evident if you stand behind her and her formerly pristinely white graduation gown. Oh my God! Every woman's nightmare! That is just what has happened. Quickly thinking, I sidle up to Shawna from behind to cover her backside.

What to do? I quickly chat with both her dads, who have been so awesome under such crisis as this before. We punt. Dave takes both girls to the reception *(sans white graduation gown)* with her dark flowered skirt as camouflage. It's not noticeable. This way Shawna can still enjoy the fun, and you can't see anything on her skirt, thank God! Wayne and I whisk away her now less-than-pristine graduation gown and take it home for a hopeful, instant spot removal. She will have to wear this same white gown on stage at a following ceremony the next day. Along the way, Merlyn offers many prayers to the Gods of fertility and to the Gods of Laundry soap, to spare Shawna this small, yet very embarrassing predicament.

"Out, out, out damn spot, out I say!" I chant over and over as the cold water runs from red to pink to light pink to clear. Thanks be to the Gods of polyester! The gown now hangs out on the porch, flapping in the summer breeze without a care, its' sad story erased.

Shawna's life has never really been easy for her... or for any of us involved with her on the day to day. Yet we adapt and muck in. On today of all days, when we wanted her to "be just one of the typical high school kids" I was mortified to have her picked on as a Karmic Jest.

We averted the eye of harsh and blatant community scrutiny once again today, and I thanked both Dave and Wayne for being such awesome mates and fathers and for helping me with such indelicate dramas as this over and over through the years. It takes a village, they say, and they are SO right. It also helps when you pick good mates to get you through these nightmare moments and then make them magical again.

The Purple

So now, our sweet Shawna, beautiful graduate-to-be, with Down's to boot…gets herself ready for bed before her big day tomorrow.

But horror of horrors, she can't seem to find her Barney doll! He is her nightly purple friend of nigh onto 15 years. She sleeps with him every night tucked under her arm. *(If you were to really look and analyze this particular Barney and scrutinize his features, you would say he has a perpetual smirk. It's from years of being squished and loved and kissed and rolled on in the night.)*

Jesse finds the doll and says, "Here he is!" and whips Barney across the room to her.

Shawna yells, "No! No! Careful of his eyes!" Jesse and I look at each other whimsically,

"Be careful of his eyes?" We burst out laughing. Yes, this Barney is special.

As I turned out the light after this big day, Shawna is now asleep. Barney is sitting at the ready, keeping careful vigilance over her. I kiss my big girl graduate-to-be and whisper to the heavens, "Yes, careful there. And God please bless Barney's eyes."

Barney says nothing of note, but remains ever watchful there, on guard over her in the purple darkness, keeping her safe and smiling his perpetual sardonic smile.

Pomp Under the Circumstance

We get Shawna up to the high school well in advance of her graduation ceremony. She looks beautiful and we left her with another group of similarly dressed future graduates. Then our little family went and found our seats in the now crowded auditorium.

Yesterday, the vice principal took me aside and told me that when all the kids rehearsed for the ceremony, there was some hesitation when Shawna was supposed to get up in line for her diploma. So, he advised, would I "<u>PLEASE</u> work with her, and remind her that she needs to get in line right after the name "James C. Strife" is called." I promised I would, and so I started the actor's game of memorization with her in earnest.

"James C. Strife... James C. Strife... Shawna, it rhymes with LIFE... get it? James C. Strife."

And so we practiced and practiced, in the car, at the house, before dinner, before bed, upon arising in the morning.

"Shawna, what's the kid's name you follow at the graduation? James C. Strife."

"Yeah, mom, me know," sighed a very perturbed teenager. She knows what she knows, and I should trust her, was what I inferred from that heavy sigh.

Onto the main event…The band starts to play "Pomp and Circumstance," the graduates in blue and white enter, and we all stand. The graduates file in on each side of the auditorium, and go up the stairs on each side of the stage, meet their graduating counterpart, hug or shake hands *(or high five if they had the energy)* and then they go find their seat.

"There goes Shawna!" we say as we proudly watch her go down the aisle at a good clip *(which is a good sign, as she is usually very pokey).* Up the stairs she goes, hard for her, but she does it pretty well, one deliberate step at a time, even in her gown. Then, we apprehensively watch Shawna sort of get lost on the stage, fumbling and looking around for her chair instead of finding her partner first *("sort of symbolic of most of these graduates feeling lost," I muse).* Shawna has obviously forgotten that she is supposed to meet her other graduate counterpart for a welcome on stage before she sits down. *(I start to fret and bite my lip.)*

Then I see Shawna's grad partner get her attention. He gives her a little "come hither" motion and thankfully she finds her way to him and they give each other a big hug. The audience watching all this goes wild with support for her! What an awesome kid he was! I heave a sigh of relief and gratitude for his kindness. Most of the crowd is aware of Shawna and her disability as we all live in this small town and we are all acquaintances it seems. They know her. They know the mountains she's had to climb. They are being very supportive.

After what seems like forever sitting through speeches, some good, some bad, some ridiculous, comes the part we all came for. The important final 15 minutes of an hour-and-a-half ceremony, the handing out of the diplomas!

Of course, Shawna's last name begins with a "U" so we have to wait longer. I bite my nails, all the while I'm sending her telepathic messages that mostly consist of, "James C. Strife, Shawna, LISTEN for the words, "James C. Strife."

The names roll on and on and then the magic moment comes! The vice principal says... "James C. Strife." *(I hold my breath)* And Shawna continues to just sit there, oblivious and unconcerned in her cap and gown. *(Oh God, please have mercy)*. Several kids get up and get in line when their cue is called. Time ticks on and Shawna continues to sit unaware. Other kids now line up behind her. I now know *(as does the vice principal)* that Shawna has totally missed and messed up her position in the receiving line on stage. I can't imagine how it will all turn out well now, and I fret and bite bleeding hangnails, as my fingernails are all well trimmed down to guitar-playing length. I am sitting in between Shawna's dad, Dave and my husband, Wayne. "She's way out of turn now," I whisper hoarsely to them both. Visions of confusion and an apparently lost Shawna on the stage in front of the whole village haunt me. *(Egad! Is this how it will all end? Why does life always, always have to fuck everything up? I am totally beseeching God now)*.

Then there is a pregnant pause in the list of names. The vice principal motions to Shawna, someone next to her nudges her to attention and then we all hear;

"Shawna Rose Underwood." *(I hold my breath.)*

The Queen then rises from her seat and picks her way delicately down. It is an extra special entrance for an extra special little lady. Everyone sees her cute baby picture and her senior picture being flashed up on the overhead projector screen. When everyone sees that it is Shawna, that they are waiting for- they all go nuts, clapping, cheering and hollering!

Previous to this moment, I thought I would cry. But all I

really feel is relieved, proud and happy. Now we see her getting her picture taken with the principal and gripping her diploma.

Then she gracefully waddles back to her seat like the Queen she is.

(I really think that Shawna was royalty in her last life. No, really. Like it's some sort of karmic lesson she must be learning in her current life. Yes, she is presently carrying this disability about. It must be her chosen way to learn dependence on others, in a necessary way. I am positive that in her last life she was indeed a QUEEN. She probably ordered everyone about in a master/servant relationship. Now, in this life, she must need to learn the lesson of reliance and doing without. Or maybe she must learn how to do the easy things with a little more perseverance and determination. I know this because I am her mother. Past lives die hard. Just watch her try to manipulate you to get her things, or do things for her, like the Queen she was. She'll ask for a glass of water with a flippant wave of her hand, expecting all the while that you will bring it on a golden platter. "You have legs, my dear," is my usual reply).

But Shawna is certainly Queen for a day this day! And a more empathic monarch you will never find! I swear if there is a person in a room that needs a hug or some love, Shawna will find them and she will touch their life somehow.

There is a party for after with a DJ, teachers, friends and family to share conversations, laughter, a buffet of too much food and presents! Some of Shawna's friends are from her special-needs classroom; they come in wheelchairs with nurses, or they come walking deliberately on braces or crutches. They all dance *(some in wheelchairs)* to the infectious song, "I don't want to work, I want to bang on the drums all day," and take turns popping balloons on the dance floor and eating cake and ice cream. It HAS been a good day. Good enough for a Queen.

The Bad Word

Let me preface this story and tell you that I love my daughter, Jesse, so much. Really. She's a good girl. And for good and for ill, she's a lot like me. There are always some rough moments when you raise teenagers. Here is one such story a long time ago.

It was a hot summer day when Wayne and I broke down and gave up on thinking that we were actually going to have the time to sheet rock the girls' bedroom. We called for help. Help came in the form of our big, burly friend Ben and his strong friend Tyler. They came...they saw... they sheet rocked. It was all up and the first coat of mud was on in about six hours. We paid them and we were all happier for it. How'ere, they tracked sheetrock dust and chalk *(as is to be expected)* all over the house. This particular morning I had a small window of time to use before an afternoon gig *(Pirate Show)* so I tried to get going early. I had so much to do in so little time. I needed my girls to help me, but getting the girls going on the first day of summer vacation was the trick. Once in the room up there it was so hot, I started the negative self-talk which turned into full scale bitching when no one came to my rescue. So finally, I yelled, "Jesse, please get up and help me clean, sweep and mop your room this morning!" But Jesse isn't really a morning person, she's always been a night owl even as a baby. I admit I didn't like the job of cleaning up the workmen's mess upstairs, the room was hot and it was steamy in there. Jesse appeared at the doorway.

"What do you want?" she groggily asked while rubbing her eyes.

"Can't you help me up here? It's your room, after all," I said peevishly, *(heating up with one of my hot flashes)* sweat beading up on my face and shoulders.

"It's done, leave it for later," she drolls.

I looked at this almost grown beautiful child of mine, and start berating her with gibes, insults the likes of which a good mother never would do. Words like "fat," "lazy," "ungrateful," "unmotivated" and "how are you gonna get anywhere in life doing this shit?" spewed forth out of my lips. (I'm not proud of this moment. Just telling you honestly…) This whole tirade took maybe four minutes of time, but was enough to sear into my daughter's psyche for eternity. I became the textbook Freudian Mother Monster.

I continued, "Well, it's not done, just look at it! There's lots left to do! If we do a little at a time, it'll get done." I say as a drip of sweat decides to run a rivulet down my face and drip off the end of my nose. "Can't you DO something?"

"Well, I can't sheetrock if that's what you mean," *(she is starting to sound snotty)*. We went back and forth a bit, my hormones and the stifling heat ramping up the emotions. I was quickly morphing into full scale bitch mode.

"The sheetrock's all done, you can sweep, can't you?" I threw the broom down at her. *(Granted, I was not "adulting" well at the moment.)* Like-mother-like-daughter, she sounded like an exact mimic of me and added some more snit *(along with the appropriate sing-song voice of sass) to* the mix, "*Why no,* I can't sweep, I never learned *how.*"

Nice Mommy now morphed into full scale Evil Cinderella Complex Mommy who picked up the broom and said, "Ok, enough! Get the hell out of here! I'll do it the fuck, myself" and started sweeping.

My teenager turned on her heels to go and, as leaving the area (that I told her to leave), lobs her direct cannon fire volley by saying under her breath, (but loud enough for me to hear...)

"Yah, well... at least I'm not a... cunt."

(PAUSE)

*(*In retrospect, I feel that it was at this exact moment when I went insane. Yes, I am quite certain of it. Let me preface it right here that I don't believe in child abuse. And Jesse is a smart, great kid. Oh, there were days during my divorce when she acted out, and she had a few spankings when she was younger. This wasn't like that. No. Now *Psycho* music erupted in my head. This was going to be an all-out catfight of the century. Dogs barking in the neighborhood, people calling 911, children crying, cars crashing....you know, like that.)

Flinging the broom down, I came whipping out of that hot, stuffy room meaner than one of the Wicked Witch's flying monkeys! Sporting "Raptor hands" *(as Jesse described them later),* I came from out of the blue somewhere with some sort of Banshee scream searing the hallway. *(It's said that you only hear a*

Banshee scream just before someone is about to die.) My new impromptu plan was to kick her ass down the stairs. I had on shoes. But she's bigger than me now.

Jesse's whole plan was to survive the imminent wrath of a wild woman that used to look like her mother. It was a good plan. Jesse planted herself at the top of the stairs like a tank, with one arm bracing the stair railing and the other arm bracing the wall and wedged herself against the incoming onslaught. I came flying at her so she had no choice but to go on the defense. She grabbed a fistful of my hair and held on tightly all the while I flailed around and beat her about the head and shoulders.

I cannot begin to tell you the sailor language that this Pirate Merlyn spewed as I beat this sassy whelp of mine for a bad cuss word. Ironic, I know. I was aware of the irony as I beat her and it sort of spurred me onward.

I called for help from Wayne *(intermingled with more sailor-style wording)*. I suppose I probably could've gotten a hold of myself, if it weren't for that shit-eating grin she was wearing this whole entire time. I am not sure what broke up the cat-fight. Could've been cold water from a goddamn garden hose for all I know. In another world downstairs…in a galaxy far, far away….Wayne had been on the phone with a business call when WWIII broke out upstairs at 8:30 a.m. on one bright and sun-shiny morning in Mayberry.

The next thing I remember is Wayne telling me to calm down in the kitchen and stop bitching at everyone. *(READ: He took her side)* "Did you hear what she called me?!"

"It doesn't matter, you have to get a hold of yourself, honey, you are the grown up here, and …blah…blah…blah." *(I never heard the rest. I blocked it out. He took her side.)*

I went out on the deck with a cup of coffee to try to calm down. I looked up at the sky and begged the Gods to help me figure this all out, because I definitely couldn't. After I was done shaking, I did what my mother would do. I went upstairs and finished the job and mopped the room by myself. An old wive's cure: Pine Sol used as pain-relief medicine. Jesse sat on the front porch and I sat on the back deck for an hour. We didn't speak. I went and got lunch for Shawna and myself, but not for Jesse or for Wayne, because I'll be damned if I was feeding traitors!

In an hour or two, Wayne ended up buying Jesse lunch. *(Read: He bought her lunch! I decided to not speak to him ever again.)* Wayne and I had a gig that afternoon and drive an hour each way. Intermittently I ranted, cried and pouted the whole way there. We did the gig. A Pirate Show. All the wee children wore their pirate costumes, and they were perfectly wonderful children, and we laughed and gave marker tattoos to the kids and sang our scabby little hearts out. *(I thought...How perfectly piratical! Singing a toe-tapping jig with dagger malice in my heart...Plotting mutiny all the while...side glancing murderous thoughts, whilst singing murder ballads, yet smiling with my face, with fingers crossed behind my back. I felt like a pirate for REAL.)* And because we are professional musicians, **no one knew that I was even upset**.

Back at home, life became civil. Jesse apologized for the bad word and I apologized for going ratshit crazy. But like Humpty Dumpty, it's been a lot harder to put it back together. The thing that really upset me the most about this fight was that it was just a word. A single stupid word. A vagina is a wonderful thing, it is sweet and necessary. A female's "little kitty" is adorable. But the word "cunt" has such a bad connotation. Weird.

WHY?

It's just a word. I think it must be the hard "C" sound, followed by the resting slope of the "N," finally snapped off by sharp "T" sound. Short. Hard. Like a gun shot. But the really fearful thing about that word isn't the word itself. No. It's the wild image of a Insane Woman on a Vengeance Mission. Authentic, but out of control. Be afraid of THAT, my friends. It's NOT the silly word itself. I've made peace with the word ever since. It's an awesome word, though, best used rarely, as is the energy that makes her a reality. A wild woman is a powerful thing indeed, but that uncontrolled, wild energy is anti-productive and can be destructive to relationships.

The Bat Visitation

Wayne and I went to bed with Monty, our doggie, at our feet. At the precise hour of midnight *(how cliché ....but true)* the dog went out into the hall and started quickly pacing back and forth. His toenails clicking on the hardwood floor, back and forth, quickly back and forth. It roused me from my sleep. I wondered what the hell he was up to. Did he have to go out? No. Back and forth. He paced back and forth. Then I heard a bump over the sound of the fan. Then something fluttered into our room.

"Wayne, I think we have something in the house, a huge moth or God forbid another bat." *(Yes, this would be the third one in three years. Hey, how lucky are we?)* I peered into the hall, without my glasses on. In the moonlight, it was barely visible. "Swoosh" then "Swoosh" again. "Yup, it's a bat all right."

"Shit" was the first word Wayne mumbled. He was just waking up. So now I knew why Monty was going back and forth, he was following it, trying to catch it!

"Well, go out into the other room and open a window for it to find its way out. They can't hurt you. They have SONAR" said my brave husband.

I replied, "Me? Why not YOU? Nice try, but it sounds like a manly-man job to me." I pulled the covers over my head. *(Hey, if I have to do all the cooking and cleaning around here, I have this option! It's like the "Law of Tit for Tat" or something).* Heavy sigh from Wayne.

He proceeded to pull on his robe *(although not nearly quickly enough under the circumstances, if you ask me)* and he gathered up his nerve to go out into the skinny hallway to dodge the pendulum swinging bat. It was like trying to jump in on a game of Double Dutch! Just judging on when he would jump out, jump into the hall and turn the corner and go down the stairs. Finally he saw an opening, and deftly entered the dark, active, airstream in the hall. He walked about five steps when I heard him scream.

"Are you ok?" I asked hopefully, with feigned concern in my voice, I was trying desperately not to laugh.

"Yeah, it just hit me in the head!" *(So much for the sonar theo-ry.)*

"REALLY?!" I said, and supported him by immediately closing the door behind him so that it would not come in and get me. I lay down safely on my bed with my dog with my courageous husband out trying to dispel the vermin. After awhile, I heard Wayne say something from downstairs. "I've got the downstairs door open, is it gone yet? The mosquitoes are really getting thick." I opened the door a crack for air, and peered out into the darkened hallway.

"Whoosh." Then a couple seconds later, "Whoosh!"

"Nope, he's still here. I think it's really disoriented, as it just keeps going in circles in the hall out there. It hasn't ventured anywhere else. Turn on a light downstairs so I can see what it's up to."

Sure enough the bat was continually hovering, still swooping back and forth, back and forth. Lost, so very, very, lost. Monty and I watched the antics peeping through the safe three-inch-wide door opening. *(It was much like you might watch a street side drunken brawl safely from your bedroom window. You can't stop watching it, you don't like what's happening, but you'll be damned if yer gonna get involved in it!)*

After several minutes, I tell Wayne, "It's taking a rest and hanging upside down on the wall over the window. He must be really tired Hey! Bring up one of your whoop-tie-doo flashlights with the big beam on it and we'll be able to see it better." Wayne proceeds to bang around downstairs in the dark, trying not to wake up the girls.

"Oh God." I swallowed hard.

"What do you mean, "Oh God?" said Wayne coming up the stairs. "What's it doing now?"

"I can't believe it. Eeewww. It just sort of gymnastically crawled with its elbow wings somehow up into the molding in the wall over my sweater closet!" *(Silence... while I got the willies thinking of that for a minute).*

"Oh kewl. Thankfully it must've been a dead end, cuz he's coming out now." Wayne comes up and shines the flashlight on the bat hanging upside down on the wall molding. "Oh, honey, he's just a baby, he's so scared, just look at him!" I say as we look at this adorable, heart-pounding, mousey-like, soft-brown, furry, wild, feral, probably rabies-laden, sharp-toothed creature.

"Why don't you catch it in something?"

"Like what?"

"Beats the fuck outta me."

The sweet little lost bat has now had enough of life in the obnoxious limelight, and decides to do something really amazing. We watch incredulously, as it crawls up under the tight ceiling molding and go directly into the attic. GONE. Pondering this feat of disappearing magic I hesitate, and then said, "God, I didn't think there was enough space for him to get in between in there, did you?"

"Nope, me neither," said Wayne shaking his head.

"What do we do now?"

My brave husband advised, "We go back to bed. He'll either find his way out, or die in the rafters." *(Yeah, like that thought is comforting).*

"Come on Monty, you are sleeping with us as an alarm system." We go to bed and fall asleep with the sound of the occasional wee scratching in the ceiling tiles in the hall. We never saw the bat again.

But we think of him often.

Testosterone On Wheels

One day, Harry arrived breathless with happy news for me: "Honey! I just bought us a replacement for the blue van!" *(What I need to tell you here is that we own a car, plus three, count' em, three vans, and this would currently make number four.)*

"Another van? Why?!"

"This one has a .... *[Pause for dramatic effect]* a RAISED ROOF!" *(Insert angelic hallelujah chorus here.)* "I can nearly stand up in this one," he said. "You will be able to stand totally straight, it has lots more room, so it will be great for music gigs, changing into garb and camping and, YES, honey, *[he says this next bit sort of anticipatory and conciliatory]* I'll get rid of the old blue van too.... *[and quietly he adds]*....right after Josh and I finish stripping it out for parts."

Here is where I will tell you of my husband's fetish. Chevy Vans. *(Ooh baby, ooh baby!)*

I think over the course of his life he's had like twenty of them. Their undeniable and desirous wiles include: Interchangeable parts. Steady. Reliant. Rugged. And the last three have had.... BEDS in them! It's a stud's dream! Remember the 1970s song, "Chevy Van?" Yeah. Seems that it's Harry's theme song. *(I better stop sexy talking like this; I don't want to push him over the edge if he reads it.)*

I don't know what it is with men, I guess once they find something they like and understand, they buy fifteen or twenty of them. Strip them naked and keep their parts safe in a box. Ready. Available. "Just in case" they ever need it on a whim or an emergency. *(Oh, how I'd like to be able to do that to some men... sorry, daydreaming now.)*

My first husband did this very same thing with Karmann Ghias. We had about SEVEN in a row along with their subsequent boxes of parts, spare doors and windshields. Boy, howdy, do I know how to pick men. Ah well, I suppose women do this same thing too, in their way, what with finding an outfit that makes their body look awesome and then buying it in every color....

But surely I digress. Back to the new purchase.

"So, want to go for a spin with me, babe?" *(Do I really have to?)* "I warn you.... it's a little rough." *(Ah there it is. The Alarm Bell Rings. Now, when a man says, "It's a little rough" be prepared for a dirt camp in the hills of Appalachia.)*

"The seats are a little wonky, too, but, hey, no worries! I'll just switch them out with the ones from the blue van. It'll be great.... *[Disclaimer]*...When I get it fixed up."

OK, so after this incredible PR build up, I go out to ride in his new chariot. He dances out the front door to the van. I open up the passenger side door and a thick acrid smell of cigar smoke wafts out polluting the crisp fall night air.

"Ugh! The last owner must've smoked cigars like a bloody chimney!"

"Huh, is that what that smell is?" My husband bats his eyes, projecting feigned ignorance.

"Oh yeah, that's what it is," and I climb in and wonder how the hell I am going to fix it. He took me for a ride all the while recanting the joys and wonders of his new purchase. "It's got a tow package. I can nearly stand up straight in it. It has SOLAR panels!" *(I think he's hyperventilating now)* "Which will be great for gigs and camping. All wood trim, we have all this extra room with all these compartments, a kicking stereo, LOTS more room when the seats are out for when you and I travel long distance, and the bed is bigger....blah, blah, blah." He chatters on, not realizing how surly and quiet I've become. He also doesn't comprehend that I don't even want to touch anything, much less lay my bare ass down on it.

"It just needs a little TLC, honey, really not much, just some brake lines, fuel lines, gas tank, tune-up, windshield wiper pump, thermostat, outside paint job, you know, the usual."

I wasn't ready to settle for "the usual."

So I said, "Alright, give it to me. Brass tacks. How much did you actually pay for this manure spreader? Cuz that's what it fecking smells like."

"Three hundred bucks." He took me out for the ride at night. Brilliant of him, I must say. It was dark.   I go out in the morning to survey the real story. I understand now why he took me out at night. It's a nightmare. Not only is there a yellow cigar film stain on all the wood trim and glass, but there is grime and mystery stains on the faded upholstery. MYSTERY STAINS. I am sure that in the history of this van, <u>no one with one drop of estrogen </u>has ever been in it. And IF there ever was a woman in this thing? She didn't have teeth. And no hair, neither...most likely fur...or wool...Yeah, yeah, that's it....Just a guy and his sheep. Out tooling around, seeing the world, spittin' tobacco.

It was obviously a MAN's vehicle. A BACHELOR man's

vehicle. An OLD bachelor man's vehicle. Make that an old bachelor FARMER man's vehicle. With what I can only imagine are...tobacco... and spuz stains. On freaking everything! I mean, on the carpeting, and yes, the walls too, and, holy mother of all that is good and clean, even on the ceiling!

All the guys at the mechanic garage have given Harry the "He-Man Testosterone Recycling Award of the Year" for all his swapping out of parts of these vans. They are amazed and impressed with his innovative ideas! I think that more than likely they're happy he's spending all his folding money with them. It's positive reinforcement for their garage. I mean, just think of it! The GUYS at the GARAGE are impressed! He's been walking around like a rooster crowing and preening his cockscomb!

The next time he sees me, I am in the van, with my third bucket of steaming Murphy's oil soap, rubber gloves, rag, carpet shampoo and a scrub brush. I am wearing a permanent grimace and occasionally muttering things under my breath and spending my time saying things like:

"Oh fucking God. How gross!" And... "He'll be freaking' lucky," and "Bloody feckin' nasty," or the ever popular, "IT HAD A NAME." But mostly there were just utterances of "Eeeuuuww" *(and THAT was when there was hair attached).*

It was a beautiful day, though, and after awhile Harry pops his head in the side door of the van, surveys the surroundings and smiles an appreciative grin. "Oh Merlyn, honey, that looks awesome! It smells sooo much better too! You are the best wife in the world! I love you SO MUCH!"

"Don't even come near me, you...you... MAN," I say in my loudest voice.

"C'mere, honey. Come give me a kiss." He puckers up.

I protest: "Oh hell, no! Well, wait. Maybe after I friggin' boil myself down with hydrogen peroxide, anti-bacterial soap, and use a nit comb just to feel like myself again," I say as I scrub the walls and squeeze out the sponge.

He admires the work done and asks, boyish like a kid at Christmas. "Well? So...What do you think?"

"I will absolutely NOT drive to Florida in this thing, or stay in it for two weeks with you, without different seats being put in and totally new carpeting. Period. *(I wave my wet, dripping yellow rubber gloved finger around dramatically for effect.)* I go on, "And as far as the bed goes, I will not ever, EVER, lay down on it, unless somehow it gets hermetically germ sealed in plastic with an air mattress on top of it with NEW SHEETS."

He smiles that wonderful, wicked, wry smile and says, "I knew you'd like it."

The World According to LARP

Harry and I play a lot of gigs as "theatrical musicians" which means that we get dressed up in costuming for certain events. I should probably give you some information about people who have fun, "pretending" and playing dress up for fun or profit in the field of re-enactment:

There are about 5 kinds of re-enactors:
1) The top echelon featured slot is the **Historical Re-Enactors.** These folks are the real deal.

They are usually Civil War buffs, Revolutionary War, or French & Indian war historians and well; they don't feck around with any of this "Play" stuff. History is important to them. They try to be as authentic as possible and live within the re-creation of the time period that they are portraying. Their uniforms are made with the appropriate weight fabric and the buttons are authentic reproductions. They live, cook, and camp in the 1st person and for the duration of their event. They also don't seem to have much fun, a sense of humor either as, "War IS Hell."

But these folks are accurate with their history and I will give them that! They are very good at being "information lecturers or 1st person hosts at forts and missions. I adore it when they drill, march in step and blast off REAL cannons too! They also really appreciate our music, and I love them for that. Merry Mischief music adds an "air of authenticity" that is quite palatable to them.

2) The next down from the top are the **SCAdians**. SCA is short for the "Society for Creative Anachronism". They take the "Best of the History" award.

They pick and choose what they like about a certain time period and try to exemplify it to its best degree. It's like living history but without all pestilence and disease. A lot of SCA people are VERY particular and some can be quite snobbish about what they do, what they wear, how they fight, live, act and behave in court. They count stitches in their garments and will tell you how perfect their garments and recipes are… *(But please don't always get too sucked in. I also happen to know that some of them buy fabric at Joann Fabrics. Oh the shame of it all.)* The SCAdians Mecca is called "Pennsic" and it is an annual pilgrimage to an instant mega-tent city in the middle of summer in Pennsylvania and many go there to live the life, shop, have fun, battle and even do commerce. It's liken unto the Burning Man of the Renaissance World.

I don't know a lot of SCAdians who have a boisterous sense of humor. It seems to be gauche to guffaw or find things humorous, unless it is a play on words. Their humor is more dry and cerebral and randy. Some SCAdians would rather be RIGHT than have fun. But there are the many that love a bawdy ballad however, and I aim to please them in that area.

I will give them several big kudos, though: Thankfully they are keeping the finer arts alive and well and brought forward for us to continue to enjoy. (Sewing, needlepoint, calligraphy, heraldry, fencing, etc)

They have LARGE collections of garb, most of which has been loomed or made by hand. They can be big Garbaholics. ("Garbaholic" is a word I made up regarding: a person who owns or is addicted to buying/making/acquiring lots of costuming. I am a Garbaholic and damn proud of it. And many SCAdians are Garbaholics and damn proud of it too. Ask them. They mostly likely MADE the chainmail they are wearing).

And another awesome thing about SCA people. Man oh man, can they COOK! Their dinners and 10 course banquets are a thing of beauty! And all served on wooden trenchers and in silver platters fit for a King. No shit. Really. The KING is there and you need to serve him.

I fell in love with a drink called "Hippocras" that I was turned onto at a SCA banquet *(at beautiful Winter Solstice gathering)*. I will make it but first, I have to order some odd ball spice called "Bird of Paradise" from Pennsic or get it online from someone with no teeth in India in order to make it… but honey, I'm going to, because it would be WORTH IT.

I have a lot of SCA friends. I admit it But there are also a lot of SCA people who won't socialize with me… because…

I am a………

3) RENNIE. "Rennie" is short for "Renaissance faire goer" *(either one who works on the faire circuit or one who is a "playtron"- a ticket holder who develops a character and goes faithfully).* Rennies are more laid back than SCAdians. Having been at both kinds of events, I will say that I think Rennies have way more fun in my honest opinion. While SCAdians are particular and unadulterated with pure form or historical fact…Rennies love the renaissance time period of history and mix and match their garb without being too anal-retentive about it. If they like it and they think it works…it's good for them. They can be big Garbaholics too.

Rennies have a bawdy sense of humor! They know that "This isn't the Renaissance" and they are glad, because they happen to like flush toilets and antibiotics, thank you very much. They are just playing and they do it with an accent and a trunk full of garb, and they hope you will play too!

They can be Scottish, Irish, English, Spanish, French, Turkish or Pirates.

They can be of nobility, merchant class, or the scum of the earth beggars and thieves. They are thinkers and doers and many have lives in professional occupations. Yet these same real time librarians or computer programmers or doctors WILL drink and dance in the rain half naked. They love good music from the authentic, to sailing shanties to the bawdier realms. They appreciate our harmonies and weird sense of humor too.

Rennies will let me pick food off their plate and give me sips off their ales and wines and they will offer you 10 different flasks of alcoholic beverages of your choice.

I love Rennies. Rennies rock my Ren World. And hey, I'm a Rennie.

4) LARPERS. "Live Action Role Players" are another strange being. They are playing a "game" and immersing themselves in a role for sometimes whole weekends at a time. The "PLAY is the thing" with them. They know its play and they truly love to play! They can be big garbaholics too. Their roles can be one of an animal, science fiction space character, historical figure or fantasy figure. They will have a name, dialect and they will sleep in their garb and live and breathe it. They can be Orcs, Kings, Knights, Fairies, Elves, Trolls, Wolves, Cats, Vikings, Vampires, Dogs, Zombies or ethereal Steam Punk Time travelers. It's all about the GAME. If you can fit within the game, and/or logically explain why you are doing what you are doing or where you are or what you are wearing…you are AOK. You just have to package it well.

Oh, and you HAVE to have a BFG. *(Big Fucking Gun)* Or Axe… Or Hammer… Or Staff…. Or Sawed-off Automatic Machine Gun…Or Savage Pike….Or Bow & Arrow…

Or Shield and Mace….Well, you get the idea."WEAPONS R US."

Real LARPERS fight with boffer *(pretend/padded)* weapons and run around in the dark in the woods killing zombies, vampires or werewolves. *(Of course the way I heard this from one of the LARPERS was that they beat up the Trekkies :) I've seen that myself. I wouldn't feck with a mad Larper. He doesn't have a phaser. He has an ax.)*

Even if they are foam covered for safety's sake.

5) Last but not least are the **TABLE-TOPPERS.** These are the REAL gamers.

This is where it all started from. Like D&D. (**Dungeons & Dragons**). They can be intense and take their game VERY seriously. They can live within their board game. Sometimes they get so involved it's like "Geek Raging" *(This is where grown men yell at each other in Klingon or Elfish and get pissed off because someone used a magic weapon that wasn't sanctioned and usurped someone's super power and now someone else is PISSED and won't speak to you ever again)* kind of thing.

Some table toppers LARP….. and some absolutely DO NOT.

It is hard to tell if a table topper LARPs or not, because the ones that DO NOT Larp, may also wear garb at the table! The only way you will be able to tell for sure, is that they never leave the table. They are generally younger, single, heterosexual men without girlfriends. They order in pizza, beer, 'Code Red" and chips and continue playing all through the night. It's is Dungeons & Dragons in its' hayday.

So now you know the different types of Fantasy players. Is that all clear as mud now?

Traveling to Another World

We have packed up, loaded and trekked off to another world to a LARP *(Live Action Role Playing)* Renaissance faire to work this weekend as wandering minstrels. We started very early this morning, in preparation for the trip, packing garb, food, clothes, costuming, trip necessities, guitars, drums *(all tools of our trade)* and RAKING out Harry's van at 10 a.m. for an 11 a.m. departure. We are traveling in Wayne's conversion van. I was blessed with an epiphany during all this:

"I swear that I know why the Gods made women," I muttered to my daughter Jesse as I helped getting Harry's van

ready to go. "It's so men wouldn't SHITE themselves to death."
Then more oozed out. "He's like this. Remember those newspaper clippings of people who died in high rises in New York
City? They had catacombed themselves over the years into
their apartments. They only found out that they died after their
newspapers backed up to the point of obscuring the door. And
when the landlord finally pried opened the door, they had to
excavate the person out of the apartment using archeological
tools and implements to dig through their accumulated shite."
Then I whispered quietly and looked both ways, "They only
found the dead person by the smell."

"Boys" was all that Jesse said. We both nodded our head.
I kid you not, I had to CRAWL into the van over wires, gear,
dirty sweatshirts *(of which he wanted to wear again, I said, "NO"
emphatically, and let the sweatshirts stand by themselves in the laundry
room..."Splurge and wear a clean one!" I barked),* I climbed over old
newspapers, tech manuals and mysterious sound system parts
to even GET to the back seat where our bed was destined to be.
(Why, God, why?)

Rather than spend my breath swearing, I just tried to focus
on cleaning and vacuuming the van, whilst Harry was hauling
crap out and putting it God knows where *(I'm sure I'll find out
later).* We did finish, amazingly so, in nearly the allotted time
*(which is why he always saves this crap to the last minute. It's like that
old saying, "Do you know why a dog licks himself? Because he CAN.")*
After the van was cleaned, loaded for bear, and after five hours
driving later, we are here, parked in the middle of a dark field,
in our cozy Chevy conversion van, in the rain, somewhere in
Massachusetts. We are dry, safe and sound, well fed on salmon,
stuffed mushrooms, baklava and wine after finishing an amazing meal at Zorba's Greek restaurant. I am stuffed and feeling
no pain from the several lovely glasses of Cabernet I had with
dinner. I am looking forward to singing next to him tomorrow
*(it was really sweet that he bought that amazing dinner, as his makeup gift
for our hard work and travel).*

On the morrow, we will be a part of this new baby faire,
put on by a LARP group. It is a neat place and grounds, with

a nice tavern, and they are really trying to utilize the space and rolling grounds and woods. We shall see what the morrow shall bring. More rain methinks. Lots. At least that's what the weather man doth say. We have cloaks, music, bad jokes, limericks, smiles and hugs to give others. For our fortification, we have wine, a short walk to the privy, a box full of food and a dry, comfy, luxurious bed *(albeit an air mattress with sleeping bags, but still, it is private and clean)* to share together...just us. It is quiet, safe and sound in the woods and I am with my handsome man. I also know he is naked under the sleeping bag. I think we will lull ourselves off to sleep, with the rain pitter-pattering on the roof of the van, the smell of pine trees and perhaps making love in a rocking van here in the woods of Massachusetts. I don't think the other campers all around us will mind. They are probably aliens, trolls or wookies anyway, and, well, it is the custom here.

Next Day- Remember when Luke Skywalker, Hans Solo and Chewbacca go into the space tavern bar of multi-gifted and cultured aliens? It will be like that here tomorrow. Anything and everything is expected to be sighted from: Renaissance lords and ladies, flitting fairies, snake people, angels *(dark and light)*, knights, Irish step-dancing children, hobgoblins, cat people, wizards, vampires, pirates, furries, sorceresses to, well..... Elvis.....*(there seems to be always one KING who will "be in the building")*. It will be wild. Or "wylde" as the case may be.

We awoke at 5:30 am to a driving downpour rain and discovering our recently erected picnic tent was down for the count. It was suffering from fatally twisted poles and bent-frame disease. Fuck. There would be no hot coffee this morn on the Coleman stove, methinks. Nor any dry clothes for the day.

Standing *(sort of)* bent over in the van, we put on clean garb, assorted accessories, drank some V-8 straight from the can, ate the leftover salmon and rice from last night for breakfast, *(still delicious)* donned guitars and drum and hoisted cloaks over all and started the trek up to the faire site on foot. The pasture and paths are ankle deep in rain water and muck. The day feels like your typical, soggy, grey day in Mordor.

And around here, not only could I imagine Orcs jumping out with their bloody, threatening blades and nasty teeth...but I expected them too. It is a Live Action Role Playing group here, remember? **It could happen.**

For the most part, all the staff, performers and supporters were in very good spirits. We all played the day as seasoned rennies do, which is just plain happy to be there. All garbed up for the occasion, speaking in our versions of Celtic accents and singing boldly and often, with good hearts. Harry and I saw hobgoblins, lizard men, angels, pirates, demons, vampires, fairies, nobles and peasants just as I predicted. Later, we were amazed at the savage sword and dagger demonstration, here where violence is practiced, and realized that most fights back then were not the lengthy up-and-down-the-staircase choreographed duels we've all watched with Errol Flynn. Rather they were savage, well fought, dexterous and quick. For the off-time evening delights, the management invited all the performers and volunteers to meet back at the tavern for free victuals. And a "buck off" ales. Of course we went.

I had scoped around the shire earlier in the day, hoping to find the best chess player around, so that I might find a challenger to play against Harry. You see, Harry is a really fine chess player. I found a willing challenger, and they set up the beauteous giant chess set. The chess board itself is the size of a dance floor. Rather than have Live chess players as pieces as many faires do, this faire had purchased a most beautiful teak chess set of gargantuan size. The queen chess piece was literally as big as a third grader. Then Harry and the other chess master went at it. It was really most interesting to watch the strategy of this chess duel with its ponderings, the missed mark, the weighted musings, the stroking beards, the havoc, the carnage, and the turn of the game back and forth. After a nail-biter of nearly an hour's time, Harry conceded the game and was in his glory to finally play someone who matched him.

Then we joined another couple of new to us musicians who introduced themselves as Jay and Abby, "The Harper & The Minstrel." We really clicked! The four of us played popular music after hours for everyone till late in the evening. My absolute <u>favorite</u> part of the night was playing a ripping Scottish bodhran to Led Zeppelin's "Ramble On" *(which sounded awesome, if not a bit of a bizarre instrument accompaniment choice)* and also singing four-part harmonies to Emerson, Lake & Palmer's "Lucky Man." We were all serenaded by each other and ended up giving hugs and sharing pints all around. We dubbed each other "most excellent bards" *(which is the "Ren" equivalent for the drunken declaration, "I love you man")* and patrons bought us several rounds. The music and camaraderie totally made up for my soaking, squishy sandals, Harry's sodden leather boots and our now-over-burdensome cloaks from the heaven's pissing down on us all day and night.

The next morning was still wet, but the day was much kinder. We sold baskets of CDs, *(and saints preserve us!)* we made a rogue's deal for a couple of authentic reproductions of Blackbeard's and Calico Jack's pirate flags! I also begged Harry to buy a beautiful, new tunic to match his amazing, blue eyes, which he did. We belted out verses and banged drums and guitars. We forgot some words. We made up others. We were happy to be with the people smitten with us there, and we were asked back for the next year's faire. Got paid for good work.

We drove home happily and safely, with Ren tunes in our heads, recanting and singing the old faire standard, "Roll the Old Chariot Along" with our newly invented, yet apt verses:
"A pair of dry shoes wouldn't do us any harm" and *"A wee nip of rum wouldn't do us any harm"*...Which of course, they didn't.

We set back off for the same fair in Massachusetts the following year. We threw in the costuming, popped some cheese, crackers, fruit and a big bottle of wine into the camper, tossed the instruments above our heads onto the bed of my sister's RV. Dorothy's camper sits on a Toyota base with a small underbody and bigger camper on top. Dort says that it resembles "an ant carrying a cookie" in its size and shape. We sang a cappella most of the way, trying to work out new arrangements for this year's songs.

We found our way here again and have parked the camper on the faire grounds. We are settling into faire life for the weekend. It is dusk, and we hear a mixture of wild birds, crickets and the hum of the thruway not far from here. OK, well, you have to use your imagination, OK? The other campers are mercifully quiet, as this is a work night for those of us who actually work the faire day. The air feels and smells really sweet here in the woods tonight. It was a very hot traveling day. The camper is cozy and comfy. We are content.

The next morning dawned kindly with sunshine, blue sky and puffy white clouds. There were "Boffer Tournaments" at certain times of the day. *(A "boffer" is a pretend/play weapon for some of these role-playing games. They are usually covered in styrofoam and are not considered dangerous, although they can sting)*. This is where the LARPers run out onto the field with boffer weaponry and "any unsuspecting gentle with a weapon that isn't peace-tied, and has said weapon in his/her hand is FAIR GAME." As per the game book. It is quite the sight to see, with ren folks running about with their sturdy, pretend, whapping weapons chasing each other about, dueling, slashing, doing fancy foot work, even with the Queen in their midst, who was barking orders as to who to kill and who to guard.

It is a wee bit surreal, to say the least...but fun and entertaining. There were also sword demonstrations, the Vikings of Vinholm camped up on the hill, a Shakespeare "Reloaded" play *(which has elements of modern movies within it, like "The Matrix", highly unusual, but pretty clever nonetheless)* There was also the lovely fun of singing and playing music, which is the primary love of our lives. There is so much fun to be had, being together and just singing and bantering, and being onstage together. We sang a magical song to some wonderful tarot card readers and one named Lady Diane actually ran up to me after one song, and said, "I have to give you this!" and gave me a huge hug! She said, "This is for the lady dancing behind you when you sing. You have the most amazing voice, and I can see a spirit behind you, a lady much like yourself, and she is.... well....dancing and twirling and enjoying herself so much!" "Interesting. Hmmm. It's probably just me dancing with myself. When I play I feel so alive and happy and whole." I say.

A fun point of interest was at five bells, the Sheriff of the Shire came running into the Miner's Tap Tavern *(where we were just happening to have a pint, what are the odds??)* The Sheriff ran in and said, "Every able bodied man with a weapon come now! There is a rampant giant troll lose on the shire!" A TROLL??? Well, this we had to see! We grabbed our mugs *(can't forget the beer for God's sake and careful not to spill it!)* and ran to the front door, just in time to see 25 warriors of both genders, trying to take down a 12-foot troll! He had a red, demon face, horns, long legs and a savage sword. It was an intense fight, until the troll fell. He was declared dead by the Sheriff and the Queen herself! Much rejoicing commenced! *(Crowd murmurs "yaaay!")*

After that, we happened upon a man and woman in the field of vendors. We saw them and they approached. He was wearing a deerskin fringed kilt. Beaded, even. It was beautiful and comfy looking. The lass with him was sweet and shy. Harry looks at me, and says, out of the blue, "Let's play 'Lakes of Pontchartrain' for them." I look at him incredulously, cuz it's not a song of the time period we are in, but instead, I went along with his intuition…and went with the flow, regardless… we let the Muse guide us. So we played that pretty 1800s song at the ren faire and bent the rules. While playing I noticed the man had walked off a ways away with a friend who interrupted the song…then we both realized that the man was crying. Crying about our song. When we finished the song…the man turned around, with tears rolling down his manly face, and said: "I'm sorry to have turned my back upon you when you were playing, I wasn't being rude, it's just that I was so overcome with the song. See, I am from Louisiana, and I lost family and friends with Katrina, and your song, hit so close to home, I couldn't keep it in. I lived around Lake Pontchartrain, and I love it there." And here I was, wondering why the feck Harry felt compelled to do that damn song! The man from Louisiana, himself, was the reason. The emotions that poured from his face told the real story of his heart.

I have learned to "Follow the Muse." You never know who you are being led to speak to, or why, but there is always a reason. We are now traveling west and homeward, leaving behind, Trolls, Orcs, Fairies, Goblins, Vikings, Roman Centurions, Rennies, Scots, Larpers, and Gypsies.

Well, not all gypsies are left behind, as Harry and I are still traveling home together.

Free Bird

It was September 2001 and we were in Bushnell Park in Hartford, CT. Harry, Ron VanNostrand and Dan Cleveland and I played "Mark Twain Days" for the "Connecticut Yankee in King Arthur's Court" portion of the festival. We were to be the Renaissance music for wandering and to be the gathering crowd act just before the joust.

There we were, all dressed in our minstrel best, awaiting our turn for our music part. We were waiting on the dais under the tent on stage, before a couple thousand people, along with a Falconer. This huntswoman was going to give one of her many demonstrations with her birds of prey.

While waiting there with my minstrel friends, instruments tuned and at the ready, I struck up a conversation with the Falconer as she stood there with her gauntlet glove holding the beautiful, but hooded, sharp-taloned Peregrine falcon. "What a beautiful bird. So lovely. May I pet him?" "Sure." I stroked the feathers of the bird's back. The bird's sightless hood turned in the direction of the intruding pleasure of my petting hand. "Oh, he's SO beautiful, so soft!" I looked at the birds' feet shackled by tether to the Falconer.

I continued, "Interesting. Can I ask you a weird question?" The handler shook her head approving it. "My name is Merlyn. I love birds, especially Merlins and all falcons. Here's my question: 'Aren't you afraid that this wild bird will just take off on you and just keep flying sometime?" *(Coincidently, at that precise moment, the bird cocked its hooded head in a quizzical manner. It looked as though it was thinking a thought it had never thought before. Like "Huh! Really? I could DO that? I never thought of THAT before.")*

The huntswoman said, "Oh No. My birds are <u>highly trained</u>. They respond to my commands without wavering."

I went on in my Devil's Advocate voice, "Yes, I'm sure they are, but they are, and always will be, wild creatures. No matter how highly trained they are. I would think that one day, it would just say "to hell with it" and fly off and do what's instinctual when it has the chance to keep flying….instead of always returning on command."

(When those words left my lips, the bird cocked its hooded head again in my direction. It seemed to say, "Huh. Well, how about THAT! What a great idea. I'm breaking out the next chance I get!")

The four of us even noted how funny it was to watch the bird "think" about it. The Falconer disregarded our humor, as she was just then called up to do her demonstration. She walked out onto the joust field with her wireless mic on, and started giving her information. She walked and talked about her highly trained bird holding it on high. She then released the falcon to the delight of the crowd!

And guess what happened?

Yup. The bird immediately flew straight up into a nearby tree and WOULD NOT COME BACK. I swear to God it was as if the bird had internalized my words and said, "Yah, thanks Merlyn! You rock. Why didn't I think of this before? Woooot! I'm a FREE BIRD! I'm outta there!"

The handler was unruffled. She then spoke almost the same words that I had just said moments before verbatim, "We have to remember that these birds are still wild. They are, and always will be wild creatures. No matter how highly trained they are." She went on justifying the birds' naughty behavior while Harry, Ron, Dan and I laughed and laughed backstage. Coincidence? I think NOT.

I admit, I did feel a bit guilty for inciting the bird with a wicked adventurous idea. I figure my intuition had either picked up on what it wanted to do all along, or the bird had already decided that with the support of my questioning that his time had come. It was a sign by God.

The handler tried and tried to make the demonstration go well. She twirled her lasso of tender meat treat around and around for quite awhile. The bird just flitted from tree to tree, deciding which tree it liked the best. The wild bird totally ignored its owner. After awhile, the trainer decided that the embarrassment of her show had reached abysmal proportion and came off the field, "left the stage" as it were, leaving the bird laughing in the trees.

Warning announcements were made at the festival which stated, "If you have small children or small pets, please keep them close to you, as the bird may think that they are prey. Please be advised and be careful."

It was hours that we watched the handler troll through the crowd swinging her tasteless lure, trying to convince her bird that he really wanted the captivity treat. The bird was not sure it wanted to come back to her. Ever. The handler refused to talk to me for the rest of the festival.

But what had I really done? I had voiced the animal's secret freedom wish. The bird listened and acted on it. It was the funniest thing that ever happened spontaneously and I have witnesses to this day of this conversation and resulting yet amusing catastrophe.

I am glad the bird did take off. It gave us all hope in throwing off our own shackles of limitation. It was more than coincidence. I spoke to a wild thing, and it listened! I was a Bird Whisperer!

The bird proved that sometimes you just have to spread your wings and feel freedom! Even if only for a short time and a short flight, the resulting stand up for your rights can be truly exhilarating. For yourself...and also for everyone who sees your power.

The bird eventually did come back hours later. But not before a lot of small dogs and toddlers got the word to be on the lookout for a menace from the sky. And not before we minstrels enjoyed the thought of that feathered blind hooded bird getting a wicked notion and pondering his own freedom while in his tethered bonds.

In the end, the falcon **DID** choose to go back to the bonds of captivity and the slavery he knew, rather than embrace the unknown aspects of freedom.

Unfortunately, a lot of humans choose to do that too.

All's Faire in Love

Something that I have learned in many years of being a minstrel, playing guerrilla theatre as it were, is that there are levels of patrons and fans too. Reactions to street musicians runs the gamut. We've played at so many venues. From Celtic fests, roaming mall entertainment, farmer's market, casinos, schools, libraries, restaurants, jails and mental institutions where they lock YOU in as well. We've played churches, taverns, street festivals, erotic arts festivals, played on houseboats and trains along with our work at Renaissance faires. I've found that most people fall into these categories:

• **Ignore the Minstrel. Just keep walking, make no eye contact and maybe they won't see me**. *(I'm sure mimes get this reaction a lot too. If you are this kind of a patron, you usually have children in tow and may say to the wee one, "Honey come away from the musician. We have to go home and watch TV." I really hope you change your mind about live performance and let your kid stick around, because the child is obviously mesmerized and is interested. Maybe you'll have more fun if you stop your hectic pace and check it out for five or ten minutes. Risk missing your rerun. You may be surprised at what fun you can have.)*

• **Notice the Minstrel, and just try to act normal and don't stare.** *(But really, thank you for stopping! And it's OK to stare. We're paid to be this weird! Enjoy the weirdness.)*

• **Notice the Minstrel but openly scoff at them while walking past and making guffaws, mockingly play your air guitar or clap out of time on purpose to try to throw the minstrel off time.** *(First off, my rhythm is pretty solid, so you really aren't fucking with me. You just look like an* asshole to everyone around you. I usually just internalize this abhorrent reaction to my sincere creativity, talent and energy with telling myself at the time that, "Hey, dude, I'm getting paid to be this weird at this moment and you posers are not." i.e., "I win, you lose.") Personally, when I see a street performer while I'm out and about and not currently working, I usually stop for a few moments or a song, and try to give them a "thumbs up" for the effort and the courage it takes to dare to suck. Go ahead. Get dressed up and try it on some busy street corner someday. It takes balls.

• **Notice the Minstrel and stop and tell the minstrel your life story and usually while the minstrel is currently singing.** *(Hey, I'm good at multi-tasking, but dude, really. I'm working here. And I'm singing loud. Why are you carrying on a one-sided conversation with a singing-engaged performer? Have you forgotten your medication? Do you have a grip on reality?)*

• **Notice the Minstrel and stops and watches and sings along and claps.** *Sometimes they offer tips too. Especially nice if patron can carry a tune and knows the song being performed. This patron can be just passing by in a moment's time on a transient journey or may stay for a whole song or set. They enjoy you totally. You feel like they "get it." Minstrels LOVE YOU.*

• **Notice the Minstrel and is sincerely appreciative and supportive of the Arts.** *These folks usually get on mailing lists and buy every one of your CDs. They soak you up and you soak their loving energy too. It may be the catalyst in some portion of their life and they may be inspired by your music to pick up an instrument and start learning finally how to play it. This is how I personally got inspired to play, by becoming smitten with a musician and it drove me to hours of practice and braving the stage myself. Minstrels LOVE YOU and NEED YOU.*

• **Notice the Minstrel and then becomes enamored.** *They become an Uber-fan and starts dressing like you, buying Chevy vans to match yours, going to every event on your calendar and may even have a Shrine of you in their home. A little unnerving, but flattering. Just please stop before you start stealing my underwear. It's wacky and I really miss that pair.*

• **Notice the Minstrel but goes on to become some of your real true good friends.** *They may even offer to help roadie. They often ask you to learn special music that would be perfect for you in your repertoire. You ROCK.*

Like I said, it runs the gamut. At many Renaissance faires around the country, we are often called on to be the "Wedding Minstrels" for the frequent marriage ceremonies. It is a pleasure and an honor to be admitted to this very special moment of people's lives. Over the years, Harry and I have seen our share of weddings and vow renewals. Some have been breathtakingly beautiful! Some have been so perfect and sweet. Some, well, not so much. They really run the gamut of all kinds of ceremonies, religious, secular, magical, civil. They also run from the sublime to the ridiculous.

One of my favorite sublime weddings of all time was for Rick and Anita, who were having their vows renewed. Rick was profoundly deaf and he signed all his vows to her.

Having raised my daughter, Shawna, with what they call "total communication" *(using both sign and spoken word together),* I was able to understand a lot of what he was saying. Anita welled up happily with joy and pride at her husband. I was personally very touched by this show of ultimate devotion and acceptance and perseverance. In the years hence, this family has grown to be good friends of mine. I don't think I have ever met a more angelic yet real couple in my whole life. Rick sometimes "sings" on some of our songs with us on stage by signing the words. It is how we met. It is a reminder how can teach others how to communicate better.

But all weddings are not alike. The wildest of all Renewal Days had us minstreling down 75 couples from the front gate to the Chapel. That's like riding a wild octopus and making sure everyone stays together and not lost, all the while you are walking with jingles on your feet and playing and keeping time and singing for about 200 people in a long line to China. We packed them in the chapel like cattle that day and it was what I think a Renaissance Rev. Sun Myung Moon mass wedding would've been like. Not your ordinary romantic wedding gig, that's for sure. Thankfully, since this over-booked day, that particular faire put limits on wedding couples per day.

I will tell you of a few more individual weddings that you may find interesting, fun, unbelievable or even annoying. Stories included here are from all over the country and from the last 16 years of us working at several different fairs. They really happened. Really, really. My writing takes a vernacular turn here to incorporate the language of "Ren Ease." Enjoy.

The American Baptist Wedding at the Pagan Festival

Harry and I arrived early one Sunday morn to a Renaissance faire to help the wedding with music and ambiance. Whilst all seemed well and good, guests were hither and amiable, Harry and I noticed that no one was really talking. *(Odd, for a festival wedding day, methinks?)* After Harry's booming voice gathered up the family, he proceeds with a town-crier type proclamation of a "Here Ye! Here Ye!" type greeting. The guests all then circle all up around the couple in the courtyard to listen to me as I recite a sonnet with a garland rope encircling them.

Harry then boisterously heralds all to: "Partake in this ceremony and festival day with Feasting! Dancing! Good ALE! Huzzah!" And he held up his mug as a grand gesture! Which went over like the proverbial fart in church. Silence. The sound of crickets was deafening. So, sensing the odd non-reaction, he then encouraged them to shout, as one, "Cheer for the couple in one Grand HUZZAH!"

"Huzzah," *they mumbled.* And then it dawned on us. No one told us they were a bunch of Baptists! *(READ: "ix-Nay on the eer-Bay.")*

Well, we got them all to the chapel, on time, and were settling in the guests *(who, I must say were all like deer in headlights. Evidently, some of the guests found it distasteful to find themselves at what they considered a "pagan festival" on a Sunday morning during church hours, instead of actually being IN church...they all looked so, so guilty and skittish. It was just "wrong" somehow to them.)*

No one spoke*! (I still thought this was the oddest thing for a wedding congregation...we had no official clue why, but only conjectured as to what the real problem was...)*

The Justice of the Peace started the service. It was all the usual and sundry stuff until it veered into a long service and I was certain we were now on a particularly righteous path. Remember, I've spent my time in many a church and could well read the signs. A friend of the family was called up, and he started a deep and droning Christian sermon of 20 minutes or so. *(FYI~ That would be considered a very long sermon for this type of service at a Ren Faire on a festival day, where folks usually want to have a short service and get right on to having an adventure at the faire).* The man preached intensely on "Love." I'm sure we've all heard those inspired words of 2ⁿᵈ Corinthians many times and the very same sermon before at many weddings. But by now, I have put two and two together and came up with a basket of loaves and fishes. These folks were all "saved." Which is fine, but now I have to punt with my choice of music for the recessional.

So, after the man sat down and the couple were wed and kissed, and turned to us to "sing them out" of the chapel, I had to do a pre-emptive avoidance of an incoming missile tune for our guests. We usually sing the fun old song "Three Jolly Coachmen" with the chorus chiming "Landlord, fill the flowing bowl until the cup run over, for tonight we'll merry, merry be, tomorrow we'll be sober." *(Yah, probably not the best choice for tee-to-talers.)* Fortunately, I see where this sermon is heading, picked up the signals of their spiritual leanings and quickly switched the recessional song last minute to something tamer. I caught Harry's attention from across the chapel and signaled the new song to insert, "Star of the County Down" and we punted. Thankfully, we didn't get lynched. It satisfied the congregation.

But now it is time for the toasts! We go to help the serving wenches pass out the fluted glasses with something bubbly for a toast to the newly wedded and their guests. It's now all of 9:30am. I handed a glass to one of the guests and she recoils in fear of decadence of the offered goblet of champagne, "Oh! No! I don't drink!" (then adds) "What is it?"

I tell her calmly that it "is most likely a sparkling wine, but I will go and check for thee."

I ask the serving wench "What be in the glasses, love?"

She looked at me with a tired worn-out expression of dealing with many a bridal wedding issue and says, in a bland voice, "Birch Beer."

"Birch Beer?" *(to toast with? Well OK then. When in Rome we go with the flow, and I am now very happy with my intuitive recessional song choice!)* I go back and hand the skittishly temperate woman a bubbly glass of wild and crazy birch beer. She accepted it like a chalice from Heaven. Whatever. When in Rome and all.

But here's the good part. Why would a strict family wedding be chosen to be celebrated here, of all places, if they weren't into any of it? Well, evidently the bride and groom had been to the faire before and LOVED it. It was their day. They were going to give both of their conservative families an eye-opener, whether they wanted one or not. All of their guests were "virgins" to the faire and had no idea what to expect. The new couple were giving them a gift of a new perspective! *(Naked dancing and coupling in the streets, mayhaps? No, wait, that's the cast party.)*

Before we get ready to leave this anti-bacchanal wedding reception for our real workday to begin at faire, I traditionally always give a toast as a gift for our parting words. *("This toast was especially satisfying under the circumstances" I think wickedly to myself, and happily will pull their leg.)* We have everyone raise their glasses of birch beer for a "Mischievous Toast from Merry Mischief."

"Here's to lying, cheating, stealing and drinking!" *(I imagined some of the ladies getting the vapors and swooning onto fainting couches)* and as we looked around at the faces of the shocked and disbelieving, I smirked and gave the rest of the toast: "If you lie...may you lie together...If you cheat...may you cheat the devil!" *(Waves of relieved looks spread through the crowd, men wiped their sweating brows, and women stopped fanning themselves wildly)*. I continued, "If you steal...may you steal each other's hearts... And if you drink...may we all drink to your good fortune! HUZZAH!"

I tell you, it was like pulling a tablecloth off a loaded table successfully. Voila! A heavy sigh of relief came from all the Baptists in one unison collective breath.

The brand new Mr. and Mrs. went hand in hand laughing all the way to their honeymoon carriage and lusty *(and now legally and family sanctioned)* wedded marriage bed.

As my friend, Michael, who is King at many a faire says: "I wish you a hot bowl of soup and a warm bed...or...vice versa... if you can get it."

The Clueless Hordes of Zombies Wedding

This particular wedding morning, Harry and I arrived in plenty of time to check in with a faire office to gather information for the ceremony that day. Our office friend, the wedding planner, is smiling the familiar painted-on smile folks in customer service often wear on these occasions. "No one has RSVP'd for this one," she worriedly admits, "So, the bride said 'to just make up as many packets with tickets as possible and they'd pay for them all at the end." *(No one RSVP'd? How unusual, don't you think? I'd never heard of such a thing. I mean, are they breathing? None?)*

We go outside to find, meet and greet the wedding couple only to find a large group of folks milling about, aimlessly amassing and shuffling here and there clueless for a wedding. We make the bold heralded announcement, "Aye, Good Morrow! Hast all those gather-ed hither for the wedding checked in with the office, to get your tickets/packets for the faire?" *(They all looked at us as if we had just uttered Swahili. Blink, blink, blink.)*

A dazed look ran throughout the crowd. We repeat the announcement and some guests wake up just long enough to shuffle off slowly to the office. *(I swear I almost imagined someone say "braaaainssss"...)* I spy a well-attired wedding guest likely of some importance and go up to grill her for information. "I say, love, are you on the family side of the bride? Or the groom?"

To which she informatively replies, "Yes." *(Yes? Mayhaps she misheard heard me, so I repeat the question.)* "Nay, lovey, are you on the bride's side or the groom's side?" This time she answers back a little peaved with me and says sternly, "Yes!" Finally, she says petulantly, "I'm the mother of the bride." *(EUREKA! We are getting somewhere! Huzzah!)*

"Ah. That's grand!" I say. "I be looking for the blessed couple of the day. Wouldst thou say whither the bride and groom are hither?"

"Yes, they're here." *(AH! Fer feck's sake, mother, where are they? I screamed in my head.)* She never did say, and trailed off to do something… motherly, perhaps. After what seemed like eons, we did finally find the bride. Both the bride & groom were decked out in garb. That's cool.

Onward, with continually late-arriving guests, we give reminders to all the lost souls that we will be starting soon, and we continue to send the wandering anonymous guests to go and check in at the office. Again and again we remind them. We have also been given one additional job now… it is the ridiculous and unwarranted task of Harry escorting fecking droves of adults to the privy. *(I mean, really, didn't you see the ones in the parking lot when you parked the car? Didn't you go before you left? Never pass up an opportunity to pee, is my motto. I wondered how they missed this lesson in kindergarten).* Add to this lovely unruly scene is the handy addition of twin coolers of beer that they have dragged to the wedding procession and are now popping tops off of and drinking from in the line waiting to go down to the chapel ceremony at 9 a.m. *(the faire Head of Security squashed that one when he heard all the pop tops go off in unison.)* We finally set off, nearly a half-hour late, with nearly 100 guests in tow, to minstrel down to the chapel at 9:15 a.m. *(sadly sans twin beer coolers but grateful everyone had peed their car beers before the beautiful ceremony commenced).*

Once the clueless hordes and shuffling minion of guests were finally there, I now realized I had yet one more job. I had to set up the entire service. No really. Neither the bride nor groom had thought of that, nor of what they wanted, what'ere, until this final minute, and then? They left it all in my hands. "Whatever you think is best" they told me. (*Blink, blink, blink.*) "What'ere you want to do is fine. We don't care." (*I'm thinking, "Ye don't care a whit about what happens here at your own nuptials? Ah, well, so be it." I could've called for flaming torches and dancing Popes and they would've been alright with it. Hmmm. dancing Popes. I sorta like that festive idea.*).

Soon, they were all wed and it was done. But it was then that we found out that this particular couple had been living together for 17 years before deciding to marry today. Think about that for a minute. 17 years.

The groom's friends were all dressed in mourning clothes. "He made it this far...why did he do it?" they sobbed into their beers. "Why buy the cow when you can get the milk for free?" was uttered more than once. And they weren't the only ones neither. The bride's lady friends, all telling the bride, "Why buy the pig just to get a little free sausage?" Their chant seemed to be: "Another one lost, lost, lost." They all shook their heads sad and knowingly so.

This time, I winked at Harry and we DID launch into and sing our chosen song, "Landlord, Fill the Flowing Bowl until the cup runs over, for tomorrow we'll be sober!" Because at this wedding, they had Mimosas, which was very cool with us after all the work we'd put in. I could use a drink about now. The alcohol must have sparked something within them, too, for now, they were all of a sudden completely awake and actually had personalities! Now the zombies were all coherent and kind enough to place a large mug brimming full of champagne topped off with a bit of orange juice, in our hands, afore we started our day at the faire at 10a.m. Yes, thank you. Thank you very much. I love zombies.

We, however, felt as if we'd put in a full day by the time we got to opening parade! And indeed we had. By 3 of the clock, that very same day, the groom came to one of our afternoon shows, stumbling drunk, incoherent, off his arse, and his bride was nowhere to be found. She'd been missing for several hours and was finally found puking drunk in the privy on her big day in her wedding garb. Just think. They waited seventeen years for this ceremony. Hmmm, maybe some things are worth waiting for? And maybe, just maybe, they might've rushed this one.

The Stingy Scot Wedding

Now mind you, I love Scots. I am one. Me very own Grandad fought in the Scottish Regiment of the Canadian army in kilt and all. My older sister once asked him, "Grandpa, did you wear a kilt in the war?"

"Aye, I did, lass," he said. She continued, "What did you wear under neath there?"

He replied, "I canna tell thee, lass, but it sure were COLD."

We all jokes about Scots and their tight purse strings. Oh, the parsimonious Celtic darlings that we be! But this one takes the cake *(or Shortbread, as it were)*.

We arrived to gather up the good gentles for this morning's episode on The Wedding Channel at the ren faire. The bride and groom were ready and waiting in their matching tartans, beautiful, handsome and all set to go get hitched. I go to the office to get the last-minute details.

Well, amazingly enough, it seems that the wedding couple did not pay for ANY of their guests entry to the renaissance faire for their wedding, but instead, had asked them all pay their own way in! *(I mean, ye have t' admire the brass ones on those parsimonious Scottish darlings!)*

But it did not faze any of the guests a whit. For being a Scottish family, most guests came prepared and unruffled with their Wegmans' half-priced coupons for reduced faire entrance. *(Always the resourceful ones, aye?)*

So as to not be showing any out and out blatant favoritism; the bride didn't even pay for her own aged mother who came hobbling on a cane in her kilt. Scrooge would be right proud o' her Scottish heritage for sure. No matter. I saw that the old lady had a cane and looked like she wasn't afraid to wield a shillelagh.

I can totally understand tight purse strings, but this I couldn't fathom: There were no cake to sup, nor was there any drink neither! I mean just think on that, me laddies and lassies! Nothing to drink at a Scot's wedding? No haggis? No short-bread? No pints of dark stout to toast with? NO WHISKEY? May God and Robbie Burns have mercy on their tartaned souls!

The All-the-World's-a-Stage Wedding

"All the world's a stage,
And all the men and women merely players:
They have their exits and their entrances;
And one man in his time plays many parts."
    ~Shakespeare ("As you like it")

This particular wedding was indeed a production. It had a stage plot, script with lines for various characters, props, a town crier *(complete with a southern drawl)* and a big finale! It seemed as though this whole wedding was choreographed. The bride, groom, attendants and the town crier each held a massive ten-page script for the whole service *(which they read from and couldn't pull their eyes off of for the entire time, trying to keep their place.)*

Once Harry and I got the wedding guests and the bridal party to the chapel and were in the process of singing their beautiful processional music, the town crier couldn't wait for the finish of the song. *(READ: He jumped his cue.)* He interrupted the processional ballad mid-song and started yelling in his perfect "Cat on a Hot Tin Roof" Southern drawl and it sounded like this:

"Hare yay! Hare yay! Y'all gather round, now right-chare, for the wedding "Nup-she-alls!" Enter Justice of the Peace!" *(That's right lovies, he actually read-out-loud the blocking directions on the script for the Justice's entrance).* Harry and I looked at each other askance, smirked and tried desperately not to laugh, *(mayhaps this was the inevitable comic relief part?).*

There were many props *(goblets, candles to light, a picture of some dead relative and of course, the inevitable prop malfunctions that always go with stage plays. Like, the picture of the dead relative was "not happy" and kept falling over at the most inopportune times. Definitely a message from haunted stage theater lore, if you ask me)* and all the props had their share of energy in the wind at the oddest moments.

During the actual ceremony, there were missed cues, muffed lines, the sound of shuffling script pages and the whispered prompts of words from another with their finger on the correct page coaxing with lines. No one seemed to be actually living in the moment here, but all were reading along like a play rehearsal before first night. I mused, mayhaps a coach, dress rehearsal and some practice would have been warranted for a production of this magnitude? Emotion? Well, not much, no. All the actors *(I mean, the wedding party)*, were more concerned with reading off the script and turning pages back and forth trying to find their places.

To her credit, the bride did have her "lines" memorized. The groom was lost, sadly, but he made a valiant effort and tried to follow along anyways.

Example: "Do you take this woman to have and to hold forever forward, so help you God?"

Groom: "Hold on...Where am I? What page are we on? Page 8? Oh thanks" *[shuffles papers, finds line with finger and then reads]*, "I DO."

At this wedding too, there was no wedding cake, nor anything to toast with *(I must say here, I feel that a wedding without a toast, from special friend or loved one is like a day without sunshine). And really, what kind of a play is it, without a cast party?)*

Oh! In all stage plays you must have special characters!

One of the guests was in a wheelchair; she was the bride's sister. She played the part of The Diva. We had taken certain extra pains to make sure that the bride's ample sister arrived safely down to the chapel, as we do for everyone with special needs. We are gentle and happy to be inclusive of everyone that is in need.

How'ere, whereupon chatting with her afterward, this "disabled" guest said that she "could walk perfectly fine but chose not to" as she had a "respiratory illness." *(Which she punctuated with a smoky exhale of her third cigarette in 15 minutes).* However, her 60-year old, frail, skeletal-thin husband *(who had, to his credit, muscled her big frame down the perilous rocky and bumpy path)* asked if he might "borrow the dividing ropes from the chapel seating, to 'haul her up the hill with a bunch of my strongest guys."

I said, "Nay, sir, it is not up to me", and rightly discouraged them from their burly adventure. We left them pondering how they should indeed hoist her arse up to the top of the faire grounds. *(I mused that mayhaps it might be good for her if she could haul her own arse up the hill instead of finishing her next smoky treat. Did I breathe a word of it? Nay. Instead, I just smiled and was my sweet consoling self. It did, however, all remind me of theater rigging, stage hands and opera divas in the end. I almost felt compelled to shout, "Hey! We need a roadie over here and bring a winch!" to no one in particular.)*

The oddity of the day though *(as if this weren't all odd enough)* was that the bride and groom chose to "pay extra" for their wedding party to attend the joust *(READ: a fight...oh how romantic)* and to sit up above the dais over the Queen and her court. Evidently, according to the jousters and tech folks, the wedded couple and their entourage made quite a hullaballoo up there, hooting, hollering, stamping and otherwise overloading the old catwalk. In retrospect, this must have been their big "finale" at the end of their wedding production.

The only thing that was missing was "a bit with a dog" to round the whole thing out into a Shakespearean comedy. So instead of wishing the bride & groom, "Good Fortune to Ye!" as we did, in retrospect, we probably should have said "Break a leg!" or "Bravo!" or "Author! Author!"

I just hope they autographed their program...I mean, their marriage license.

The Virtual Wedding

This wedding was totally arranged by the groom *(Read: Not the bride).* I will affectionately call her –"She who never spoke."

The bride was all of *maybe* 5 feet tall and 90 pounds soaking wet and who seemed to be along merely for the ride. I am not even sure she knew anything about what was happening. I am guessing that they met online in a chat room. Really. Why do I think that? They were both totally pale and wan *(probably from spending years in the glow of computer screens in the dark)*, and I am sure they wanted a wedding that was, mayhaps, reminiscent of some medieval-themed virtual computer game.

Here at this particular faire, however, there were no trolls to kill, no dragons to slay, nor damsels to save *(saving for her grace, the bride)*. After all, we are at a Renaissance Faire. Not a LARP. And there IS a difference, as you now know.

The bride was visibly wracked with fear and shaking violently *(or was having a mild seizure brought on by some wizards gamer spell)* during the whole ceremony. *(I was wondering if she'd really ever been out in public before with real live people before?)* The bride and groom stood a total three feet apart for the whole service. They never touched or held hands or even looked at each other *(which I felt was tragically foreboding for an omen)*.

Then, suddenly, the Justice of the Peace announced that they were wed, and it suddenly occurred to the bride right then, that there was to be a kiss involved. *(I thought for a moment that she would swoon).* They leaned their upper torsos toward each other *(from the same three feet apart)* like Lego dolls that bent forward only at the waist and innocently kissed, briefly, for seemingly the very first time, for two seconds. Yup. In front of God and everyone *(however, thankfully for them, their pelvises were still a very safe distance apart from each other so no one was violated)*.

Oddly enough, this wedding had the luxury of a fine sit-down meal and drinks for feasting for after! It must be all those bonus points and accumulated Lindens from Second Life were cashed in for the occasion.

It was a storybook wedding by the book, but it was very much The Groom's Day. It was he who was arranging the event, taking the compliments, shaking hands and ordering everyone hither and thither about. He was quite in control. The bride, how're, looked like she was a deer in headlights and would keel over in a moment or two suffering from no air. Mayhaps she was bewitched in some Dungeons and Dragons enchanted spell? I dearly hoped someone had informed her that there was to be a wedding night involved later that ee'en and all that it would entail.

Ah well, no worries. Maybe their avatars would work it out for them virtually on screen later when they played the game on their matching computers in different rooms. Or maybe they would begin to live once they found their private "on button" between the sheets in their real time bedroom? However it happens, I dearly hope that when they reboot after this stressful day is done, that they will be in sync and online with each others' hearts and that this was no fatal error.

The Beautiful Dress Wedding

We arrived on yet another grand sunshine morning at one Renaissance Festival to gather the gentles and wedding party to go to the chapel. The groom and his groomsmen were all waiting and dressed in renaissance garb. Someone in the family had made all their wedding outfits, which were quite lovely.

How'ere, there was something amiss. Originally, I thought that the most fancifully dressed man there in blue and silver standing grandly with the wedding party would be the groom. But no, it seems not. The groom's attire was not the most fancy. He, instead, was dressed as a peasant, in the exact same outfit as all his groomsmen. *(How silly of me to assume his outfit would be different.)* But the real question remained. Where was the Lady of the Hour?

"She's hiding in the storage room with her Ladies-in-waiting. She doesn't want to be seen until the last minute." *(Ah)*

So! Harry stays with the modest groom and all of the guests and I, the lady minstrel, go to seek out and find the bride and see to her comforts. There is a waiting lady guarding the door. I knock and say in my best approximation of Renaissance faire language: "Good day, may I come in hither? I be Merlyn, your minstrel this day, and would bade spake with the bride." I am reluctantly granted passage to the secret chambers. As I enter, I surmise that all of her Ladies in Waiting are also likely dressed in beautiful renaissance garb. My eyes then fall on the beauteous Bride. And I really couldn't believe my eyes.

She was wearing the BWD *(Big White Dress)*. You know the one. The traditional, huge, many crinoline layered, white, netted, sequined, lace draped, puffy-sleeved, low-cut, cost a ransom, babe-a-licious wedding dress. With a train. A long train. With beads and pearls *(I shit you not)*. And the finishing touch was the high-heeled, white, beaded, satin, spike-heeled pumps. *(I immediately thought, "Oh my GOD. Gasp! Has she never stepped foot onto a faire site before? Eegads! Does she know where she'll be traipsing? Honey, its sensible shoes terrain out there!")* Instead I managed an honestly breathless, "You look beautiful my dear! " *(She really did. I am still quite shocked and grieved for her now white dress and the pounds of silver that will shortly be ruined all for naught of a bedraggled keepsake...not to mention her most surely future sprained ankles.)*

But it is now time to be wed! So, as not to be seen, we set off, separately: Harry, the Groom, Groomsmen, and all the guests in one minstrel train and the other train consists of me, the Bride and her ladies who will traverse down to the Chapel on a separate path.

And all the while I sing and play and minstrel her and her ladies down to the chapel, we are dragging this bride's pristine, white, beaded, sequined, long, virginal train over dirt, stones, sticks and the occasional mud puddle. *(If you ask me, it's really quite a perfect thematic symbol for the life of marriage, aye? I mean, we all go through some shite at some point during our married lives, as will this dress doth know in the here and now.)*

Gingerly the bride steps all the way to the chapel and teeters dangerously in her high-heeled, white, satin, beaded, stilted pumps over muddy rocky terrain, dragging her train daintily through the muck and mire, whilst maneuvering past the greasy turkey leg booth and rough-ish ale houses, game houses and pillow fight until we get her to the church on time.

The service was lovely. They are in love or in lust, *(It's really hard to tell the difference sometimes).* The groom was knocked out by her and she was smitten with him. So all was well there. Their plans were that they would all be staying at the faire until only 1 p.m. and then going to a "big reception elsewhere." Someplace "nice" the Bride said, "for dancing and a big sit down dinner and eating on china plates."

It is 9:30 a.m. when we finished their service. By 10:30 a.m. the groom and his men had all eagerly changed into jeans and T-shirts to enjoy the faire *(and to escape their garb which had set them apart and so noticeable to other faire goers)*. But the bride, how'ere, was still in her beautiful dress at the hour of noon, getting her kudos, although she was looking a bit bedraggled, and that goes for the gown too. In sooth, that dress will tell a tale at the end of this day! It shall be forever noted by its indelible tale-telling stains. Every picture tells a story, don't it?

The County Route 7 Adventure
(subtitled: The Ren Wedding Detox)

A minstrel's life can be a thing of beauty, living by the muse. It can also be arduous and full o' peril. What with the missed pints, the rare but real cheap inn owner who wants to duck out the back rather than pay up for the music already played, or the many perilous long journeys that we face on empty pockets, sore fingers, no sleep, not to mention the flying surprising guitar strings that could kill or maim you.

Case in point: We played a lovely Renaissance wedding recently. It was a most lovely summer day, although savage hot and humid. The bride and groom were obviously in love and a match, and the plans for the reception were grand indeed. The food was delish, the people pleasant, the ren faire folk singing along to every ballad, hoisting a pint to every drinking song and snuggling in on every love song that Harry and I brought forth. The "Wailing Wench" ale in the keg did flow, and *(bonus)* the keg was placed right next to the band. Handy, that. There were loving gifts given to us by the wedding couple, who are big fans, and we seemed to be well liked by the guests, for the most part *(considering that half the guests had never been to a Renaissance faire, Irish Fest nor heard many of these songs!)* And all was well.

Except that after the wedding pictures were taken, and the bridal party came back into the reception hall, the bride, well, she looked ILL. And by that I mean, she was definitely not well. She was over heated on this extremely hot day. It could've had something to do with the two corsets she wore *(one for a bodice, one underneath it for a corset),* adding to the heat of the sweltering day, the lovely satin wedding dress and bloomers underneath. The bride refused to eat or drink a thing all day, most likely due to nerves, though she was reminded often by her bridesmaids and friends. She was looking pale, indeed. As the day wore on, the Bride was almost done in. As for the actual reception, due to the bride's ill health, all was up in the air. She was not merry, but white as a ghost. The dinner postponed a bit in hopes that she'd rally. She did not. The toasts to the happy couple were non-existent as they rushed the bride, in her white wedding regalia to the emergency room during the reception, which had yet to begin!

Harry and I, as the wedding minstrels, and the amazing best man, all rose to the occasion and we did our now-absent-groom friend, right proud. The best man was truly the awesome man to have as Leader In Charge. We smiled and made all the guests feel at ease, comfy and happy under the stressful circumstances. The restaurant hostess, Harry, the best man and I were a power quartet which held the wedding reception together with bailing twine, staples, chewing gum, toe tapping ditties, and bad jokes under the circumstances. The Wailing Wench keg flowed free, the guests all still managed to have a good time, even if the wedding couple were not present at the reception. This was odd to say the least

The bride *(now at the hospital)* did perk up in a short time, once fluids were introduced intravenously and she survived her wedding day! Hopefully, that's the worst of it that her marriage will have to endure. After the guests had been fed and watered, however, we loaded out all the minstrel gear *(speakers, amps, mics, cables and other sundry items)*. We continued to tap the keg ourselves *(no sense in it going to waste)* and were being handed several glasses of the finest Irish whiskey. Oh the tragedy of it all. Harry and I were encouraged to go to the next spot on everyone's itinerary, which was the campground where all the "Rennies" were to be partying after the wedding, to continue the fun.

Now, it DID sound fun. And Harry and I both wanted to go. But Harry also had another commitment thirty miles away to pick up another rental system that evening. Unbeknownst to me, it was rented and stowed in a bad part o' town, and he feared it being stolen and irretrievable, if and when he eventually DID return for it. So, thusly, he was antsy to get back, and secretly he did not want to go to the after-wedding party. But, being a man, he did not tell me all that. Instead, into the minstrel van mobile we went, following the well-watered, but still happy and drivable rennies twelve miles away to the campsite.

As Harry and I got in the car, we were finally able to be alone and compare notes on the day. We commiserated on this or that, such things as: the late arrival guests, the wedding crashers without invitation, the distractions of children trying to climb out the second story windows for fun, the frantic bridesmaids, the unfortunate swooning bride, the worried groom, the confused wait staff asking for direction, the drunken handsome men singing and fondling me as I played guitar, *(and while they also while sang off key right in my ear),* all the while we both played and sang without dropping a note or a chord. You know, Band Stuff. But we did thank the Gods it was over, we were compensated in full, and we were watered and fed. So all's well that ends well, aye?

That's when we started to expel some of the day's events and rehash it all. Suddenly, Harry took a left turn and left the caravan to travel along without us, without a word, he took up both our cell phones, turned them OFF, and said, "We're going HOME."

"Home?! I thought we were following everyone to the party?" Sullen silence as he gripped the steering wheel. So, what did I do in response to this? Something logical. I took his phone and I threw it back into the back seat to be swallowed alive in the mass of racks, cables and instruments, all of which he refers to as "gear."

It sort of went downhill from there as we dispelled the negative energy that we had been forced to soak up, but had yet to channel it off of us and ground it. We had evidently, absorbed it, and smiled through it, and unknown to all there we seemed to have risen above all day's wacky problems. But looks aren't always what they seem, are they? I nagged Harry about not going to the party and bitched about not knowing about having his other commitment. Harry growled at me. I crabbed back. Harry sulked and continued to just DRIVE without speaking. And then came the ritual combat dance: Slowing down the van, Harry had enough of the nagging and says, "Do you want to get out?"

I said, "Do you WANT me to get out?"

He says, "Do you want to get out?"

I say, "Do you WANT me to get out?"

He says, "Do you want to get out?"

I say, "Do you WANT me to get out?"

He says, "Do you want to get out?"

I say, "Do you WANT me to get out?"

Then Harry says: "I don't give a FUCKING SHIT WHAT you do." *(Bingo! We have a winner! A tie breaker!)*

I say, "FINE!! Let me out right here." He stops the van abruptly. I grab my purse and my cell phone and exit the van with a flourish and a hard slam of the van door. Harry drives off down the road for his a-waiting gear.

Finally, there is peace and quiet and birds are singing. I am on what road? …hmmm…where am I? Oh, there's a sign that says, "County Route 7."

But *(ahem)* where the fuck is County Route 7? I have absolutely no clue. I'm in Oswego County somewhere, which is NOT my county of residence. Beats the hell out of me. All I know is that the horrible red demon man driving the van is gone. Ah. Deep breath. Relax. I am well. I am walking! I figure if I just keep walking, someday, somehow, someway, I will be home, or at least in somewhat recognizable vistas. I once participated in a Jerry Lewis Walkathon and walked 25 miles in one day. I can do this. It's a nice day. "Any anyways, I'm fat." I could use the exercise. My phone rings. It is a rennie friend at the campsite, the one where we were supposed to show up.

"Where are you?" she says.

"I really have no idea," I say.

"What do you mean, you have no idea?"

"Um, Harry dropped me off somewhere on County Route 7 to walk home".

"WHAT?????!!!!! We're coming to get you!" she blurts.

"NO."

"Oh, yes, we are!" Off phone in the background I hear her yell to the party around the campfire, "Hey! Everybody! We have a BIG PROBLEM. Harry has deserted Merlyn on some bumfuck country road! We have to go find her!" To which I hear a sort of low groan and laughter from the campfire bunch there and overheard their words of, "Not again" and "Where the hell is County Route 7?"

I reiterate, "NO. Oh, HELL NO. I'll be fine. I'll find my way home. DO NOT COME AND GET ME. I will walk as far as I can or I will hitch, or I will sleep in the woods until morning but I WILL get myself home. I can do this. I am woman! Hear me roar! What are a few thousand mosquito bites to a frontier woman?"

"No, we are coming to get you."

"NO, DON'T!" and I hung up pretty sure they couldn't trace it. I walk a mile. It's a beautiful evening. I will just walk off this stress. I am positive Harry will be back or I will find my way home. Either way, FUCK HIM. I continue to muse, Jaysus. Why does the world always have to jump on everything? Can't I kill my husband in private?! *(I feel like that song says, "I've acted out my love in stages, with 10,000 people watching." Everything I do is seen by a million people it seems.)* I appreciate them being so sweet and they are dears to be concerned, but now I've ruined their drinking time as well. Good God. Christ Almighty, I could use a drink myself…why oh why didn't I pack a goddamn flask?! FUCK.

And then…Up the road…..Here he comes. Yup. Right on schedule.

Enter Round 2 of the Combat Ritual:

Harry is coming back to get me.

He pulls up and rolls down his window, "Do you want a ride?"

"Are you gonna apologize?" I ask.

"FUCK NO." he says adamantly.

"Then NO THANKS to the ride. I don't want to ride with someone who "doesn't give a "fucking shit" about me."

"FINE." he says.

"FINE." I say.

"This is your last chance." He dangles the tasteless carrot.

"No thanks, asshole, I'd rather WALK than ride with someone who doesn't care about me." He turns around and drives off fast towards home, about 25 miles from here. I wave goodbye to him with both middle fingers in the air with my high-flying birds overhead. He puts his left arm out the window in a similar salute goodbye.

Ah….love. "C'est La Vie." Oh, Pat Benatar, the fighting rock' n' roll minstrel would be so proud of me. Only SHE knows what I am going through. I walk some more. Love is indeed a battlefield. It really is a nice night, even if I don't know where the fuck I am. There are NO cars on this road, here in Jesus Radio Land. Not one vehicle has gone by in a long time.

After about 20 minutes pass, I get a text. Ooooh, look… It's from Harry. I'm all a quiver. (NOT)

It says: "I love you. Do you want a ride?" I don't answer. I come up over the hill, and there is his van parked in an old closed gas station. He's obviously waiting for me. I quietly walk by, see that he is laying down sleeping in the van. He's tired. Poor baby. It HAS been a hard day. Asshole. I walk PAST the van about a quarter of a mile and then I call him.

"You texted?" I say.

"Where are you?" he asks.

"AHEAD OF YOU." I say triumphantly.

Round 3 of the Combat Ritual Closure:

He drives up and says, "Just get in the van, sit down, and shut the fuck up."*(He's so romantic like that.)* We both try to remain quiet, after a bit of posturing, although, quietly, I am inwardly screaming psychic profanities at him, throwing hexes and damning him to the nether regions of Dante's ninth circle of hell. We go home. We are safe.

In the interim, a posse of half-drunken rennies has been sent to God knows where, to look for missing Merlyn, and with me, destroying all their drinking time, of which we should have been a part.

But life goes on. Dawn brings great lovemaking (i.e. make-up sex) in the morning with all the previous days' events purged and forgiven. Yes, flushed and dumped out and smeared all over some back road in Oswego, NY. Aye, it can be perilous being a minstrel, but it has its rewards.

Like, at least now I know where the fuck County Route 7 is.

The Wedding From Hell

Last but certainly not least, I give you this most amazing wedding. It started with us turning up at the faire office to find the groom-to-be dressed ONLY in a pair of Red Hot Chili Pepper silk boxer shorts *(he obviously felt like hanging loose)* and a pair of dirty army boots. He was a shorn, buff muscular man who also happened to be drunk at 8:30 am, *(most likely from the kick-ass bachelor party the night before)*. The King of the Day had no teeth in his head and was quite happily animated for his wedding day to come. His bride-to-be was nowhere to be found as she was "bringing his outfit." *(or I thought, mayhaps had R-U-N-N-O-F-T?)* His thoughtfully kind, but embarrassed best man said, "Hey dude, where are your teeth? Did you leave them in the car? Can I go get your plates for you?"

The groom replied, "No. I know right where they are.

I'm not wearing them on purpose. If she wants the REAL me, she'll take me as I AM, because I'm an ASSHOLE. See?" And he then turned around and showed us all the tattoo that he had chosen to etch across the top of his broad shoulders. It read: "MR. ASSHOLE." In INK.

OK then. This is when I wished that I, too, had already started drinking. This was definitely going to be a wedding to remember!

So, my next quest was to find the Justice of the Peace. I see a man dressed in the black robes of a judge. He's hard to miss as he has the distinctive green Maori tattoo across half of his face. I introduce myself to him, "Hey Ho, I'm Merlyn, and are you the clerk for the service?" *(Hoping for an actual name introduction I stick out my hand to shake).* He shakes it and only says, "Yes."

Alright, I'll try it another way: "Aye, and what shall I call thee this day? Your Honor? Esteemed Judge?"

"Erik" was his only deep voiced short reply. Erik is a man of few words. We waited a long time there with them. We chat and find out that the groom had "just gotten back from Iraq" and was proud that he was "a hired mercenary for a business there on his third tour over there." He also bragged that he "loved to kill" *(oh my).* I tried to make some polite chit-chat *(without making any sudden moves to spook the groom into any rash decisions)* while waiting and asked him "Is this your first wedding?" To which the groom-to-be said, "Nope, and it ain't going to be my last, neither!" And he and his best man laughed and laughed. *(OY. Now how's that for faith in true love on your Wedding Day, my dears?)*

We continued to wait for the bride. I figured she must have justly cold feet and wasn't coming. At least, I hoped like hell she wasn't coming for her sake. I mean, what was the woman like who was gonna marry this guy? I couldn't wait to meet her. All the guests were there, though, standing around waiting with the half-naked groom. It was getting way late to start, so Mr. Asshole, *(hey, I didn't name him…)* Erik and all the guests set off down to the chapel on the faire grounds, while Harry and I waited to escort the bride *(wherever she was)* and her father down to the chapel.

She finally did show up, and she was indeed a vision. She was a very well-endowed woman indeed. *(Read: HUGE tracts of land in a big white dress.)* She too, sported some highly visible tattoos, which the wedding dress was chosen to show it off to its best angle. The Queen for the Day had an ugly demon tattooed nicely and prominently displayed on her neck. The demon had its tongue sticking out, which sort of tickled her jugular vein.

Alrighty then *(hmmmm…maybe this WAS a match after all?)*

Harry and I started our minstrel duties and melodically walked the bride and her father sweetly to the chapel. It was time to start the ensuing nuptials. We played the loveliest version of "Greensleeves" while they proceeded to walk up the aisle. When they were almost up to "Erik," and our song was nearly finished, *(but not quite),* the father of the bride stopped, turned around and faced us at the back of the chapel and hollered us while we were still singing the final chorus "Greensleeves was all my love, greensleeves was my delight…" and right then he bellowed: "FREEEEE BIRRRRD" and gave us a thumbs-up.

(SO. She's marrying a guy like her dear old dad. I get it now).

Well, hopefully it would be a happy union, but I wasn't sure if everyone was in agreement about this match. For when the part came in the service and Erik said, "Is there anyone here that forbids this marriage for any reason? Speak now or forever hold your peace," there was a flurry of coughing from the bride's side of the chapel. There was a lot of loud hacking and spewing that sounded like *"(cough cough)* Asshole!" and *"(cough)-*No fucking way! *(cough cough")*, and "*(cough)* Mistake!" In sooth- I swear to you it is the truth. The groom only beamed in hearing the knowing cacophony of his bawdy friends and family. Erik plodded on ahead regardless.

The couple got hitched. I wondered if they would pump out a bouncing-baby-larvae someday soon. Ah love!

At this wedding, how'ere, they did water us well with alcohol, *(God Bless these thoughtful Devils!)* and both the bride and the toothless groom were happy as clams with our part for their service. And for their part, they both seemed to be quite smitten with each other. I was really glad of that. I'm always happy to see love and lust united.

But wait! There's more: Later on that day, Harry was summoned to the joust field because this same Groom from the sidelines during the joust, had called out one of the jousters for a duel! He wasn't kidding. This was his day to shine! He was going to take on a Knight! "Mr. Asshole" reared his full potential to the crowd's delight and to the jousters' dismay. The joust was upstaged by this kilted wild man with fists and it was all in good fun for him. Harry knew all the jousters and they knew that we'd just dealt with this couple in the morning. Harry turned the whole thing around with some humor and the groom had his fun with the knight *(who now was amused and not as paranoid about this self-destructing half naked kilted maniac on his wedding day.)*

The bride too, had some fun on the shire herself. She had decided to give everyone at the Washer Wenches show a treat with a show of her own. The bride had upstaged that show and dropped her wedding dress halter top and flashed those big, booming, swinging tracts of land at everyone at the wash pit. The men in the audience were delighted! Wives slapped their husbands for drooling gape-jawed and wee nursing babies got hungry at the sight of those luscious big baby bottles. The Washer Wenches were thrown for a loop, but were improvisational savvy performers and instead included this moment with some bawdy banter in their show! As I said, it was a day to remember!

A couple of years after this connubial day, Harry and I ran into this same couple again at a different faire. They were still married! And yes, they had indeed pumped out a litter. Self-proclaimed "Mr. Asshole" was contentedly pushing a baby stroller and Mrs. Asshole was pleased indeed. They seem really happy. Somehow…someway, they had managed to settle down and had become a nice, normal family of civilized law-abiding tattooed devil spawn.

This is what I learned from this fun and outrageous wedding. Love, like personalities, comes in all forms. So, don't dismay if you are single and haven't found your perfect mate yet. This wild, loving, odd couple proved to me that there is someone out there for everyone. So, there's hope for you too.

Bewitched by the Tombstone Moon

Jesse and I left a restaurant at 10 p.m. after joining friends for late dinner after a long day working at a Renaissance faire. I put some motor oil into my car, as it was smelling hot when I arrived earlier, and now I drained what little oil there was left in the can into the crankcase. It needed more oil, but I figured it could get us home with that wee bit of lubricant. It was my little clown car, the Ford Aspire, and it was also really low on gas. But then again, the thing ran on fumes. Heading out of town, I remembered that I had take Rt.104A, so I veered back onto Route 104A to follow my way home, assuming I could get back to where I started out from. Seems logical, right?

Jesse and I were happily chatting and recanting tales of the day's festivities, when all of a sudden, Jesse exclaimed, "Oh, Mom, look at the moon!"

It was the weirdest, strangest, and creepiest moon we had ever seen in our lives. *(Once, I saw a blood-red moon at 3 o'clock in the morning that nearly gave me the willies.)* This moon was worse. This one was florescent piss yellow *(like you'd been swallowing Vitamin B kind of yellow)* and it was OVAL with a straight-edge bottom. I said, "Eegads! It's shaped exactly like a tombstone!" Jesse swallowed hard and said, "That looks wrong, just plain wrong" *(Now I figured that there was some bending of light around some clouds and shadows, but for whatever the scientific reason, this moon truly was OVAL.)* About at that very same moment, we realized, with horror, that we were lost.

"This isn't right," I said. "I don't want to be in <u>North</u> Sterling! I think we missed our turn." We were lost.

Lost in North Bumfuck.

At night.

On a dark black road that stretched out seemingly forever and ever. Out on a country road with no one up at this ungodly hour of 10 p.m. With very, very little gas. With no street lights, no intersections of note, no gas stations. And a bizarre moon lighting our way to boot. "It's OK, we'll be alright," I said to Jesse, not wanting her to hear the trembling in my voice. "I'll just go back to where 104 and 104A join and start over."

And so we did. I glanced at the gas gauge every so often, and prayed that my little clown car would just keep on snorting the little bit of gas in it and keep going down the road. We started back on the path home once again. We noted land-marks along the way and commented on the oddity of the moon. After turning left here and right there, we wound up... right back where we had been about 15 minutes before! In North Sterling. *(A feeling of unsettling panic sort of eerily welled up and gripped us both.)*

"Oh shit, this can't be right." Turning around again with even less gas, we try it one more time. Back to the beginning and change the outcome, I mix things up by turning right here *(where I previously had turned left)*, and I turned left there *(where I previously turned right.)* A short time later, we wound up...right back in North Sterling!

Jesse's intuition was screaming, "You should not be here! Something is going to get you! LEAVE NOW!"

Me? I could imagine a hand on the outside of my door handle, just like in that creepy scene from <u>The Twilight Zone</u>.

"Mommy, I'm scared," said my 20-year-old *(who, by the way, isn't daunted by intense Stephen King novels or bloody-slasher movies.)* Panic rose in me and nestled at the back of my throat and my hair tingled. I realized I hadn't been breathing deeply or much at all.

"Me too, honey." I told her. "I just want to get us home! I don't want to run out of gas way out here in Bermuda Triangle-land" at night! Where the fuck are we?!" I shouted at the sky and shook my fist at that crazy, weird, yellow tombstone moon! It seemed to be mocking me.

"OK. Look, this is what we'll do," says a determined Jesse

as she directs me off the beaten path *(an even worse idea, in my opinion)* and we follow signs for the elusive Renaissance faire out here in the middle of Jesus, not too far from nowhere-land. After miles and miles of dark twisting roads, strange landmarks, dangerously dipping gas gauges, creepy thoughts of us abandoning our out of gas car in the strange moonlight to wander back roads for fuel, while no one knows our whereabouts, and the subsequent thoughts of faceless serial killers on blind alleys, me trying bravely to hide my welling tears and churning stomach All the while with my Jesse girl, sitting there quietly- trying to be brave....and that damnedable creepy tombstone moon.

UNTIL…A FOX crosses our path. It was just then that we went past an intersection that we recognized.

"Oh thank God!" Jesse wanted to go one way, but I knew better. "I know where we are! I know where we are!" I nearly jumped for joy! Now the bad news, my car was now on less than reserve, we were still in North Bumfuck and the likelihood of a gas station being open at 10:45 p.m. was slim out here in Hooterville, where they roll up the streets at 9 p.m. sharp.

"I know where there is a gas station. PRAY it's open! But it's kind of far…" I sigh, gripping the wheel with white knuckles. I imbue my gas tank to will itself to live off fumes for a bit longer. We do not have cell phones at this time. We have no way to contact anyone and there are no houses for miles. Finally, we pull in to the gas station parking lot. Only partial lights flicker within.

"Go and check if they are still open for business, Jesse." I felt sick. I was shaking and nauseous. She went in and indeed, they were just closing, and the clerk was cashing out the register but thankfully we could be their last customer of the night! Jesse came out. After scraping together my last $7 for gas, she'd chatted with the attendant and thanked him profusely for still being open, and told him we'd gotten lost <u>repeatedly</u> on 104A in North Sterling.

"Yeah, that happens a lot, it's weird on that road" he said. *(You're telling me brother. You're preachin' to the choir here.)*

So now we had gas, and even though I still felt like throwing up and was still shaking with residual fear, we were on our way home! Huzzah! Waves of relief washed over both of us. We would live to tell the tale and not have to wind up on the headlines of the daily newspaper! "Two local women found dismembered in North Sterling."

We looked back up and gazed at the moon once more. It was now a perfect, beautiful, round white moon. With no hint of its former self. "Yeah, like, ah, that's weird. Why is the moon not the Yellow Tombstone Moon anymore? It looks like a regular moon," we both muse in the dark. I guess the Boogeyman must've given up on catching us. We quickly re-named Route 104A to the beastly name of Route 666 A.

Relieved and even more tired from the stress, we pulled into our home driveway. I then told Jesse what I'd realized earlier *(but withheld from her)* for the entire ride home. I didn't want to jinx us anymore than we already were. I had accident-ly driven without my license that night. My license was in the garb in the van that Wayne had driven home. "Oops," I said with a sheepish grin.

Jesse then said (with a smidge of horror in her voice), "So, you had **no I.D.** on you? Mom, my faire I.D. was also in Wayne's van. Good God. Yeah, like, you know why? That's so no one could easily identify our bodies after all. The moon KNEW, eh, Mom?"

Reluctantly, I realized she had a point and I shook my head yes.

When Wayne got home, we told him our story. Jesse said, "It was the weirdest thing, like *something*, cosmically kept getting us lost in the same circle, round and round, over and over, even though we went a different way EVERY time. Something or someone wanted us to get lost in North Sterling, and have us run out of gas and wander in the dark, then kill us or some-thing."

Wayne said, "Wait a minute. Did you say, North Sterling?! Hey, wasn't there a girl murdered back out that way a long time ago…on…Route 104A? Yah, that's right, now that I think of it."

In a moment of epiphany, Jesse said, "Of course there was! It was probably right where we were, and the same point that we kept coming back to. I bet today was even the anniversary of her death!" We looked at each other and felt happy to be alive and considered kissing the ground.

So I looked up fox in my Animal Totem Cards- the blessed animal who crossed our path that night-and then helped us find our path home.

FOX - The family protector. Keeps families together and safe. An excellent talisman for those traveling far afield. Associated with camouflage. Uses silly tactics to maneuver to safety.

Thank you, Fox!

An Apple A Day Will Keep The Doctor Away

Harry and I got invited to perform at a banquet for a follow-up meeting at a big apple festival. We had been booked that weekend of the festival and the committee really wanted to get us in to entertain them. The evening's festivities were a bit of a drive away, and they wanted us to come in Erie Canal. They would give us our fee and dinner. *(Bonus! Minstrels have through the ages sung for their supper)*.

We got to the fancy golf-club facility and many committee members were there, having drinks and appetizers. It was nice, chatty and friendly. One elderly man was quite animated. He was going from table to table and was the man of the evening. He was 85 years old, the guest of honor and one of the founding committee persons who put on this annual fall apple festival. They'd been hosting the event for about 40 years. We were to perform after all the members had given their quick committee reports at the podium. Dinner would then ensue while we were performing. It was a good plan for a fun evening.

We waited on the fringes of the group, while each and

every leader handled their portion of the event. The evening ticked away. Only one more speaker was scheduled before we were to go out and sing. It was the old man who was the gadfly that we had met earlier. He went up to the podium and everyone applauded. It was his night! He was dressed sharply in a suit, and he had a gleam in his eye. He was a pistol, to be sure!

The elderly gent proceeded to make everyone laugh while he regaled the group with stories of the apple festival, its early days and how important they all were, and how much fun he'd had over the many years of service. They were all on a voyage together, sailing the seas! Then, in one grand gesture, he raised his hand in a final swoop and DOWN HE WENT. Out like a light. Dropped to the floor. ????????

Oh my God. Was he…..DEAD?

Several people rushed to him. Was there a doctor in the house? Yes, there was. Harry, in his infinite roadie wisdom, ran to the bar and had the bartender call 911 immediately to bring an ambulance. Harry came back to me, waiting in the wings, both of us flustered, while a circle of people enveloped the old man down for the count.

"What do we do now?" I asked my mate.

"We wait and see what happens, see what THEY want us to do." He said matter of factly. "If they want us to go on, and chill out the audience, so be it. We can do this. We can make the evening better for all here if that's what they want. It will soothe them. We can start off with the song "Johnny Jump Up" as planned."

"Ah…No, we can't." I said.

"Why not? It's a song about cider and cider is from APPLES." He was trying his best. I wisely ran through the lyrics for him.

"Harry, darling. NO fecking way. The chorus to that song, IF you remember, is: "He fell to the ground and he did not get up.' It's hardly an entertaining song under the circumstances."

"Oh, shit. You're right." We sort of chuckled in embarrassment and from under the stress. OK, so we were getting a bit punchy. It was stressful to say the least. The pressure. The tragedy that had just befallen and then ALL eyes were gonna be on us to save the nice evening…and we were in a predicament! Hot water to follow such an act! But then again, maybe they would tell us not to play. There was that option too. But then, the awful demon reared its head and a voice whispered in my ear the ugly truth, "Yes, but if that happens…will you get PAID?"

(Ooh, Merlyn, how DARE you think such a callous thing at a time like this?) But there it was. We had to laugh at that too, because it was so plainly truthful! The fact of the situation demanded decorum, respect and compassion and yet here we were, wondering about money and the time we'd spent getting there, and the not knowing made us giggle to relieve the stress. Sorry about the old man though…really we were…but, oh hell! What was to happen?? How the fuck were we gonna save the day?

The ambulance came in. The old man went out. He was alive. THANK GOD. Like a Pirate Captain he fell during a melee. They had carted him out to sick bay. The fray went on without him. Unbeknownst to us, we found out later that this was to be his last participation in this festival, and he was excited to be named "Man of the Year." We also did not know that he was so excited that he could not eat much all day and when he got to the dinner party, he downed several cocktails in anticipation of his public speaking. So…he had a drop in blood sugar and he was toasted. But no one knew. He was a true professional and he was an old man, exhausted and drained and gave his all. The cocktails and the stress were too much for his good old heart. And then? We get the word from the host.

"You're ON." (gulp!)

"We now present….Merry Mischief!!" *(Feeble applause ensues from wrung-out over-stressed audience members. Crickets. I hear crickets.)* So we stepped up to the plate.

We soothed, we coddled, and we ultimately made a warm fuzzy and helped the evening recover. We did NOT play "Johnny Jump Up." Sometimes you really have to throw out the set list. I figure it's more like the Pirate's Code anyways, more like "guidelines." Sometimes you just have to adjust the sails, go in a totally different direction at the last minute, and hope the Captain lives to tell the tale.

Vikings Attack

We pulled into yet another renaissance faire campground for a gig, and parked our RV, affectionately named, "The Cottage." We tried to find our stages in the dark and mark the times we were scheduled to play the next morning. We found out when the morning meeting for performers was held and we went home to the cottage to rest, settle in and prep for the magical weekend ahead.

At the end of our following faire day we went back to the Cottage, popped off the bodice and boots and found that Vikings had invaded. Complete with horned hats, they were partying on into the night right next to our camper. We attempted to settle in for the night, and at the point that I was just dozing off...Harry, snuggled in next to me, quietly said, "Do ye think they could say 'fuck' any more times in a sentence?" After listening, I agreed. I was impressed to hear that the word "fuck" was being used as an adverb, verb, adjective, noun and pronoun, and these Vikings made it an art form. I felt bad for our other minstrel friends in the pop-up tent next to us, Jay and Abby, who had their 10-year-old, Kimmie, asleep *(hopefully)* right there within Viking stabbing distance. Surely, Kimmie was getting an educational earful. The Viking party went on into the wee hours, as Vikings are wont to do. *(Really, just replace the longboats, barrels of mead and chests of treasure with Chevy's, coolers, flasks and pizza boxes. and you have an accurate picture here.)*

Unbeknownst to us, the true Viking party outside was yet to commence there in the campground the next night. It started out lovely and melodious with a guitarist singing to his party of revelers with some popular contemporary tunes, southern rock mingled in with some Viking ditties. Like the old favorite, "Burn that Saxon village down, boys, burn that Saxon village down."

And all was well until the "Norseman from Hell" arrived complete with his wood war paint on, shouting obscenities of which my pirate ancestors would be proud. We heard him coming from across the campground. His gregarious greeting to his Viking compatriots of choice was:

"FUCK YOU, all you fucking fuckers!" at the top of his lusty lungs. To which the group grunted back a similar response. Obviously, this was a sentimental gathering of like-minded individuals.

Harry and I were both sure at that moment that Armageddon would occur just outside our door. Were they mad? Were they happy? Were they just shitting around? We couldn't tell. (Inside their camper next door, Jay and Abby also wondered the same thing. Was there going to be a row? Would someone pull a dagger? Slash their pop up tent and kill us all?) Mercifully, the Gods made it rain. Nay, it started to pour.

"Ha!" we mused. "That's sure to wind up and finish the party!"

But we forgot that Vikings in rain are like ducks in water. Fowl ducks that sleep *(eventually)* on a soaked truck bed with a blue plastic tarp as a drunkard's blanket. But wait! There's more! The Valkyrie had yet to arrive. She came in the wee hours of the morning, her Viking garb jingling and chainmail clanking, all summoning her arrival. Then, she too, raised her voice in salutation addressing her Viking mates: "Hey, you cocksuckers, where's the beer? You all fucking owe me 10 bucks, so goddamn fork it over! Give me some beer! I've been drinking fucking Jameson's at the bar all night for $4 a shot. What? No beer left? Goddamn you, you fucking fuckers! Come on, let's go get some more! I'll drive!"

I lost consciousness and finally fell asleep after that. And, I think, so did they. Or they left in their longboats to go pillage more ale.

But in the morning next to the cottage the dripping tarped Viking truck bed remained moored there, complete with bare feet hanging out over the edge of the tailgate. We had to marvel at their courage and stamina in the cold morning air. Our friend Jay, Harry and I stood within inches of the cold bare blue feet, and as we chatted in regular voices, I mentioned that I was tempted to hang a toe tag off one of the big toes sticking out off the truck myself, and label it "Sven Doe." But we, the minstrel neighbors, *(being professional drinkers and old festival/party survivors ourselves)* were all content with knowing that they would all indeed suffer from ale- head. This was guaranteed to come, after they vomited and blessed the ground or the blessed privy on this fine morning. And we smiled knowingly and did what we thought would make them as comfortable as they made us the night before, by making as much loud noise as possible as we went off to our early work day.

Later on, at faire, I saw a patron wearing a black T-shirt with white lettering that said: "Fuck you, you, fucking fucker." I looked at him, grinned, pointed to his shirt and just asked one word: "Viking?"

"Fuck, yah!" was his perfect reply.

Sleep Disorders & Other Sundry Items

I don't know if you've been on a long trip with a loved one before, but after about three weeks or so on the road they really start to get on your nerves. I know I am on Harry's nerves, the way he barks at me. Maybe it's the crowded living space, the tight schedule or the lack of sleep. And he's definitely getting on my nerves as well.

For instance, when Harry gets very exhausted, he has this habit of sleeping on his back, with his arm overhead in an inverted V over his face, covering his eyes. After awhile, as his sleep gets deeper and deeper, his arm gets tired, and so it starts to droop and bit by bit it slimpses over, closer to me, closer, closer, until it bonks me, sleeping Merlyn, smack in the head. Whereupon I sort of drowsily wake up and move his arm down to rest quietly upon his belly. Repeat. About twenty times a night. Needless to say, my sleep gets disrupted, but he continues to sleep! After awhile, I admit, I have less and less patience for this kind of behavior. In my sleep deprived state, over and over again just as I start falling back into REM sleep, I get a little punchy. I actually start thinking that it is a subconscious passive-aggressive move on his part. Like, he's doing it on fucking PURPOSE to deprive me of MY sleep. Granted, normally I wouldn't think this way, but after many times of getting woken up by someone bonking you on the head, you get a bit paranoid.

I have sleepily considered and daydreamed of ripping his arm off and beating him with it and throwing the bloody stump out the window while he sleeps. But surely I digress. Anyone who has been married for more than ten years would understand my dilemma.

On one hand, I love him and would do anything for him. On the other hand, I, too, am exhausted, and deserve some sleep and rest. I didn't even mention the restless-legs thing that happens. Now this only happens when Harry gets very exhausted, on some of these roadie gigs where he works 24-hours round the clock, and you can get TOO tired where you can't sleep or when sleep is just plain weird and I truly understand that sleep disorders are born of such need.

Take the restless-leg thing. He will lie on his back, happily snoring away, and props his leg up to rest flat-footed on the bed, so his leg is now in big "V." After awhile, his leg must get tired and so, again, it starts to slimpse down, inch by inch by inch by inch, until I think he will just straighten his leg out and lay it down. But NO. When it gets to this point of almost relaxing it to a straight leg, he bends his knee back up into a bent position and the whole process starts over again. Repeat. Ten or twenty more times in a night. So, after awhile, I just take my foot and nudge his foot and straighten his leg out to lay flat. Done deal. It's either that, or I have also sleepily considered ripping his leg off and beating him with it and throwing the bloody stump out the window. Sleep-deprived people can get a bit strange and I would say that possible violence at the slightest provocation at 4 a.m. is a real likelihood.

My first husband, Dave, God love him, had a sleep disorder and because of it, I don't think I slept soundly for the whole 17 years we were together. He would have nightmares and sleepwalk and talk. Once he dreamed a nightmare where I was stuck in a piece of machinery, and he would try in his dream to save me by extracting me from the jaws of steel. But in actuality, he was in a sleep trance, holding my sleeping body physically tight around the waist and trying to stand up and pull me. I woke up in the death grip of a sleeping giant squeezing the air out of me as I became groggily aware of my imminent death. While it was certainly honorable that he was dreamily saving me from certain peril, it was also the sound of him screaming and running through the house at 3 a.m. and hollering obscenities while monsters chased him that was even more unnerving. You can get a bit punchy after awhile of this.

Like, I had to laugh when I read that Willie Nelson's first wife tired of his drinking, his latent drunken stupors, and his constant affairs and actually did something amazing to him as he slept. She folded the sheet around him as he lay passed out on their bed. She sewed him up in that sheet one night, with little tiny fine stitches, totally engulfing him in closed pocket of a death shroud…all the while he was drunk, sleeping. When her sewing project was finished, she then calmly went into the kitchen, took a broom out of the closet, walked back in to the bedroom and proceeded to beat the living crap out of him, clubbing him with the stiff belt of the broom handle about the head and shoulders. Now that's what I call a well deserved and symbolic wake-up call. While I'd never do such a thing to any man, much less to someone I adore, you have to admit that to someone sleep-deprived…

the idea has merit.

A Riddle & The Amazing Answer

Question: "What wheel on 'The Cottage' (our RV) can you absolutely NOT drive without?"

Answer? "The STEERING WHEEL." That's right!

Harry and I are on our last leg of "The Cottage's Maiden Voyage Tour" and all has been well. We have bonded with the RV and we love it right well and have told it so.

We've also been reading a tremendous book on the trip, called, *You Can Heal Your Life* by Louise Hay *(positive affirmations to draw good into your life)*. I read the book out loud to Harry whilst we have been driving this whole trip. It blew us away with its amazing truths and positive influence on us. We've been doing a lot of the affirmations and adding in the changes to our belief system ever since we started the book. Some of the most important affirmations in this book are: "I approve of myself" *(said many times a day, it sinks into your consciousness)*. "Everything I need is provided to me" and "Success comes to me easily."

So, this morning, we woke up at the West Virginia rest stop at 4:30 a.m. and got driving by 5:30 a.m. Drove thru West Virginia, Maryland and then stopped for coffee in Pennsylvania at a McDonald's at 6:30 a.m. Harry pulled into the parking lot into a parking place and THE STEERING WHEEL CAME OFF IN HIS HANDS! We stared at each with a WTF? look on our faces. We busted out laughing hysterically! OK, so we were a bit punchy before coffee at that hour. But it was obviously a gift of the Universe! Why do I say that?

1) It could've fallen off at any time before this on our 3,000-mile trip...or when going down the highway at 70 mph! But it didn't! It fell off IN A SAFE PARKING LOT while we were backing up slowly and facing out.

2) It fell off in a parking lot...NEXT DOOR TO AN AUTO ZONE! *(How handy!)*

3) As we were sitting there amazed by the circumstances:

a) We didn't die!

b) Things could've been way worse!

c) The Universe is really providing everything we need, just as the book said and we could actually attract what we need!

Just then, to ram it home...and to prove the instant attraction thing even more-so, the Universe added a bit of humor to the already stressful situation by letting this next thing happen:

4) A tow truck pulled up right next to us and parked. We busted out laughing again! How perfect is THAT? It just floored us by the synchronicity of the Universe and also the humor it provided.

5) We got coffee, breakfast burritos and waited an hour for the Auto Zone to open, by reading the paper, listening to classical music and finding the tools in the camper that Harry would need. He also looked over the project and made some plans.

6) Harry went inside to Auto Zone promptly when their doors opened at 8 a.m. and THEY HAD the exact parts and horn for this 29-year-old vehicle!

7) Amazingly enough *(and totally unusual)* Auto Zone fronted Harry the parts and tools *(to make sure they were right before paying for them)*, and Harry came out and put it together! Just like clockwork! It is now 8:30 a.m. and we now have a steering wheel that works and a working horn again! *(A bonus here too, is that the horn hadn't worked the whole trip down!)*

But the best part is this: We didn't die! *(I know I said that before, but it's worth repeating).* And plus we didn't have to drive home from Pennsylvania steering with ½ inch wrench on the nut *(great for right turns, but a bitch for left turns).*

8) Bonus boon! Before the steering wheel fell off we had just parked in a McDonald's parking lot. This had its perks! For one, it has COFFEE…and a bathroom inside! *(Always a plus after morning coffee, breakfast burritos and stress of your vehicle falling apart in your hands before 7 a.m.).*

So I say, "The Gods are good, Mimsaab!" What a wealth of treasure available to those who believe it will come. Because it can happen. This whole trip has been proof of it! Symbolically, the steering wheel riddle this morning proves to me that we can readjust how we "steer our life." We feel that we are back on the right course now and "Steering in the right direction." HOME.

A Minstrel's Dues

I love to sing and play music, oh, yes I do! Harry and I have sung for parties, festivals, big stages, faire lanes, weddings, pubs, schools, libraries and restaurants. It's all good. But there is a time when the talent comes hard-pressed. It is when we are asked to sing for a funeral of a friend. I have found this to be THE hardest job that a minstrel could ever do. It is an honor as a minstrel and a duty as a friend. While I was not able to sing nor eulogize either of my parents at their funerals *(I couldn't. I just couldn't. Chatty, outgoing Merlyn could only cry those days…)*, I have had to sing at five of my dear friends funeral services.

The way that I was baptized into this charge was the hardest of them all. My work friend, Lisa, had set up and booked Merry Mischief to sing at her wedding in May in the spring of 2002. We happily agreed and she wanted a bunch of Irish music, and so it was booked.

But when the tragedy of 9/11/01 happened, Lisa, being in the Red Cross, flew to NYC to help. Whether she was exposed to radon gases, pollutants or she was already cooking a cancer, I don't know. But in February of 2002, Lisa became quite ill and doctors had determined that her liver and kidneys were full of cancer. She died quite suddenly the second week of March. It happened so fast.

Her body went to be autopsied because of some of the odd and sudden events that surrounded her death. Her fiancée' called us and asked us to sing at her funeral on Saint Patrick's Day in March…instead of at their upcoming wedding in May. It was tragic indeed. And of all songs in the world to pick, he asked us to do "Danny Boy."

I've already told you that I am a psychic *(we all are, if we choose to listen)*. As Harry and I drove to the funeral home that morning and were preparing ourselves to sing that heart ripper of a song to a room full of mourners, something amazing happened. He and I were riding in our car and Harry turned the corner. There. There sitting at the light as we turned, was Lisa! She was driving a red sports car. Harry and I both saw her.

"WHAT?"

"Did you see that?" Harry asked me after he turned the corner. "YES. It was Lisa!" I said in disbelief. "But she's dead. We're on the way to her funeral!" Harry said back to me.

"I know. I think we just had a vision. That wasn't really Lisa. It couldn't be! It was just the angels telling us that she's moving on. And in a sports car no less! You GO, Girl! She's off for new adventures and she really isn't here with us today. She won't be at the funeral, honey. She's got other places to go." I said and those words just rolled off my tongue and I'm not sure where they came from but the reasoning and symbolism made us both relax.

At the appointed time, Harry and I got up to sing "Danny Boy" and stood with our backs to the closed coffin. We looked out at a sea of grieving faces. I started the acapella notes to the song. When my emotions got to me, and my voice started to crack I decided to look at the wallpaper border on the wall by the ceiling, instead of the grief-stricken faces. Somehow, we did it and got through it and it was the absolute hardest minstrel job I've ever done.

Later, after most of the friends had left the service, Lisa's father and fiancée came up to us and thanked us for what we did. They also told us something amazing. "The autopsy wasn't done in time. Lisa's body wasn't here for the service. That's why the casket was closed. We didn't tell anyone before the service as we wanted her to be present in their hearts for her funeral."

So Lisa really WASN'T there. But we already knew it. The Angels and Lisa had told us before we arrived at the funeral home! She had sent a message of Love and Hope and Happiness and of Service to Others.

Since this first funeral, I learned a great truth: I never, ever sing at the front of a church for a funeral. We sing from the back or from the choir loft but never in front of the audience. It's just too fecking hard. At times like this, "It ain't about you" is my motto. It is to add ambiance and comfort and hope for the bereaved. I also know now too that usually the deceased isn't there either but has been called on to other places. But they surely are happy and appreciate you singing for their family. And if you really listen to the signs, they will send you messages that say so.

Merlyn & Harry Do Their Taxes

Aye, life begins when the goddamn taxes are mailed. Let me tell you a story. I've ranted about doing my taxes before. Personally, I would rather have someone else do them, as I used to *(I think I'd personally rather take a bullet than be a tax preparer)* but somebody special came into my life. YES. A genius, eccentric, masochistic man who actually LIKES to do his taxes. Harry. He loves to do taxes. *(Isn't that like the sickest thing you've ever heard?)* And he MAKES me do mine. As of March 29, 2008 we entered the promised land of *"Time to do the Taxes."* A misty, magical land filled with mountains to climb, mucky mires to trudge, and sink holes to avoid, with the reward of an **Intensely Glowing Golden Welcoming Mailbox** at the end of the treacherous hero's journey.

An altar was set *(a card table for the purpose in the front room).*

Special illumination was arranged *(a desk lamp because I am fucking blind)*

All the financial papers, receipts, calculators, rulers for grid paper, pencils, pens, multi-colored highlighters, and other such dedicated "Holy Things" were placed lovingly in reach for the special high Holy Days that lead us to the "Culmination."

Aye, this day of all days. The Most High Holy Day of all. **APRIL 15ᵗʰ.**

I prepared and readied myself by laying out the Communion items. I opened a beer and set out the leftover dish of Easter candy. I proceeded to involve myself and work myself up with the Universal Prayer Chant to begin this magical event: "Fuckin' taxes. Jesus! I hate this, what do you mean 'if line 3 is more than line 17 multiply the smaller number by your birthday' WTF? Oh, great, I fucked it up. Shit. Harry?! Goddamnit! I need another clean copy. Fuckin A. SIGH. There. It's done.

HALLEHUJAH!!! WHAT? I forgot to include, 'Cost of goods' ? Jaysus F'in' Christ, I need a shot o' whiskey. FUCK ME. Oh, you bastard IRS. You and your mother, and a big pointy sharp stick. Tallying. Oh hey! That's kewl, it's less to pay than before! YAY! I'm done! Wooo Hoooo!! I'm gonna INK it in. Look good to you, Harry? OK? An error?! Somebody get me a goddamn knife cuz I'm gonna kill myself and we'll dab up the blood with the Schedule C and send it in as payment. Time for another fucking beer. *(Merlyn opens dark ale).* Oooh, look, see? Right here, here's the spot on the form where it says, 'Insert kidney. Sign here with drip of blood.' You fucking cocksuckers."

Well, you get the idea. I feel more like the sacrificial lamb to slaughter. But not Harry. No, Harry is the High Priest of the event, and he revels in this time of year and he is in his GLORY. He puts on his Special Vestments. His blue fuzzy robe and slippers and starts the coffee IV.

Harry's chant is a bit different. He goes like this:

"Honey? Have you seen the box of tax stuff I had right here? OOOOH, here it is! *(Harry does a happy shuffle and picks up a box full of receipts, worksheets and column paper).* Ahhhhhh, *(angelic chorus breaks out and a golden beam from heaven shines down upon the box),* and here, here are the instruction booklets! *(read: Bible).* Hmm. Oh, isn't that interesting? They've changed line 27. Hmm. I wonder why? Let me read the bible, I mean, the instruction booklet. Wow, that's amazing. I'm so excited! Oh honey? Can you go online and research something for me? Oops. I messed that bit up. Oh goodie. I get to do it again! I feel horny. Let's fuck five times in celebration that I get to do the 1040 all over again! Uh oh. Honey? You made a mistake right here on this line. You better do it all over again. God, Merlyn, but you look so hot when you erase. But wait, do that after we fuck again first ok? There. That's great! Mmmm, yup, just like that. Put the amount right there on line 20a. Yah, mmmm, that feels nice. We are doing great! Isn't life fantastic? We are doing so much better than last year! Hmm. I can't find a whole month of receipts. Dammit. Hmm. How about a quickie? Ohhh look! See? You are lucky for me! I just found my receipts! That's great!

Let's fuck again. OK. I think we are done! And look, right here! Here is the spot that says, 'Sign with drip of blood.' Wow. They love me! Let's give 'em a quart instead of just a drop just to say 'Thank you for everything, Love Harry,"

PUBLIC SERVICE ANNOUNCEMENT: "The Intensely Glowing Golden Welcoming Mailbox Lunar Eclipse is: (drum roll, rrrrrrrrrrr).

THIS NIGHT. MIDNIGHT. Harry will see you there. He will wait precisely for the Bewitching Hour to insert our Offering of Holy Papers and Coinage to the God of Calculation. Amen. Blessed Be. Shalom. Signed, Name of Tax preparer/Date."

And TOMORROW the world dawns fresh and clean! And life begins ANEW.

Virgin Roadie With A Hint Of Lipstick

When I call my mate by his name, Harry, he is a minstrel. But when I call him by his given name, Wayne, he is a roadie and an IATSE (International Association of Theatrical Stage Employees) Union member. Today, after all these years of being the mate of a union stagehand, he FINALLY called me in as a permit worker on a big stage call!

I may not be big-boned or burly, but I'm a farm girl for Christ's sake. I have scythed hay, dug ditches and mucked out barns full o' pig shit and horse manure, and to be perfectly honest, I've taken down bigger fellahs than me in a fight, so why not?

Not that I ever really WANTED to do this kind of work, mind you. I haven't. I'm not mechanical. To tell you the truth, I've avoided it like the plague. That is probably why Wayne has not pulled me in before, as I'd rather have teeth pulled. I told Wayne when we first started dating, "I'm not gonna be your MULE. I'm not gonna cast my withers carrying fucking gear."

Yet I've loaded, unloaded, and reloaded our Merry Mischief gig stuff over a 1001 times. I've set up mic stands, light stands, carried heavy snakes *(cables wrapped 'the RIGHT way'),* lights, all sorts o' things., But when it comes to being an 'all-out-bust-ass-lift-this-anvil-and-tote-this-ton-o'-bricks-horse,' you can find someone burlier or another person to help me! The money's not THAT good to do that kind of damage."

I've heard the tales. The real late nights, Wayne crawling home broken and punchy from being up round the clock for 24-hour gigs, the bruises, the pinched fingers, the horrid, randy, mean-ass crude crew, the tales of accidents, broken fingers or lost hands, nuts, and well, the odd…ah… death. The tales also run the gamut of the "hurry-up-and-wait" scenario where you are paid to sit on yer arse, sleep in the carpet room in the cat-acombs under the theater then dash to the "Balls to the Walls we'll make a record tonight on the out, by Jaysus" calls.

So, after being on the opposite side of the mic for the past 10 years, I'm going to join the ranks of roadies out there and do an "Out" tonight. A "Major-Rock'-n-'Roll-many-tractor-trailer-loaded for- bear-smoke-em-if-you-got-em-'Out' at the New York State Fair. Load out starts at 10 p.m. It's an 11 tractor trailer pack up event. I've already heard today from him that this particular job is what roadies affectionately call a clusterfuck. See? I know the lingo. So, oh boy howdy, I'm just soooo lookin' forward to being a part of the "spitting, swear-ing, mean-ass, overworked, overtired, roadie party" tonight. Hopefully no one will fart up the tractor trailer as per usual. Thank God there's whiskey for afters!

One good thing is that Wayne is a crew leader tonight, and I'll probably get put on his team, because he knows what I can and cannot do. I do have a couple of roadie skills, so hopefully they won't have me climbing trussing or lifting really heavy speakers. Bonus also is the fact that my roadie husband can bark like a vicious dog and I'm sure will protect me if I get cornered by wild frothy rabid, randy roadies or worse, union stewards.

I already have a nickname. My name of Merlyn will be perfect and work magic for me, because I know that roadies love their nicknames They have awesome roadie names like: Country, John Glen, Sparky, Mouth, Nipper, Stinky *(guess how he got his name?)*, Pickle, Doc, Dreamy, Checkers, Batman, Meatball, Crash *(you don't want to know how he got this name… and neither does the insurance company)*, Box Car, and Pope on a Rope for all that I've met. I love how all these names make me imagine that we are all a demented, weird, industrious family of dwarves.

Hopefully I will come back with all my fingers. I need them to play guitar. But just because I'm putting on work gloves doesn't mean I can't put on my game face, complete with a little makeup. I'm naked without my lipstick. So it's lipstick and work gloves for me. Hey, there might be cute guys there.

Cue the roadie theme song! Jackson Brown's "The Load Out."

Now roll them cases out and lift them amps
Haul them trusses down and get'em up them ramps
'Cause when it comes to moving me
You know you guys are the champs
But when that last guitar's been packed away
You know that I still want to play
So just make sure you got it all set to go
Before you come for my piano"

Maybe I'll even get a crew shirt from the band. That would rock.

Bats: A Dark Night

One night, Harry, Shawna and I curled up on the couch together to watch a movie. Harry had rented, "I am Legend" with Will Smith. I like Will Smith. Well, about a half hour or so into the movie, it started to get creepy. I do not like scary movies. I said, "Eegads! Rabid RUNNING zombies! Euw. This is too scary for me, I'm going to bed. Shawna, I don't think you should watch this movie either." My brave Shawna confidently said, "Me love zombies."

"OK. You are an adult. You guys suit yourself. I'm off to La La Land. Hopefully NOT to dream of sprinting zombies."

And so I went upstairs, turned on the fan, laid down and fell asleep instantly. My bed sure felt grand. Then I awoke with a start. I heard a "chirp" sort of noise, sort of familiar, but not really a cricket. And it was LOUD. "What was that?" I wondered.

Then I peeled my eyes open and perked up my ears in the darkness. Ah yes. There it was. The unmistakable sound of fluttery leather wings and the dim sight of an erratic flying object. Oh fuck. Another bat! It seems that every year, about this very night, we get a bat in the house. It may be familiar, but it is still unnerving.

"EEEEEKKKKK!!! HAAAARRRRYYYY!!!!! THERE'S A BAT UP HERE!!!" His voice, downstairs, echoes back, sort of calmly…"Actually… there are TWO."

"TWO?! Oh, God!" I pulled the sheet up over my head, heart pounding. I could hear it flying around in the bedroom, here and there. Harry yells, "I've got the front door open. He'll leave soon, one just did" *(mild sigh of relief)* Then no sound. *(It's getting sort of hot under the sheet here. So, I just crack the magical protective cover enough to get some fresh air. *sniff* I cover back up quickly)* Silence. Maybe it's gone? *(Oh, wouldn't that be grand!)* Then I feel something on the bed….oh so light. Ah, it's probably nothing. Probably just my silly girl imagination. No sound. Silence. Maybe it IS gone. *(So, just to be sure, I fluff my sheets to prove the bat is NOT on the bed with me. I give the sheets a quick snap!)* Then I hear the SOUND OF A FLYING BAT AGAIN. "AAIIEEEE! ACK! IT WAS ON THE BED WITH ME!!!! WAYNE!!!! Please come up here and turn on the hall light! It's gonna get me, I know it!"

(Now on an aside, let me tell you the way I feel about bats, snakes, spiders and… fairies for that matter. I think they are all goodly creatures. They are good for the environment. All that. But NOT in the house. Bats and snakes both fucking freak me out and for the same damn reason. They are UNPREDICTABLE in their movements. They are quiet and stealthy. You don't expect to see them and BOOM! There they are! Suddenly flying overhead or weaving between and under your feet. Not there… and then… THERE! You have to avoid them or climb a stairway to heaven with your

heart beating on your eardrums. Bats are erratic. They don't go where you think they will. They have those beady black eyes. Or maybe glowing RED. Eegads. They creep me out.) Harry comes up the stairs, so bravely, and says, "Just clap your hands. They live by sonar and sound waves."

"Yah, I remember the last time you said that," I say. And then I remind him of the bat that hit him in the head while it was supposedly using its sonar. "That will surely attract them," I muse with quivering voice. "No. They are smart creatures. It'll find its way out."

"Here he comes!" I say, as the creature continues to fly around upstairs looking for his mysterious and elusive exit. Harry walks out into the hall…and BLAP. The bat nails him square in the head.

(Insert sound of Harry screaming here)

"Oh, you li'l fucker!" he says as he brushes said "smart bat" out of his hair. Both Harry and bat exit room. *(The sound of muffled laughter emanates from the under the sheets as I continue to live and breathe there.)* All is quiet. "I think he's gone," Harry says awhile later as he climbs into bed.

The next day I asked someone how their night was and if they saw anything unusual. He replied: "I saw 'Batman: The Dark Knight.' and you? You do anything?"

I said, "Something similar. I saw 'Bats: The Dark Night' too."

Fight Over the Squab

Let me start this story by saying that I love my dog. He's great. He's fun and cute and smart and silly. He's a good friend. I love him with all my heart. He's my bud. But like all "domesticated" animals, they can be instinctual "survivors" *(Read: Thief)*. One time he pinched and ate two and a half huge, hot-out-of-the-oven chicken cordon bleus right off the kitchen table. He then proceeded to lie around for three days with a swollen belly, lethargic and spewing the worst damn gas a creature could ever have. I think it was the ham plus cheese added to the mass quantity consumed. He paid for it with a bellyache, but good God, he was a vile creator of noxious fumes and, we all paid for it.

Anyway, the other day, I was having a bad day. It was the Autumnal Equinox, and it was a topsy- turvy kind of day. First off, I got some bad news in the form of an unexpected huge bill in the mail, Harry stood me up for dinner *(being the absent-minded professor that he is),* and I didn't feel all that well to start with, as I said before. Very late, and mad, I had given up the ghost of waiting for him any longer and decided to eat my beautiful special dinner without him, not knowing when Shawna was gonna be home. I fixed my *(now solo)* plate for dinner and settled in for a quiet evening. Roast chicken and salad and a movie. That should cheer me up, I thought. Well, just as I was sitting down on the love seat, Shawna comes home early from her group activity. Yay! I won't have to eat all alone, and I'll have some company. I put my plate down, go to answer the door to welcome her... I turn around, (you can see what's coming, right?)

Yes, Monty is at my plate, face fur all over it and is now gobbling down my chicken in three great huffs and gobs. Chomp, chomp, chomp. Right there in front of me. I rush to the dog, which startles him, and he drops the chicken *(ptu!)* out of his mouth. I turn to yell at the blatant thief, and unwisely, he turns and snaps and snarls at me and shows me his teeth and his shining eyes blaze and his black fur stands up on the back of his neck like Cujo. At ME! Yet HE was the thief! Now he's protecting his ill gotten gains?

(On a quick aside, do you ever remember "sassing" your mother? Saying that last, awful, horrid, amazing "wish you hadn't, but did anyway" comment to her in a fit of anger? It was a beautiful terrible thing when it came out of your mouth. Do you remember the look of complete shock that crossed her face, just before she beat you to death? YAH. That's the face I had on my face just now.)

My cute, little sweet, doggy snuggle puppy to whom I had given everything, is now bolstered against me, digging in his heels, in complete defiance with sass on his whiskered face, basically standing up to ME with his canine teeth barred and channeling Cerberus and posturing, "That's MY chicken, BITCH!"

This was also, coincidently, the exact same moment when Merlyn opened her glowing can of Whoop Ass.

"Don't you snarl at me you ungrateful cur!" I howled as I beat that dog silly. I think I even put the boots to him when he showed me his teeth and wouldn't back down. I was going to teach this uppity canine who was BOSS, Goddamit! *(It's sort of like Bill Cosby saying to his kids, "I brought you into this world, I will take you OUT.")* There was a flash of teeth, a scratch of claws and an utter, brazen anger. *(And by the way, Monty acted out that way too.)* I don't know if it was the bad day I was having, or the fact that Monty hadn't been minding me as well as he should have the past couple of weeks, or the fact that he has pulled this stunt before with stealing food *(he recently ate a whole cake off the table in the middle of the night…I wondered why his beard was sticky in the morning. It's a wonder he didn't go into a diabetic coma).*

Anyway, for whatever reason, and with great glee and abandon, I threw myself joyfully into the confrontation of the epic battle: **"Savage Pirate Captain Merlyn vs. Monty the Schnoodle of War."** It was a battle well played by both of us. And I WON.

"Put that goddamn dog outside. I barked to Shawna. "I don't want to see his face for a couple of hours! He can cool his jets out in the dark." Shawna was shocked. She had just witnessed this ferocious battle of man and beast, must've wondered, what would Mommy do next?

I went over to the chicken, still lying abandoned on the carpeting. It was still warm. The lemon herbs, so decadent and savory, scented the golden crusty skin. I scooped it up, took it to the sink, checked it for tufts of Monty's black fur, carefully washed it off, and then?

I ate it like an animal, savagely devouring it over the sink. I let the juices run down my chin as I tore the flesh with my canines and ripped the skin and licked my lips. It was savored with the glee of rewards of a fight well fought.

I WON, Goddammit. **I WON.**

Pondering HRT and Cream Gravy

"I really need to get control of my life," I said, as I pulled into the McDonald's drive thru. "May I take your order please?" came the voice over the monitor. "A double cheeseburger with extra ketchup, a small order of fries, and a… diet soda." I know. A stupid diet soda. Not that it is for less calories, I just don't like how sweet regular soda is.

Why am I eating this shite and soda at all?

Because I just came back from my annual checkup at the gynecologist's office. When I was young, Mom would always allow me a special treat for being a 'good girl' at the doctor's office. Especially if I had to get a shot or I experienced something upsetting while I was there. The appointment today was for my annual pap smear and the everlasting re-order of my "anti-swelling" birth control pills. All was well. I am healthy enough, but stepping on the scale, the nurse started adding the lead weights at the 150-pound mark. What the Christ. It's disconcerting. Granted, I can still get into MOST of my garb. Yet, like some heartsick cow, reading a Cosmo, I WISH to be thinner, but totally understand and accept the fact is that I was raised on farm cooking for the heart and soul.

Food=Love. Homemade sauerkraut, pork hocks, ales and the ever delicious cream gravy made with real bacon grease and from the cream that had settled on the top of the pitcher, which was then served over side pork and potatoes with horse-radish, for God's sake! It's not like I have a choice on what tastes good or not, because of it. I was pushed into the realm of tasty decadence. It was an easy promiscuous slide of the taste buds at an early age into being a foodie. I have never had much of a "sweet tooth." No, I've always had a "salt tooth" and a "fat tooth." Not much has changed. It's an acquired taste. Give me salt-and-vinegar potato chips over cake and ice cream any day. Give me bitter ales and sour whiskeys over sweet wines and liqueurs. Give me venison jerky over candy. I like men the same way. More tough as nails and a bit sour and salty, rather than sickly sweet.

When I went through my divorce many years ago, I made major shakeup changes in my life. I controlled every morsel of sustenance. Every ounce of food chewed, every drop of liquid I swallowed, every step I took was counted, and every moment of my day was accounted for. I had myself scheduled on a daily plan for aerobic or strength-training activity. It was what kept me taking one step a time through my day and was what kept my sanity and me going forward. If I couldn't control my life, by Jesus, I could control what I ate. I got too thin. But it was my choice.

But now, I live in chaos. I live on Fraggle Rock with Harry the Doozer building his wondrous sound and solar grids made with trusses engineered of styrofoam and egg cartons instead of radish sticks. I feel like Squirrel Haven, our home, is indeed Fraggle Rock, and I am one of the Fraggles here, running from one fun gig to the next, with the last day's carted costuming, instruments and sound gear still left piled to put away. Yet, I'm exhausted and continue to make phone calls, emails and end up drinking too much so that I can relax instantly. I eat on the fly and hot-tub my aches and cares away. I'm always one step away from the Gorgs of bills, debt and home repairs. Always I am aware of the ever-present and ever-changing (yet never ever disappearing) Marjory the Trash Heap *(i.e. Harry's hoarding piles)* out back. It's enough to make anyone intemperate.

My work and gig schedule, home life, house and husband's work and family's activities are always in flux. Events and activities are planned on a dry-erase calendar, because of the changeable nature of our wild schedules. Things change on a moment's notice. I muck in on a regular basis. I imagine perhaps, in the regular world of the mundane and 'normal' person this is not the case? My life is nothing BUT change and adaptation and always at the whims and beck and call of others. I am a people-pleaser and I have mistakenly put my own life on hold for everyone else. I have no time! And now my great nurse practitioner informed me that "next year, we will have to discuss getting you off the pill, and onto Hormone Replacement Therapy."

My immediate response was? "OH HELL NO."

"Yes, Marilyn, you will be fifty, and it's time to start thinking on a different approach for you." I said, "Well, why would I want to go on HRT? It's not natural" *(says the ironic woman who just ordered soda and a burger.)* She said, "For the health of you, your system, your vagina, your colon, your hair, your eyes, your skin, overall for YOU." I thought, "Why? Will I otherwise wrinkle, dry up, shrivel, crack and blow away into dust?"

The doctor didn't answer my intuitive question but said it was something for "next year to start to think about." To me, it's like thinking of using a walker or being on a medication for the rest of your life. I don't want to be on any drug forever! Mom didn't have Hormone Replacement Therapy. But then again, hmmm, she might've had a nervous breakdown, was stressed and unfortunately acquired a dangerous smoking habit for her relief. Mom's doctor told her back in 1950s to "take up smoking. Have a coffee break and a cigarette. It will relax you." Instead, she became totally addicted and it ended up killing her.

But then again, she didn't have a fancy dry erase calendar like I do. She sure did enjoy her occasional beers, bacon and cream gravy, though. Like my mother before me, I'm thinking that maybe cream gravy should be my Hormone Replacement Therapy drug of choice. At least it's natural. Cream Gravy ROCKS and is a goddamn cure-all. It's about as close to an orgasm as food gets. Hmmm, I wonder if that's where it got its name?

The Menopausal Question
(with apologies to William Shakespeare)

"Whether 'tis nobler to be protected or to suffer the slings and arrows of outrageous mood swings, or to take medication against the sea of spermy infiltration and by opposing them, end them.

To menstruate, perhaps, no more;
and by a dying cycle I may end this womanly-ness.

Or not.

The heartache, the cramps, and the thousand natural shocks that
 woman's flesh is heir to: above all, 'tis the consummation with man that I devoutly wish. To sleep, perchance to dream, and lie in their arms, unburdened by future motherhood, and yet, to not be manipulated by chemicals, aye, there's the rub:

For in that wondrous orgasm, what dreams may come, when we have shuffled off this mortal coil of to-do lists and society's laden expectations, of decoration and of muse, or fashion and of the quest for come hither looks, must give us pause. There's the respect that makes calamity of so long a life on the pill.

For who should bear the whips and scorns of high blood pressure and the chance of stroke, just so you and he can comfortably ride bare back?

The pangs of desperate love want not to be constrained by the insolent wearing of a rubber-suit. So slippery and so ill-advised when you must needs fish one out of your so recently, well-loved, womanly depths, indeed, it does not bring confidence to the bed. To grunt and sweat and buck in love, but that the consummation of something close to a little death, only to discover the rip or tear of his cock's wetsuit gone asunder, makes us bear those ills of the pill and fly toward it like unto a wanton lover.

 Thus conscience doth make cowards of us all, and thus the native hue of resolution is swallowed eagerly in a pill, a medicinal miracle and years, many years go by, pale cast of thought of thine own health, but thinking only of thine own loins and his. Soft you now, fair Merlyn! Nymph, in my prayers, be all my sins remembered.

 All my former lovers will be regaled and thanked for bringing me to this place.

The place of the Crone and her warm, soft, wise, safe bed.

 I, after many, many years of love and lust, am following my

physician's advice.

I am going off the pill. What, methinks, horrors or blessings await me, in my natural state?

Will I, like a harpy, cry out in anguish? Will I, like a Mother turned Crone, age gracefully?

Will I wither up and dry like a cracked leaf? Will I, instead, be the nymph I always was, unfettered by the whipping of the dead horse called hormone? Indeed, I fear the coming days, for mine own self and for my loved ones. May the spirit of my will, the health of my

heredity and the muse of mine own making preserve me and mine all the rest of the days of mylife.

Anon.

Bardic Magic

We are on the road a lot as minstrels. "We drive. That's what we DO," said one veteran faire minstrel. I agree. Loading in, loading out, picking out and laundering garb, being props' mistress, musician, navigator, secretary, Indie music CD cottage business production company and booking agent all rolled into jingles and/or tie dye. You have an unusual event and need something peculiar? Talk to me. Harry and I can make something appropriate and fun happen for you.

Yearly, Merry Mischief takes a trek south to do the Fort Myers Kiwanis Medieval Faire and other gigs along the way. It's very enjoyable to us, in the middle of winter, to travel out of snow country up north to the balmy south, if even for a few blessed weeks. As we head to lower latitudes, our wintry layers of clothing from boots, hats and mittens and big overcoats are slowly peeled off. We arrive in brightly colored tops and now donning shorts and sandals. A pile of heavy dark winter clothes are baking in the heat of a hot car. Along the way south, our trips have acquired names.

2004 – The "Dear God I hope the van will make it there" Tour- This is the trip when our van's head gasket was went south on route and we went thru a case of oil on the trip. We also went thru several bottles of Absolute Citron Vodka on that trip. Coincidence? I think not.

2005 – The "Southern Acoustic" Tour- Traveling with a vehicle that had no *(knock on wood)* problems

2006 – The "All Lasagna" Tour- The trip on which Harry decided to sample Lasagna at every restaurant that we visited. And I mean EVERY freaking restaurant, from greasy spoon to French crystal

2007 – The "Titties and Beer" Tour- Caravanning and careening south with our friend, Ben Beavers. Being as it was close to Mardi Gras time, flashing was encouraged, expected and well- received. I got given the award of "Top Shelf Tits" by another musician who got a free show after tequila one night. He was most appreciative and is still forthcoming with praise to this day.

2008 – The "Cottage Maiden Voyage" Tour- The infamous trip during which the steering wheel fell off while driving

2009 – The "Kit n' Kaboodle 'Oodle of Schnoodle" Tour- Our dog, Monty-the Road Dog's First Tour.

2010 – "Santa's Holiday" Tour- This is the trip when Harry decided to keep his Christmastime "Santa beard" instead of shaving it off before we went to Florida. It opened doors for us everywhere we went. Yes, everyone DOES love Santa. Even in January.

2011 – "Fire & Ice- Circle of Life" Tour -Trip on which we drove through ice storms and saw a car-fire on the road. We experienced the tragic death of a jousting horse during performance at faire and the birth of a friend's doggie's puppies there in the same hour.

2012 – "Magickal Mischief" Tour- Complete with fairies, orbs, Harry Potter World at Universal, and a magickal spell that protected us and our vehicle and all our travel.

2013 – The "Juicy" Tour- Merlyn was on a health kick and brought her new juicer on the road and made juice for everybody. Life was good, music was sweet, and well, we realized alcoholic beverages are GOOD for you.

When we get to whatever faire we are working, there is usually a morning meeting to check in and get the last minute information from the theatre directors. They give notes on parades, specials, last minute info and all that. Morning faire meetings are different at each faire. Usually they are very early in the morning, in as close to your ren garb as you can manage before coffee, informal and impart such pertinent information to the gathered group of adult performers such as: "Stay in character all day." "Try not to be any more anachronistic than you were last time." "Party for participants in the pub after closing." Sometimes even the brutal, "Be as good as I pay you to be."

I've even heard directors admonish humorously with, "Don't piss outside your tent," and "There are no showers cuz there were vandals who fucked with the showers last year, and now we can't have showers here at the park anymore and this is why we can't have nice things."

You know…life and death shit like that.

But don't get me wrong. Ren faires can include true performers of high quality, Equity actors and classically trained musicians of wonderful caliber, to the more fanciful or the bizarre.

You can witness amazing things as paying patrons arrive as characters from *League of Extraordinary Gentlemen* to *Braveheart* to *The Three Musketeers* represented all in the same day. It's kind of like *Big Bang Theory's* Sheldon at the faire as Spock. I've seen Elvis in his white jumpsuit *(the "King" was at the Renaissance Faire)*, Scarlett O'Hara, at least three Captain Jack Sparrows and a Beowulf and that was on a single day. This is where gypsies dance and twirl and face-tattooed pirates fill the pub. These can also be people who in their real lives are accountants, soccer moms or PhD's of computer science.

But what I really love best about my job as a minstrel is when a song affects a person emotionally. We can be playing a simple song for someone, people close their eyes and they are in another world. Sometimes, they can even cry with memories or wishes. Children are moved to dance or a big burly man will shed a tear of happiness or loneliness or with memories of past lost loves. It's enough to give you pause. It always amazes me about the emotion that is evoked with melody. Hard-hearted men melt and stubborn women can be turned into instant sentimental hearts for love. It is a magickal thing! You play a toe-tapping song in a pub and grown men dance and act out the song at the pub and then leave YOU a tip of a gold coin. *(They already "paid" me by dancing)*. Groups of garbed pirates, wenches and fiddlers magically appear to sing and pound on tables and yell "Huzzah!" and buy you pints and share shots of rum or whiskey.

A bar wench came by and laid two pints of hard cider on the table in front of us. Me, being the good minstrel, thanked them in between songs and I started pouring it from the taboo plastic cup into my more appropriate mug, when my guitar slipped out from under my lap. The beer spilled the beverage all over my guitar body. I wiped the hard cider off the strings with the hem of my skirt and kept playing! I told those folks around me: "You know the difference between a violin and a fiddle? You can't spill beer on a violin."

Of course then again, there are the weirder sorts that also will come up to me, and tell me how exquisitely beautiful my feet are in sandals and the breathtaking site of my ankle bone while I play, and would I consider playing the next song barefoot? Hmmm. No.

Home again, home again, jiggity jig. Theatrical musicians have to wear many hats, literally. My garb/costume rack is varied enough to accommodate many time frames or periods. For example, at a Civil War encampment gig we strapped on our guitars, drum, and took our props *(Confederate flag, Union flag, canteen and basket of CDs. OK, so you've got to promote a bit)*. Harry wore his cotton shirt and vest, slung on his canteen and black powder pistol, and popped a straw hat on his head for the sun. I stepped into petticoat and calico skirt, lace blouse and tied a cameo on with a ribbon tie around my neck and pulled my hair back into a pony tail with a simple black satin bow. We had our limber jack doll, some other dolls from the era and enough period songs in our bag of tricks to put a temperance lady into a drunken calico swoon. To see an encampment outfitted with all the amenities of home, quite comfortably adorned really brings history home to you. We played music for men polishing their bayonets. This all in a pastoral town. A real-life moment brought forward. At one gig we sang "Shady Grove" for Union soldiers under the cover of cool leafy trees in the heat, and then love ballads and hymns for polite ladies sewing embroidery during their afternoon rest after tea. We sang for Confederate soldiers and made our limber jack doll dance jolly tunes for them. We sang drinking songs for vendors who were thirsty and needed a drink. We sang "Long Black Veil" by request from a Union soldier and made this old crusty bearded man almost cry. He loved it so. We sang a smattering of songs for a woman who'd wanted to meet us for ages, and who had "tracked us down," and we sat and sang to her personally for quite awhile. She was beaming. It's all in a Minstrel's Line of Duty.

But sometimes you get called into a line of fire. For instance, during one show, every seat under the tent was filled and it was a good-sized crowd. One woman lingered trying to find a seat, and decided quickly to sit right up front while we were singing. She sat down fast. She was off to my left down front. After a few minutes her mate came and hastily handed her a bag of ice which was put on the back of her neck. I realized then that she was overheated and sort of kept an eye on her. All the while, we are taking into consideration our show the audience, the next song, the next bit of history to offer, which verse or chorus and kept our program going forward in the heat. It was about 90 degrees, and the lady that was overheating was in shorts and a tank top, not even in layers of garb like us. And then? She went down. Like down off the chair, down onto the ground, down for the count. Of course it was in the middle of a song, and her mate was there and another woman ran for the medic.

I have found that the very best thing for us to do as minstrels during times like this is crowd control. The shift has, in an instant, gone from entertainment performance to distracting people from rubber-necking the medics and allowing the person in trouble some privacy. It's our job to keep everyone calm and peaceful under the circumstances. Another medic came running and we were still on that same song...I really forget which one it was, but I know I did a good job of it...when a nurse in the crowd joined them on the ground, asking the woman how many fingers she held up and trying to get a response, we then directed the audience to turn their chairs around to the opposite end of the tent and we played at the other end of the tent to pull the focus away from the emergency and let them handle it. It can be stressful. And then the village fire siren went off.

Let me tell you about the fire siren here in the middle of Peterboro. The fire station sits directly across from the park, in the center of town where we were. As some of you know, and those of you with scanners are aware of, no two fire stations are really alike in their distinctive signals. Some have particular sounds or variations in tone to make them discernible to fire fighters. Well this particular fire station sounds its siren for a solid TWO MINUTES STRAIGHT. I've never heard anything like it before! And yup. Right in the middle of our already medic-attending show. So I know enough not to fight something that big and loud and we "mimed" a song for a bit to show our audience some humor in the futility of competing with it, and went about waiting it out, all the while the EMT was trying to call on the phone for help. *(Harry wants me to tell you that the siren was in the key of B flat...and the decibel level was at least 110, says my expert sound man. That is the threshold of pain. And there were people sitting there, during the siren, with fingers in their ears to brace themselves from it.)* The fire truck barreled out of the station, and drove around the park fence and came. Right to our tent for that lady that who was down. *(Oh, fer feck's sake, really?)* When the fire siren stopped banshee screaming and our eardrums stopped bleeding, we started singing again to the crowd who was still so patiently with us! They waited for us to continue our show! How awesome is that? I mean, after the tragic lady's vitals were taken, and she was thusly revived, and fortified with electrolytes, and she was pronounced OK, the fire truck left, we all applauded her, the medics, and Merry Mischief went on singing. I thanked the crowd for their patience and we all wished the recovering woman well, one late arriving audience member was confused, as she was unaware there was even a problem going on right behind her, so I guess we did our job well! Several couples stopped at the main admission booth, highly recommended us to the festival, and they said they'd love to have us back again for next year. You pay your dues and sometimes it's enough. But after a day like that, you need a goddamn drink.

It was then that I had to marvel at musicians' lives: both in modern days like today, and also about minstrels back in the day of the Civil War. While we didn't have to play into an actual battle, or be caught in musket crossfire, or step over the dead and dying like the minstrels of old did, it seems we did have to remember, relive and experience some of the same issues with sirens, gunshots, war drums and the afflicted and nearly dying to make it all very real. I know that we felt like we were cannon fodder on that particular day. Who says re-enactment is all fluff and fantasy? Seems to me it's as real and life and death as it ever was, and good to know that, too.

Minstreling Prince Caspian (5/8/08)

Merry Mischief was hired to perform some of our music for the New York City movie star and special guest premiere opening for the movie, *Prince Caspian*. The only restriction was that we could not publicize or talk about the event until AFTER the event occurred because it was a private party and the press would not be notified until today, the day after.

Harry, and our dear musician friend Ron, and I set off yesterday morning, after packing a kitchen sink trunk-full of fancy garb and instruments. Ron's grandfather used to be a taxicab driver in NYC and Ron lived up to his heritage. The trip was fun because we all have sick senses of humor and are gypsies at heart and love to travel. We got lost only once, which made for a short, fun, uneventful sightseeing tour of New Jersey. The only rub about traveling to New York, was trying to get thru the Lincoln Tunnel around rush hour. Six lanes of traffic narrowing down to two, which took about forty-five minutes. But we told dirty jokes to pass the time and all was well. We got to the gig early and parked our car in a parking garage and loaded up ourselves like pack mules and found the place.

The special party was held at the New York City Main Public Library branch *(The Humanities and Social Sciences Library)* on 5th Avenue and 42nd St., NY, NY. What an AMAZING building and facility! I HIGHLY recommend you to all go to this place when you are in NY and not just to do the touristy things like the Empire State Building. The Library is filled with marble and gilt and huge sculptured lions *(Oh, Aslan, himself would be proud!)* The building is as posh and wonderful and magnificent as a castle should be! Winding staircases, rich fabrics, suits of armors, stone lions, antiquities and many treats for the eyes, including a "basement" area which has a ceiling like the Hogwarts Main Dining Hall, a fantastical starlit view of the universe!

Had fun with some of our other fun Renaissance Faire performer friends: Isaac Fawkes, Johnny Fox, Paul Garbanzo, Empty Hats, among others. We were all to be roving players for the evening and took our places and started the evening's festivities at 9:30 p.m. and played for about 1,200 guests in satin ball gowns and tuxes on three levels of the library.

Saw a lot of actors and actresses, dressed for the premiere, who walked the red carpet while we played for them. And yes, we did a little star spotting: Ben Barnes *(Prince Caspian)*, Tilda Swinton (White Witch*)*, William Moseley *(*Peter*)*, and the entire cast of the movie! But my favorites were Warwick Davis *(*who was also Willow Ulfgood in the movie, *Willow)* and Peter Dinklage *(*Trumpkin*)*.

Merry Mischief looked really good in our Renaissance garb and sounded great as we wandered around playing for these celebrities. We wound up on New York TV coverage throughout the evening as well. Our friend Ron's thrill for the evening was when William Moseley and Georgie Henley were having their picture taken …right next to Ron's elbow as we serenaded them all in the special VIP room. We had our picture taken about a 1,000 times. *(The 3 of us were pretty sure it was my very revealing bodice spillage, that, and the fact that Harry had a good hair day, and that Ron looks like someone everyone knows from somewhere… let me think, the pub? The pawn shop?)*

We finished our gig at midnight and trekked back up to the green room where catering had brought up some grand victuals for us. Blanched veggies, wild salmon, chicken, salads, apple crisp, macaroni and cheese, hors d'oeuvres, rolls and god knows what else (all the food that everyone "important" downstairs had sampled all evening). Because it was all minstrels and magicians eating together after the performance, we were all good-natured and no one got their hand bit off, everyone walked away with all their fingers and their bellies very full of gourmet food. It was not the first time that we all sang or played for our supper. Cash and checks are grand recompense, thank you! But food is ALWAYS appreciated. We are MINSTRELS, for God's sake.

Trekked out to the parking garage a block away and paid $48 to get our car out of hock for 5 hours parking and headed for home at 2 a.m. The city was beautiful on a warm spring evening. All in all, a wonderful magical musical time with two of the best people in the world, schmoozing and hobnobbing with some amazing people in a beautiful place for a fantastic story.

Thank you, Aslan. Anon for now.

Sirens: Lure of the Sea

I heard about a woman who recently jumped off a cruise ship into the tropic waters. Harry read me the news on Yahoo mail. I said, "She heard the Sirens."

"Yes," he said. I mused, "Remember, I heard the Sirens once too, but at least I was lucky enough not to act on them. Poor woman, instead, she listened and obeyed."

"Yes, I remember, "he said thoughtfully. My memory hastened back to the night when I walked onto the deck of the cruise ship on a most beauteous night in January 2000.

The night was tropical in the beautiful Gulf Coast waters. The moon was big and full and the water was smooth as glass. The festively adorned cruise ship cut the waters with little wake. It was lit up like a Christmas tree gliding through black water. Serenity and peace were there.

It had been very busy inside the cruise boat with its cacophony, hustle, bustle, games, music and lights. I needed to escape the activity as I was over-stimulated. I had come outside to enjoy the sea air, the quiet, and the moonlight on this romantic night. I mused that my current life was full of love and happiness. I smiled to myself and enjoyed the view.

And that is when I heard them. The Sirens from Ulysses' *Odyssey* fame. They called to me with their sweet entrancing voices. A feeling that sounded like a voice in my head and heart came to me. It seemed to sound like a batch of beautiful females and they sang so deliriously sweetly to me. They cooed, "It's so beautiful. So calm. So warm. It is perfect here in the deep black water of the Caribbean." I agreed. But they had planted a seed and continued, "Jump in! The water is beautiful. So warm and safe. It is velvety like the womb."

At first I denied hearing them and just watched the oceanic tide slip away and viewed the shimmering reflection of the perfect moon on the still wine dark water. The bounce of the strings of lights mirrored back up to me in a wonderland of fantasy. But I had to agree with them again, as I sighed and relaxed further with relaxation. Indeed, it was perfection here.

But the Sirens were insistent: "There is no one here but you. It's easy to climb up on the railing right there. Just put your left foot up a bit and try it. See? You are not afraid. Seasons don't fear the reaper, nor do the wind, the sun or the rain. Come on baby, you can be like they are. You'll be able to fly! Salute the sea! Pray to Poseidon with one last graceful dive! Come to us! Be a Mermaid forever! We will take care of you. You will have peace like this forever. You will be Eternally Beautiful!" I looked around for the voices. I heard "Don't fear the Reaper" so clearly, singing in my head with all those new verses.

There was no one there. It was beautiful indeed. The tropical breezes blew my hair lightly around my face. The strings of white lights that decorated the ship were so lovely on this picturesque night. The quiet night was intoxicating. The dark deep water pulled me irresistibly to it. So comforting. So peaceful. I put one foot on the bottom rail. I pictured myself climbing up and balancing on the top rail. You can be like they are. The door was open, the wind appeared...the candles blew and then disappeared. I imagined myself taking one last perfect dive into the calm still deep water. I dove in without a trace, with nary a splash. I saw the cruise ship sail away silently without me. It was warm, silent, dark and deep as I looked at it sailing away. Then I realized this decision would be forever. Forever without my love who would pine for me. Forever gone from my children who would grow up mourn and live without me.

I then became suddenly aware of my body. I realized that I had climbed up the railing! I noted where I stood. So close to the edge. So tantalizingly near to my Mermaid Swan Dive. I stepped down off the railing and I turned my back on the most luscious, deceitful, delicious calling voices of the engaging Sirens. I went back inside the ship, with my heart pounding. I was thankfully glad that my will was stronger than the pull of the sea.

The lure of the sultry, wine dark, mysterious sea.

What is your Super Power?

It was after an experience such as this last one, when I wanted to leave the crowded cruise boat via magical Sirens that I became painfully aware that my empathic sensitivities were becoming heightened. I had moments where I felt very much out of place and time. I mean, it was as if I'd received some sort of Super Power, which had lain dormant since I was small. Now all of a sudden, I was growing wings, or horns…or both. I realized that I could pick up on people's emotions all around me.

So, now I ask you to ponder something. You've magically won some sort of Wild Lottery. You get to pick a Super Power! What would you choose? If I had a choice of such gifts, I would wish for Teleportation, Invisibility and Telepathy. It must just be my way of dealing with the need to bolt on a whim, satisfy my intrepid curiosity, and see if what I'm feeling is indeed, truly accurate instead of trying to assimilate all the incoming energy and clues.

In 1998, we stopped watching television at home. It gave me jitters and the content bombarding us bothered me. We had no antennae, and so, after a bad storm we disconnected our cable service. Both of those were conscious choices. Why pay for shite? We watch videos or DVDs that we choose instead. TV makes me feel jittery and pushed to be somebody else, and to buy things I don't need. *(Hey, they call it "programming" for a reason).*

I wanted to ground my Spirit and start tuning into the Earth's cycle like some old farmer. I watched moon phases and learned them by sight. I started leading earthen services at churches for the general public. I used music, my English major capabilities, my psychic abilities and card reading along with my public speaking talents and put it all together to help people. I'd been in a lot of churches in my life. I know you have to follow each church's etiquette. When in Rome and all that… I'd been a Sunday school teacher and an aide for the handicapped for many years at certain points in my life. My love of travel and cultures now drew me to becoming a lay leader and running programs celebrating the change seasons of the earth. I wrote programs and services for May Day (Beltane), Halloween (Samhain), Christmas (Yule) and Groundhog's Day (Imbolc). I led services for Veterans Day and did Candle Magick Services for Healing the Soul. I enjoyed adding our music and my poetry to my services. People seemed to really enjoy it and get something out of it.

Often, I would guess who was on the phone before I picked it up. I would think of things in three's or in combinations. I started drumming. It became easy to pick up "vibes" from people. I would leave if the vibe wasn't right, or would follow along if magickal things happened. Sometimes I could see auras around folks. When asked, I can answer questions by pendulum. Magick had found me again, and this time I was open to listening. I felt like a kitchen witch or a healer from another lifetime. I can give you Reiki healings. Reiki to me is very much like the Laying on of Hands from the Pentecostal churches. The Source is the same to me if you call it Jesus or Universal Truth. It feels and heals just the same. It is Pure Divine Energy and it is Good.

I believe that we, as humans, are being led to plug into TV and iPhones to the detriment of our innate Inner Spirit. By tuning into them so attentively *(just watch people sometimes)* humans are learning to tune out our Divine Spirit within. As the Hindus say, "God lives in you, as you."

People are forgetting instinctual knowledge. Most folks couldn't even tell you what phase the moon was if you asked them to look at it in the sky. People are too busy texting instead of listening to their Spirit or even talking to the person right next to them. As a society, we are becoming deaf and dumb to each other and our natural world.

Shawna Leaves The Nest
(A parable about my disabled daughter's flight to Independence and Residential Housing)

This is a story about birds, chirped by me, Merlynbird, to sing you a song about my disabled daughter, Shawna, who has just spread her wings and has moved out into her very own, hard-won Independence Day. She has been both one easy and one tough little bird to raise.

She was an egg like any other up until she hatched.

A quick birth, but then, something seemed amiss. She didn't look like the other birds. She didn't look like her mommy, Merlynbird, or her daddy, Daveybird. She didn't look like her sister, Jessebird either.

She had different markings and was of a different shape in a way. But as you know, all baby birds are endearing, what with their wet bird birth feathers, their fragile, delicate bodies, their need to live and their needy babybird cries for food. So her Mommybird and Daddybird loved her, fed her and protected her from the pecks of the other birds and she grew

We taught her how to eat, because she didn't know how. It took her longer to learn everything, from the simplest things of keeping her wobbly head up and getting her flimsy birdie neck to be strong enough to carry the weight of her head, to learning how to eat, how to nurse, how to stand, how to even making her little birdie sounds. Most times, we parent birds just knew what she wanted and could read her signs and faintly flapping wings, but the other birds had trouble understanding her garbled cries. She even looked weird to some of the other birds, and she was shunned by some. They were afraid of her because she was different. They didn't know (or *didn't want to know*) that she was a sweet, kind bird and needed protection and just a little longer time to learn things.

She was a good companion to her sisterbird. Naturally Jesse sometimes grew weary of her baby sister's neediness and constant attention. Jesse would peck her head in frustration and fly off and leave Shawnabird for a bit. But when the sisterbird got some rest and calmed down, she would fly back to the nest to her little awkward sister Shawna bird. There she would smooth Shawnabird's feathers and she go back to reading and teaching her how to walk and play some more. Sometimes she would bring a twig for the nest. Jessebird taught her little sister how to be tough. The little Shawnabird needed to be a little tougher. There were bigger birds of prey out there that would easily peck her to death, if it weren't for the teaching and protection of her bigger sister bird, Jesse.

When Jesse went to bird school, little Shawnabird wanted

to go, but she was not ready. She had to go to a special bird school for awhile and to be with other misshapen birds who shared their gifts and who also needed to learn the simplest of things and how to be strong, too.

Mommybird and Daddybird worried a lot sometimes, but most of the time they didn't. They were just too busy being providers of worms and bugs and protectors of the nest. They were constantly protecting and feathering and cleaning the nest. The parents kept the babies warm in winter with their increasingly range of flight and expanding territory. It was a happy, warm life.

Then one day, the Daddybird migrated to a less stressful tree and the Mommybird pined for him. But baby birds need to be fed, so in awhile, she found another mate to help her. Together, they obtained worms and grubs for the baby birds. She would not be alone. The new mate and she sang new and beautiful songs together for all the forest to hear. The first Daddybird got lonely sometimes when he heard their songs, so then he would drop by the nest to check on the baby birds. He brought them shiny things for the nest to help like he used to. The old Daddybird and the new Daddybird didn't fight, so it was all good. They were still a family; they just lived in different trees in the same forest.

The baby birds grew into bigger birds, their feathers came in and they were beautiful. The Shawnabird's song was a bit different melody and her chirping that was most unusual, but it was nice all the same. She was a silly and fun bird. She grew plump with the grubs that the parent birds fed her, because it was too hard for her to find her own and because she couldn't fly very far or very fast.

One day, Jessebird decided to move to another tree and chirped her goodbyes to the nest and her family. She didn't move far away and came back by the nest often enough to see her Sisterbird and Mommybird and Daddybirds. Jessebird was now part of a bigger flock and she seemed happy enough and fed and healthy, so the Mommy and Daddybirds didn't mind too much. They still had the Shawnabird to love and feed and bed down with at night.

Years passed and Shawnabird learned most of the things she needed to know. The other things that she couldn't grasp she got by without. She couldn't fly far, but she learned how to flit from branch to branch and down to the ground, and back up to the nest again. She couldn't sing very loudly, but she could still sing. She couldn't fly with the big flocks, but she could fly a bit with some of the other birds that had issues. The birds with the clipped wings, or the ones with the twisted beaks, or the birds with the missing toes, they were all friends and hung out on a safe branch together and talked about life and sang their different songs, sometimes they sang together, sometimes not at all together but in a grand cacophony. And it sounded really pretty nice and OK. It sounded like a busy bunch of friends with different ideas and different lives and it had its own weird harmony. And it, too, was also good.

One day, the Shawnabird chirped to her Mommy and Daddybirds that she would like to try to live with some of the other birds and be on her own like her sisterbird. The Mommy and Daddy birds were worried. They didn't know if the Shawnabird would be able to find enough food for herself, or know when to come in out of the rain and if she could hunker down in the wind or what to do when it snowed or if she would know enough to hide when the hawk and owls flew overhead or what.

So the Mommybird sang a long and Universal song of worry and it went out into the forest. Shortly after that, word came to her about a new tree house nearby where they needed a Shawnabird. They were looking for a bird just like her to complete their new flock. There were other birds that could do some things, but not other things very well. There were mentor birds there that would feed and guard the tree and make sure the nests were safe. There are lots of these happy, safe trees around if you only look. Not all the birds are the same that live in these trees. Many are of different species and flocks, but they all live together ok.

So it was that Shawna spread her wings and flew off. With

help from her family and her new flock, they bundled up her shiny bits, her special feathers, and her books of bird calls and her coat of winter feathers and flew to her new nest. A bigger nest of her very own.

It is not far from her mommy and daddy's tree. They can almost see it if they stand way up on their tiptoes on the top branch.

The nest at home is empty now. It is sadder and much quieter, even if it is more roomy. The Mommy and Daddybirds are singing occasional sad songs for the loss of their sweet little bird to snuggle with, and they are still worried, as Mommy and Daddybirds are wont to be. But sometimes they sing happy songs for her too. And they are glad they won't have to find as many grubs and can rest quietly some for the first time in a very, very long time.

And now, the forest has some new different songs in it, sung by birds learning to sing together for the very first time, in a tree not too very far away…

Wonderings in My Weeded Garden
8/11/11

One day after faire I came home to find that my beautiful foot tall Sunflowers that were growing so well, had been EATEN. Not only that, but the yellow squash, just so recently bursting with flowers, and having given me my first delicious squash were stripped of leaves, fruit and flowers. My bell peppers were also nibbled.

Theiving rabbits!

After this, I have to say that I lost some heart with the garden.

I had ignored it a bit.

Remembering only that on very hot and dry days I should water extra. I was mad. Mad at my garden for being savaged by thieves. I had snubbed it for a bit. But today, I felt guilty and owe it the respect it deserved. I owed it my TIME and ENERGY.

I went out to commune with myself, my garden and my plants. The rest of the plants seem to be

Doing well, although, a couple of plants have always looked "sickly" yet they are still producing fruit. Previously, I had called the Co-operative Extension site when I was first worried about them and tried to troubleshoot the problem. I just continued to be a good mommy, watered them deeply, looked for pests and let them be. So this morning, after a nice long walk with my doggy Monty Joe, I got out my hoe. I rescued my garden from the weeds. It was overdue and good to break a sweat working in the earth. It now is a garden again. Although it seems to me that this garden is a microcosm of people and a bigger picture of Life itself.

The tomato plants are so big and heavy liken unto drunken sluts in the sun...they can't stand or at least they won't stay standing up. They end up leaning on their wire cage arm candy. They have much fruit to offer anyone and everyone for the taking, but instead it rots on the vine if you don't appreciate the worth of them.

The sunflowers and squash that were eaten and laid to waste, murdered by fecking bastard rabbits *(damn them to hell)* have had their wasted carcasses thrown into the compost pile. Iwas able to save only one yellow squash plant out of four. It has a couple hopeful flowers and two wee baby squash. I will pray for them.

The peppers, while savagely eaten, and almost devoured whole, still try their amazing damndest to grow, but we will probably not see another pepper. Still, like someone recovering from an addiction, I will let them try their hardest to manage a bud or flower until the frost for the principle of the thing. They need to TRY. It's good for my spirit to watch them TRY. They give me hope in so many areas of my life.

The basil is as tall as a third-grader, just as wild and unruly yet smells way better.

The sage, lavender and thyme like where they live and are

being goodly citizens and nice neighbors to each other.

The peonies are quiet, having already sung their loud riotous song last June. They are exhausted from winning "Best of Show" in the garden and deserve a rest.

The oregano and mint are fighting with everyone around them for the most elbow room. They are total assholes.

The cilantro, well, it's gone south as is the wont and desire of this Mexican parsley. It lays drunkenly gone-to-seed and takes a permanent siesta, just content to lie there with its warm buzz of tequila and lime in its salt-rimmed hedge. It bakes and enjoys the buzz of the cicadas in the trees. It curls its crispy yellow edges in the sun.

And the Coneflowers? They have on their silly, party, happy faces and they just wildly laugh and laugh and laugh.

It's really quite a garden party out here if you listen.

Double Tap Zombie

All this loveliness, introspection has led me through gardens, lawns and woods, back to the future. There is an addendum that I feel I must add to the story previously about Artie Shawcross.

The last I told you, was from my childhood, and what a terrible story it was. Thankfully Arthur went to jail. But, as with any sociopathic charmer's luck, somehow he conned and manipulated the prison parole board, and actually gained their trust. In some weird twist of fate, Arthur Shawcross was let out of prison for the deaths of two children and actually gained parole in 1987!

I take you back to that year. My girlfriend and I had run out of gas. Neither of us wanted to stay with the car or hitchhike alone. We had hitchhiked years before when we were teenagers, but we didn't really want to do it again, alone. So we decided to brave it together and try to get a ride back to her house for a gas can. We stuck out our thumbs. An older, fat man pulled over in a red, beat up truck to give us a ride. My friend got in first and I slid in beside her on the bench seat and closed the passenger door.

Once we were moving, this pasty, heavy older man said to us out of the blue: "Where are you headed?" We told him that we were going for gas.

He said, "You girls should be more careful how you travel. What if someone really BAD picked you up?" *(It was already something that we had thought of, but hadn't listened to our intuition on, under the circumstances.)*

"Well, we're glad it was you, instead." I laughed and said sort of nervously. *(Well, that was a weird opener for a stranger to say.)* My friend shot me a concerned look. She was sitting right next to him.

There was a dramatic pause as his truck chugged along, "Well, what if I reached down from under my seat and latched a pair of handcuffs on you to trap you so I could kill you?"

(Good God. What the hell kind of chit-chat was this? Terror leapt into my psyche.)

The old codger leered at my girlfriend who was sitting so close to him on the bench seat. *(Why would a stranger say something like that? It was unsettling and well, we felt immediately on edge. My stomach turned with former memories that I hadn't thought of in years.)*

My girlfriend was now uncomfortably moving away from him on the seat. Her fear made her bear down on me by pressing up tight against me so I was almost part of the truck door.

This was too weird to be true. Really, really weird. What the hell was happening here? The change in the conversation had made a palpable feeling of anxiety come over us. Our hearts had started pounding faster. I linked my arm through hers for us both to feel safer. I gave her moral support because she was in his touching range more than I.

I started feeling like there was déjà vu here somewhere. There was something really strange and oddly familiar about his voice. I couldn't place it. I searched and searched all my vibes. But I had obviously buried some past shite pretty deeply in my subconscious. I looked out the window and prayed. I wanted to be out of this truck. I wanted to be away from this weirdo. I felt my intuition screaming at me to get out. NOW. "You are not safe here," was the thought racing through my head.

All of a sudden a light bulb went off. I think I knew who he was! Was it ARTIE? But NO. No way. It couldn't be! He was in JAIL. Right? It had been many years ago when he had tried to capture me. If it was him, his looks had definitely changed much from a thin young lean man to an old fat, pale man. (He had.) It couldn't be him! I knew he was IN JAIL. FOREVER.

But here was someone acting just as weird, and just like him! *It COULDN'T be Artie. Could it?* No worries. I'll just "act as if" it is him. Just to be safe. Think, Merlyn, think. I tried to imagine what to do next. My girlfriend was now up as close to me as she could get.

I thought of something. With some bullshit braggadocio I answered this bizarre driver's frightening question with, "Well, for one thing, you couldn't catch us both. I would just jump out. I'd remember your license plate and I'd go call the cops."

"You'd leave your friend?" he looked curious with a sly grin and cackled. He obviously felt empowered in the situation.

"To save her, I would! I most surely would." I said with my biggest voice. My girlfriend was physically trembling. I could feel her shaking next to me.

"But you'd get hurt or killed if you jumped out while the vehicle was moving." *(He seemed to be calculating, blinking, and trying to work out the details).*

"I'd wait for a stop sign. You have to abide by traffic laws, or you'd get stopped yourself. I'd risk it, to save her." I pronounced, trying to outwit him.

"Yah, but she'd still be dead. I'd just bungee her to the seat and drive until I found you again."

I was prepared to jump. He saw my hand was on the door handle. I noted to myself that I was gonna take my friend with me even if she had to lose a Goddamn arm. I set my jaw and I looked at him and tried to memorize everything about him. I said out loud to my terrified friend, "In that case, we better start memorizing everything about him and his vehicle now."

I thought my friend was going to faint. I prayed she wouldn't.

With my last statement and only some more unsettling conversation from him, he obviously thought better of this risky business, and for some reason, God intervened and….he stopped and let us out!

This driver had actually done nothing really wrong but some frightening shock talk. Quick thinking bluffing on my part got us out of that hot seat. From years of living, I had recognized certain quirky behavior and called him out on it with brazen attitude, and we got away with our lives! He stopped and let us OUT!

The weird man drove off and we licked our wounds with trembling hands on beers afterward, trying to shake off his unsettling banter. Maybe he was just a weird concerned citizen trying to put the wrath of God into us about hitchhiking? We didn't know. We were just grateful to be out of that queasy quagmire. We couldn't prove anything and were justly reprimanded for our hitchhiking adventure when we told the police on the phone. No report was filed. There was no trouble with that license plate. As a matter of fact, my anonymous phone call to the police, informed me, that WE were the ones at fault for hitchhiking!

But there was just something "about him" that seemed so familiar. But that's silly for a convicted murdering felon to be out driving around, right? Silly to even think of Artie now. I put it out of my head. Somebody was just fooling with us, is all, we concluded.

Unfortunately, for other unsuspecting women it didn't go so well for them as it did for me and my friend. Artie went on to Rochester to make another life, and eventually killed many more women. He became known as "The Genesee River Strangler." He left many of his raped, dead victims in the woods or in ditches, stuffed full of leaves and grass. He drove around with one of them dead and bungeed upright in the car. He even went back and placidly ate his LUNCH while gazing at their undetected graves. This was how they caught him in the end. He would "visit" them and eat his lunch at these former crime scenes. You can read all about it… if you like the stuff of nightmares. This is one reason that I purposely don't read scary stories or watch horror movies. I've had quite enough in my real life, thank you very much. I choose life.

Some time later, Mom called to tell me, Artie WAS paroled from prison! Oh My God! It WAS him that picked us up hitchhiking that day! I didn't tell my mother. She was an old lady now. I loved her enough that I didn't want to freak her out. But I told her that want to hear it or know anything about him ever again. I didn't want to deal with the enormity of it, either. But here he was now, and all his depravity, all over the news. I felt sick. I called my friend. She nearly fainted for sure this time. I blocked the whole thing for years previous, but now here it was, right in my face again.

There was another series of tragic murders. Arty was then arrested *(after a lengthy investigation)* and he was promptly put back in prison for LIFE, this time, (THANK GOD) in 1990. When I heard that he had died in prison, in 2008, I REJOICED!

I only tell you these awful stories so that YOU and your loved ones may be safe out there.

When I asked my older brother, Chris, *(who is a born-again Christian and a kind-hearted, fair man)* about Artie all those years ago, all he had to say was this:

"Artie was a misguided asshole who decided to just kill children and women. I had a close call with him when my friend Mitch and I were hunting with my bee-bee gun and bow and arrow in Jay's woods. Artie stalked us teenage boys with a double barrel shotgun, pointed it at us while ten feet away and told us to get out of his woods or he would just kill us next time we were in there. However, the best part of this story is that Mitch and I are alive, while Artie is in HELL. Now, there's a wonderful ending to my little story. The End."

I think that says a lot.

There's nothing I can say but THANK YOU to the Gods for saving me. I don't know why some people are saved and others are not. I write this so that you will be aware. While we are taught to turn the other cheek, there are some that we should never let our guard down for.

Never, ever.

For the most part, we should love others, and forgive (for ourselves, if not for them.)

The best way to enact forgiveness is to say this (which I read in Gabrielle Bernstein's book, "Spirit Junkie"). *"I forgive you (insert name), and I release you to the Holy Spirit."*

Forgive, yes. **But don't forget**. Learn from it. Stay safe and keep your distance from evil. Again, I beseech you, shields up, lovies, shields UP.

Empathy & The Beast

Needless to say, there are things and events in my life that I've gotten clues to, and been led to ask the Universe, "Why?"

I read in the book, "Awakening Intuition" by Mona Lisa Schulz M.D. Ph.D. that some people with Epilepsy and seizure disorders have increased intuitive capabilities.

"These individuals have altered memory function, repeated déjà vu, and experience dreamlike states of consciousness, out of body experiences, the sensing of presence, internal hearing, complex vision, anxiety, panic, and feelings of doom. They have also reported seeing angels."

Ah. I get it now. That book explained a lot to me about some of what I've gone through. It seems that sometimes our "flaws" can open up passages to other realms.

For instance, one of the most wonderful things about being a musician is the fact that you can give of your total self, sing and reach a lot of people all at once! Being onstage, giving and expressing for a mass audience is the absolute best feeling. Whether it's just a song or some banter, people seem to be touched by who and what you are. It seems that they really listen and enjoy the experience you put out there. They "get you." The real you. It makes me feel like I've given my best and helped someone for their Greatest and Highest Good, or at the very least I've helped to lift their spirits for a short bit.

But the absolute worst part about being a musician is going home after an amazing grand day like that and having absolutely no one to talk to or connect with. You've given all and need refilling but no one is there. I feel like there is no worse loneliness than this, especially, in the comparison of the former grandiose experience to the quiet lonely present one, and to experience it all in a very short time frame. It's quite the pendulum swing of emotions. The difference is huge in contrast and really hard to make cognitive sense of sometimes.

Euphoria and Dread are bizarre bedmates.

But don't ask me. Ask all kinds of performers and you'll find this is a common experience.

My gifts of Intuition and Empathy help me pick up vibes from the audience. Big, wild, joyful feelings to downhearted despair of people within the crowd. Added to the feelings invoked by lyrics and melody, and you have the makings for a misunderstood ending of the day after a big wonderful fulfilling gig. Yet, I think that this juxtaposition of wide extrovert/introvert reality is why many performers have addiction problems. It's a blessing and a curse in the same breath. Most folks have no clue to what it's like except those who do this for a living.

I swear that nothing can even compare to it. High highs. Low lows. Even though they were accidental, Janis Joplin, Marilyn Monroe, John Belushi, so many... I know how they must've felt. Audience members sometimes think that entertainers are grand and they may secretly wish that they were them on stage too. "People who are entertainers have big egos," most people say and assume. Yet, those same folks have no idea how delicate, fragile and lonely the ego really is without a kindred heart at the end of the day to connect. Huge audiences...lonely hotel rooms.

Fragility, ego is thy name.

But really, a lot of people feel this way and not just performers. There is a secret part of being human that is never known to anyone but ourselves and our belief system, our God, if you will.

You have to learn how to Self-Soothe. Over the years, I have become a Seeker and a Theologian. I believe in cherry picking. It makes sense to me. We are all unique and that's what makes us the same. Many religions and philosophies are out there, and most of them have wondrous grains of Truth. I think that they all have pieces to the puzzle. It is up to each of us to make sense of our lives. There is something good in most faiths, whether or not they are your faith. It's good to learn from many points of view.

I still work with the Tarot cards I learned so many years ago. I have added Goddess and Angel cards to the mix. I consider myself to be a Healer and a Helper, and my cards are used in positive ways to bring "Poor Man's Counseling" to those who need itI've also performed music for many denominations. It's all good. I use my music to bring joy and laughter, relevance and poignancy to my audience. I try to help others with the wisdom that my experiences have given me and I try to do it with Love.

But it hasn't been easy.

I've had members of one Bible church come and make a big prayer circle in front of my tarot booth at a festival, draw a crowd and slam me as the Devil Incarnate. Then they prayed for my Soul to be saved by Jesus. What a spectacle they made! I stood there and watched them berate me to God and the surrounding crowd. Little did they realize that I, too, love Jesus. I do all my readings for each person's "Greatest and Highest Good" and folks leave my readings, empowered to be better people. *(Interesting, also to note about this experience is that I had a subsequent fabulously profitable day that same day the church people gathered to condemn and pray for me. I believe what the Universe heard was, "Help Merlyn" and the Universe did so. So, ultimately, I thank and bless them for that.)*

I have also tried to use my music and stage presence to empower folks. I've made up some chants that I get the audience to do along with me. We tell our inner selves a bunch of crap with bad inner dialog, many times daily, it seems. So why not tell ourselves something good? Something that BUILDS UP instead of tears down. I give you these mantra chants to sing-song your way to feeling better about yourself:

"I am Safe, Powerful, Healthy, Wealthy and Wise!"

"I am Smart, Sexy, Wild, Weird and Fun!"

Oh yes you ARE. And you are so much more than even that! I have come to the very real conclusion that we take in energy from others. Try to reshape it and send it back out for good. The best you can. Yes, I've made mistakes. A bus-load. But I've also accomplished many of my dreams. I will be creating other dreams that I don't even know about yet. You can too.

I continue to sing from the tips of my toes. I try to understand people, but it isn't always possible.

I had a textbook narcissistic lover once, who told me: "Not every mystery needs to be explained, and not every hole needs to be explored." He did not appreciate my intuition. I knew things about him that he didn't want me to know. But then again, he didn't want to dig and find those things about himself either. Digging hurts! Things will never heal if the poison is still within. But when you dig, you find what needs to be healed.

Sometimes, your dreams will tell you best about what needs healing work. I believe that we give ourselves answers in our dreams, if we only listen and try to decipher them. When I was a child, if I had a bad dream, I would go wake up my mother. She would make me convey my nightmares aloud to her, then she would give me hot chocolate and pray with me, so that I could go back to sleep. I think that this is a good practice. Be your brave self. Tell someone your stories. Analyze your dreams. Re-live the nightmare as well as the fairytales. Then… let them go. Let God. Ask the Universe, "What's next for me?" Move on. Move up.

Now, as the night falls, crickets buzz and spring peepers talk about the heat that built their long summer day. It is well. I am tired. As tired as if I'd been working in my father's field and garden on a hot July cicada-singing day. But I have not been there this day for Pop is long gone and his fields are now someone else's' to sow, to reap or to lie fallow and grow over in neglect.

I sit and think of him now, here on my porch, much as he quietly pondered life on his porch in his rocking chair, after his long day's work. I can see him now, sitting in his shirtsleeves and grey work pants, steel-toed work shoes, a day well done in his pocket, beer in hand, swatting the occasional fly and enjoying the warm summer breeze before the incoming rain. His vegetables laid out on the counter, corn freshly shucked now, boiling on the stove. There is a woodworking project in his mind as he looks out at his barn and fields.

My own body's exhaustion is from something different. It is from the effort of busyness brought on by my own musical and spiritual work on my path in this life, learning, growing, planting. The gift of sharing it with friends, laughter, the joy of singing for a wedding, the team work of moving gear, with sore feet and dear hearts. My day has ended with good wishes and cold ale savored in the sunshine. These good things too, my father would've recognized.

I sit here and type on my laptop, I can picture my mother. She is in her cozy kitchen, even though she, too, passed away many years ago. She is dressed in her cotton shirt and trousers and I smell her cigarette burning forgotten in the ashtray. I notice her coffee and cream and sugar in her favorite mug is predictably getting cold, while she has been called away on an idea. She is in another room. I hear her typing hastily on her typewriter, banging her idea into orderly submission. The TV in her kitchen is droning the noon news absent-mindedly while she is engaged fully with her own research project. Her scanner notifies us of events incessantly. But yet, she types on into the night.

Just as I do...

Writing this book has been one of the hardest, joyful, sorrowful, painful, enlightening, healing and most entailed projects that I've ever done. It is comes second in intensity and magnitude to having and raising my children to independence. Everything that I've written here is TRUE. I've looked at my life through a microscope. I have been brutally honest in the telling of it, so that I could learn from my experiences and mistakes. I did not bare all. Some things are best kept for another time, mayhaps, sometime, over a campfire, I will show you more fairy dust wonders...or tell more tales of these demons of mine, ones which I've yet to drag out and show their severed heads.

It was good for me to visit these stories, tell a few tales, entertain, warn, scare and instruct you, make you laugh, cry, and to ponder great thoughts about life. I know the flow jumped around a bit, but then again, that's life, isn't it? It's erratic. It's just one unrelated incident to the next. It's up to us to link together and make sense of it.

I hope that my stories have good for you in some way, and that you have found this work of words helpful.

I bid you Peace.

Works Cited

Excerpt, *Comfortably Numb*. Walters, Roger. Gilmore, David. Pink Floyd: *The Wall*. Comfortably Numb. Columbia Records. 1979.

Excerpt, (Don't Fear) *The Reaper*. Blue Oyster Cult. Donald *"Buck Dharma"* Roeser. *Agents of Fortune*. Columbia Records. 1976.

Excerpt, *The Load Out*. Brown, Jackson. *Running on Empty*. The Load Out. Asylum Records. 1977.

Excerpt, *Wade in the Water*. Negro Spiritual. John Wesley Work., Frederick J. Work. New *Jubilee Songs* as Sung by the Fisk Jubilee Singers. 1901.

Bernstein, Gabrielle. *Spirit Junkie: A Radical Road to Self Love and Miracles*. Harmony Books. Sept. 2011.

Hay, Louise. You Can Heal Your Life. Hay House Publications. 1984.

Schulz, Mona Lisa. M.D. Ph.D. *Awakening Intuition: Using your Mind-Body Network for insight and Healing*. Harmony Books. 1998.

Stout, Martha. *The Sociopath Next Door: The Ruthless Versus the Rest of Us*. Broadway Books. February 2005.

If you are interested in Merlyn's music
and hearing her duo, **Merry Mischief**

~

MP3s and CDs are available at:
www.MerryMischief.net
www.MerryMischief.fourfour.com

Made in the USA
Charleston, SC
10 August 2016